IN THEIR OWN WORDS:

Founding Fathers
speak out regarding
the vital role of the Bible
in the foundation of the
United States of America

A collection of essays
by Bob Gingrich

Xulon
PRESS

CONTENTS

AUTHOR'S PREFACE

Children should be educated and instructed
in the principles of freedom.
John Adams, 1787

I was motivated to write this book by a desire to provide my grand-children with a reliable source of knowledge and inspiration regarding the early history of their country and an appreciation for the kind of leaders who made it all possible. It is my response to those who are trying to silence Christians and marginalize Christianity, the secular humanists who say this was never a Christian nation and that the Bible played no special role in the formulation of our foundational documents and our system of government.

I believe the teaching of early American history has been both downplayed and revised to the point that people have become badly confused, especially by the twisting almost beyond recognition of the concept of "separation of church and state." This book is intended as a non-scholarly, easy-to-read early American history refresher course for people who are struggling to understand the clash of ideologies that has become known by many as the "culture war."

Many historians have labeled over two hundred of our forefathers as Founding Fathers. For inclusion in this book, I selected eighteen men I felt best represented the ideals that guided them in generating our foundational documents and the government that emerged.

The people we refer to as Founding Fathers were exceptional men supported in their beliefs and activities by exceptional women. The vast majority of these truly exceptional people were Bible-believing Christians who, because they believed in the power of prayer, looked to God for guidance in establishing this nation. They spoke often of those strongly-held beliefs.

Because many of the quotations in this book have appeared in numerous books and publications over the years, including several I used as resource material, I did not identify any single work as the source from which the more commonly known quotations came since those quotations have, through common usage, become part of the public domain. Where lesser known quotations are concerned, I did identify the sources from which I gleaned them. They appear in the End Notes section at the end of the book.

Where grammar, spelling and punctuation in quotations by Founding Fathers are concerned, I included them in their original form even though such usage may seem awkward and/or incorrect to modern day readers.

For sources of additional information on these men and their times, see the *For Further Reading* list following the End Notes.

Prologue

❧

"Though God cannot alter the past, historians can."
– Samuel Butler

We the people of the United States of America are victims of identity theft!

History revisionists whose goal seems to be to separate the people of this country from their Christian roots, are working with single-minded determination to convince unsuspecting citizens, especially those who are not familiar with the early history of their homeland, that the Founding Fathers were something other than devoted, Bible-believing Christians who fully intended that the government they founded was to be guided in perpetuity by the precepts of the Judeo-Christian Bible. As a group, the Founders believed our dependence upon God was to be publicly, proudly, and reverentially acknowledged, a belief made crystal clear in their writings and their public pronouncements. They believed King David who said, "Blessed is the nation whose God is the Lord," an oft-quoted precept among them.

In his Preface to Clyde N. Wilson's *From Union to Empire*, Joseph R. Stromberg provides this brief summation of the obligations of those who would write history: "It is the function of history and the role of the historian to help us understand who we are and how we got into the situation in which we find ourselves. Wilson writes that a historian should be clear about 'where he is coming from.' Beyond that, his obligations are to do serious research, write honest narrative and analysis, and save his individual views for his concluding sections." It would be reassuring if Wilson's words described all of today's historians, especially those whose works appear in textbooks. Obviously they do not apply to many modern day writers of history.

Our unique Constitution the Christian Founders worked so painstakingly to create is being subverted, many would say perverted, in order to marginalize Christianity and the morality inherent in its precepts. Ironically, the weapon of choice employed by the deceptively-named American Civil Liberties Union and their allies, who have become skilled in the manipulation of the judicial branch of our government in their egregious attacks on Christianity, is the First Amendment to that Constitution.

They have been unbelievably successful in undermining the traditional moral climate in America by disingenuously portraying all social issues (abortion, pornography, flag-burning, same sex marriage, etc.) as "freedom of speech (expression)" issues, a result the founders would never have accepted. Freedom of speech is a cherished right, but speech and expression are not interchangeable words. Speech is only one form of expression and the only one protected by the First Amendment. Murder, for instance, is a form of "expression." The absurdity of allowing all forms of "expression" to be protected as free speech would have horrified the Founders just as they should horrify us. Sadly, too many Americans have been taken in by this subterfuge because they don't correctly understand the First Amendment nor do they understand the clearly defined separation of powers provided for in the Constitution. Because of this lack of understanding, unelected judges are getting away with legislating from the bench, a violation of the Constitution.

If the foundations be destroyed, what can the righteous do?, the Psalmist asked (Psalm 11:3). The righteous need to take back their identity but first of all, they must understand that they *are victims* of an outrageous scam. They need to understand they are the intended victims of a campaign to separate them from their true identity as a nation whose Biblical roots are undeniable. The revisionists don't want us to remember the Biblical foundation upon which our country was built.

Charles Hodge, President of Princeton University, 1871, made a statement that we would do well to remember today:

The proposition that the United States of America [is] a Christian...nation, is...the statement of a fact. That fact is not simply that the great majority of the people are Christians...but that the organic life, the institutions, laws, and official action of the government, whether that action be legislative, judicial, or executive, is...in accordance with the principles of...Christianity.

If a man goes to China, he expects to find the government administered according to the religion of the country. If he goes to Turkey, he expects to find the Koran supreme and regulating all public action. If he goes to a [Christian] country, he has no right to complain, should he find the Bible in ascendancy and exerting its benign influence not only on the people, but also on the government...

In the process of time thousands have come among us who are [not] Christians. Some are...Jews, some infidels, and some atheists. All are welcomed; all are admitted to equal rights and privileges. All are allowed to acquire property, and to vote in every election... All are allowed to worship as they please, or not to worship at all... No man is molested for his religion or for his want of religion. No man is required to profess any form of faith, or to join any religious association. More than this cannot reasonably be demanded. More, however, is demanded. The infidel demands that the government should be conducted on the principle that Christianity is false. The atheist demands that it should be conducted on the assumption that there is no God...The sufficient answer to all this is, that it cannot possibly be done.

All of the factual information collected here is intended as a tool to help Americans rediscover their wonderful heritage; to reintroduce them to the some of the preeminent men and women who had the courage, intelligence, wisdom, and foresight to look to God for guidance in putting together our foundational documents and our systems of government and commerce. Convincing evidence is abundant that our laws, customs, ethics, and moral codes were based upon precepts of the Judeo/Christian Bible and that the overwhelming majority of those involved in the discovery and founding of the United States of America were Christians on a Christian mission. That they fully expected this country to be governed according to those precepts is made clear in their speeches and voluminous writings. History revisionists, especially many who are involved in the publishing of textbooks, are counting on a diminished understanding of early American history in general and the strong Christian beliefs of the Founding Fathers in particular to advance their agenda-driven reorientation; the public schools are one of their primary targets.

We can effectively counter the history revisionists' attack on accurate history by becoming familiar with the Founders' *own words,* thus the title of this book. I considered titling the book *History for Dummies*, but people who don't know their own history aren't dumb; they have been, for the most part, uninformed or misinformed. My second thought regarding titling this book was *Early American History for Victims of A Public School Education Conducted by People of Questionable Motives, Loyalties, and Common Sense which* seemed to be more accurate but a bit cumbersome.

I settled on *In Their Own Words* because it is important for anyone interested in knowing the truth to know what the Founders said and in what context they said it. Anyone interested in acquiring an accurate understanding of the Founders' intent will find it valuable to study the words of those instrumental in the founding of the Republic in order to shed light on how they would have viewed the present. In *Of the Study of Law in the United States, circa 1790,* James Wilson made this statement we should use as a guiding principle today: "The first and governing maxim in the interpretation of a statute is to discover the meaning of those who made it."

As recorded from their own speeches and writings, the intent of those who gave us our Declaration of Independence and our Constitution is clear. Overwhelmingly, their collective world view was Judeo-Christian; faith in God and reverence for His word as recorded in The Holy Bible guided them as they set the foundations upon which this country has risen as the most powerful and prosperous nation the world has ever known. We have an awe-inspiring early history.

Edward Everett (1794 – 1865), orator and statesman, wrote this tribute entitled, *Such Men Cannot Die:*

No, fellow-citizens, we dismiss not Adams and Jefferson to the chambers of forgetfulness and death. What we admired, and prized, and venerated in them, can never *die, nor, dying, be forgotten. I had almost said that they are now beginning to live—to live that life of unimpaired influence, of unclouded fame, of unmingled happiness, for which their talents and services were destined. They were of the select few, the least portion of whose life dwells in their physical existence; whose hearts have watched while their senses slept; whose souls have grown up into a higher being; whose pleasure is to be useful; whose wealth is an unblemished reputation; who respire the breath of honorable fame; who have deliberately and consciously put what is called life to hazard, that they may live in the hearts of those who come after. Such men do not,* can *not die.*

To be cold, and motionless, and breathless, to feel not and speak not: this is not the end of existence to the men who have breathed their spirits into the institutions of their country, who have stamped their characters on the pillars of the age, who have poured their hearts' blood into the channels of the public prosperity. Tell me, ye who tread the sods of yon sacred height, is [Dr. Joseph] Warren dead? Can you not still see him, not pale and prostrate, the blood of his gallant heart pouring out of his ghastly wound, but moving resplendent over the field of honor, with the rose of heaven upon his cheek, and the fires of liberty in his eye? Tell me, ye who make your pious pilgrimage to the shades of Vernon, is Washington indeed shut up in that old and narrow house? That which made these men, and men like these, cannot die. The hand that traced the charter of independence is, indeed, motionless, the eloquent lips that sustained it are hushed; but the lofty spirits that conceived, resolved, matured, maintained it, and which alone, to such men, "make if life to live," these cannot expire:

These shall resist the empire of decay,
When time is o'er, and worlds have passed away,
Cold in the dust the perished heart may lie,
But that which warned it once can never die.*

This book is intended as a reminder tool for those who are familiar with our history and as a primer for those who know little. For those parents and grandparents who have been looking for a way to get more involved with the education of younger members of their families, this book should be beneficial. It is my fervent hope that it will be helpful in promulgating the truth concerning the Biblical foundation upon which this country was established. I continue to be inspired with the wisdom and character of the people who, relying upon the precepts of The Bible, designed a government that has provided more freedom, more opportunities for its citizens, and a higher quality of life than any other nation in recorded history. Making certain that our children and grandchildren understand their history and their Godly heritage is one of the most important gifts we can give them.

Bob Gingrich
September 15, 2006
*Quoted in *What Is A Man*, edited by Waller R. Newell

Chapter One

Original Intent vs. Revisionism

When ancient opinions and rules of life are taken away,
the loss cannot possibly be estimated.
From that moment, we have no compass to govern us,
nor can we know distinctly to what port we steer.
-- Edmund Burke

If you don't know history, you don't know anything.
You're a leaf that doesn't know it's part of a tree.
-- Michael Crichton

Although many deny the concept, we are engaged in a *civil cold war*; an engagement that features increasingly hot rhetoric and strong passions. It is a war of ideas and philosophies the outcome of which will determine what kind of people and what kind of country we will be in the future, what heritage we will pass on to our children and grandchildren. Considering the possible consequences, it is one of the most important wars in which we have ever been engaged. An amazingly large number of our citizens don't seem to believe a "war" of competing philosophies is happening at all. This clash of ideologies has been labeled the *culture war* by those who understand the issues and realize what is truly at stake.

Culture is defined as the "customary beliefs, social forms, and material traits of a racial, religious or social group," according to one definition included in *Merriam Webster's Collegiate Dictionary, Tenth Edition*. A nation is, of course an extended social group that includes a number of subcultures but one still presumed to have overarching "shared attitudes, values, goals, and practices." To some extent, that definition still fits the United States of America. In many ways, it does not. Today, the emphasis on multiculturalism is problematic. In the past, it was not a problem because the people coming to America from other parts of world at that time wanted to be Americans. Today, they want to live here but maintain their own "culture" and speak their own language. Too many insist that we educate them in their own language, among other unreasonable and impractical notions.

Our *culture war* is described by knowledgeable observers as a contest between two basic world views, a world view being the general belief system through which we view reality. In simple terms, the contest is between 1) the Judeo-Christian world view and 2) the secular humanist world view; a battle between those who elevate God and His word versus those who elevate the theories and philosophies of man. Max Hocutt says today's ideological duel is a battle over whether God or men should make the rules; a battle between theism and humanism, which defines "the fundamental division in moral theory." It has been described as a contest between those who exalt the wisdom of God versus those who worship the wisdom of man. Even a cursory study of biographical information on the preeminent Founding Fathers provides convincing proof of the Christian world view shared by these exceptional men.

Why is the Christian world view superior to other religions and philosophies? Charles F. Baker makes a strong, succinct, common sense argument for its superiority and its ultimate truth:

The Bible avoids all the extremes and lopsided views of life and the world. Idealistic philosophy denies the existence of matter, holding that only mind is a reality. Materialism holds just the opposite extreme view. The Bible teaches the objective reality of both

16

mind and matter, but points out the ephemeral character of the phys-
ical and the abiding character of the spiritual (2 Corinthians 4:18).
The atheist denies the transcendence of God and the deist denies His
immanence. The Bible teaches both: God is all in all and God over
all (1 Corinthians 15:28; Romans 9:5). Secularism places all of the
emphasis upon the present life; fanaticism ignores the present and
concerns itself only with the life to come. Buddhism would suppress
all human desire; Hedonism would do nothing but fulfill human
desire. Manichaeism held that the human body is evil; Hinduism
teaches caste; Confucianism ignores God and the future. The Bible,
on the other hand, brings all of these extremes into sharp focus and
presents a well-rounded, common-sense world view. (1)

The *culture war* is, bottom line, a battle between our foundational culture as established by the founders vs. the counter culture
that ran amok, especially on college campuses, in the 1960s. In his
Slouching Towards Gomorrah, Robert Bork is devastatingly precise
in his description of Sixties radicalism; ". . . impatient, destructive,
nihilistic.

"Those of us who regard the Sixties as a disaster are not 'allowing'
ourselves to be divided; we *insist* on it. Opposition to the counter
culture, the culture that became today's modern [as opposed to clas-
sical] liberalism, is precisely what our culture war is about," Bork
said. "It was a decade of hedonism and narcissism; it was a decade
in which popular culture reached new lows of vulgarity." (2)

Everything about the Sixties "revolution," especially as played
out on a significant number of college campuses, was in direct opposition to the majority Christian world view and in concert with the
world view of the anti-Christian secular humanists. The distance
between *secular humanism* and *paganism* is indeed a short one.
The Founding Fathers, even those described by some as deists, to
a man condemned paganism and would have had no patience with
it. Those who attempt to draw some parallel between the American
Revolution and the upheaval of the Sixties know little or nothing
about real colonial American History and even less about the character and intent of the Founders versus the character and intent of
the Sixties rebels. A big part of the reason for the confusion is that

accurate early American history is, according to observers of public education today, poorly, if not dishonestly, taught.

While there are many fundamental issues over which the *culture war* is being contested, the controversy that underscores the entire spectrum is the pivotal, and in my opinion, phony issue we call *the separation of church state*. I call it a phony issue because it has been created by turning the First Amendment entirely inside-out as far as it's true meaning and intent are concerned. That problem will be discussed fully in the chapter dealing with Thomas Jefferson whose letter to the Danbury Baptists has been intentionally obscured to give it a meaning directly opposite from what Jefferson clearly stated in his letter. The First Amendment has been used by the American Civil Liberties Union and their supporters to make people believe the Founders meant to protect the government from religion rather than to protect religion from the government. "The framers of the First Amendment intended complete federal nonintervention in religious issues," said Thomas E. Woods, Jr., in pointing out the deceptive nature of the ACLU's campaign to marginalize the Christian religion.

There can be no doubt in the minds of intellectually honest people regarding the original intent of the First Amendment which says, "Congress shall make no law respecting an establishment of religion, *or prohibiting the free exercise thereof ...*" The ACLU ignores the italicized and underlined phrase. As David Barton points out in his book entitled *Original Intent*, "When the intent under girding a law is abandoned, then that law can be applied in a manner that is totally contrary to its intended purpose; the result can be devastating." The ACLU has perfected that premise.

As recorded from their own speeches and writings, the intent of those who gave us our Declaration of Independence and our Constitution is clear that faith in God and reverence for His word as recorded in the Holy Bible guided them as they set the foundations upon which this country has risen to power and prosperity. They believed that the safety and security of the nation depended upon our adherence as a society to God's laws and our reliance upon His protection and guidance.

"The founding fathers were students of the Bible," says John Eidsmoe, author of *Christianity and the Constitution: The Faith of the Founding Fathers.* "They quoted it authoritatively and made frequent allusions to Scripture in their writings and speeches."

As to the personal religious affiliations of the writers and signers of the U. S. Constitution of 1787, "29 were Anglicans, 16 to 18 were Calvinists, 2 were Methodists, 2 were Lutherans, 2 were Roman Catholic, 1 lapsed Quaker and sometimes Anglican, and 1 [alleged] open Deist – Dr. Franklin who attended every kind of Christian worship, called for public prayer, and contributed to all denominations." (3) Many believe there is convincing proof that Franklin became a Christian after finally resolving doctrinal questions he had harbored earlier in life.

"America is often called 'a Christian nation' not because it was founded as such, but because its Founding Fathers were either Christians or had been influenced throughout their entire lives by the Christian consensus that surrounded them," Tim LaHaye pointed out in his excellent book entitled *Faith of Our Founding Fathers.* According to LaHaye, "…Christianity is a way of life. And that way of life had so permeated this nation by 1787 that it extended its influence to every area, including the fields of law, government, morality, marriage, and business."

Former Supreme Court Chief Justice Earl Warren, certainly no fundamentalist Christian as a jurist, when addressing the annual prayer breakfast of the International Council of Christian Leadership (1954) put himself in the company of those who are convinced of the Judeo-Christian world view of the Founders when he said:

> *"I believe no one can read the history of our country without realizing that the Good Book and the spirit of the Savior have from the beginning been our guiding geniuses ….Whether we look to the first charter of Virginia…or to the Charter of New England…or to the Charter of Massachusetts Bay…or to the Fundamental Orders of Connecticut…the same objective is present: A Christian land governed by Christian principles…*

"I believe the entire Bill of Rights, came into being because of the knowledge our forefathers had of the Bible and their belief in it: Freedom of belief, of expression, of assembly, of petition, the dignity of the individual, the sanctity of the home, equal justice under law, and the reservations of powers to the people ....

"I like to believe we are living today in the spirit of the Christian religion. I like also to believe that as long as we do so, no great harm can come to our country." (3)

For this book, I have researched material pertaining to the lives of 18 of the most prominent Founding Fathers and collected direct quotations from sources which clearly illustrate their thinking where God, the Bible, government and the nature of man are concerned. These direct quotations make clear to any objective reader where the Founders would stand today, especially where the so-called *separation of church and state* argument is concerned. They would be amazed at how the First Amendment has been stood on its head by those who are determined to marginalize Christianity.

Notwithstanding the writers of revisionist history, the founders would have been aghast at the current moral state of our society and greatly concerned about the future should the current trend toward a secular humanistic government not be reversed. It is clear from their words that, had we maintained the kind of society they imagined, there would be no general acceptance of pornography protected by the First Amendment, no widespread use of mind-altering drugs, no devaluing of individual lives through abortion and the trend toward euthanasia. No single branch of the government would be allowed to run roughshod over the other branches as our judicial branch is attempting to do today.

Killing innocent unborn children would not be legal because they understood that, although the word abortion does not appear in the Bible, the ancient Hebrews and Israelites were smart enough to know that abortion is murder and therefore covered under the Sixth Commandment.

They would also be disgusted by the sorry state of public education that has left a huge segment of the population in the dark regarding early American history and the men who created the heritage from which we have benefited including the moral foundation they established. The Christian underpinnings of our culture have been censored in our public schools for at least the last 50 years, starting as part of the "education reform" of the 1930s. John Dewey, the "father of progressive education" in America, said, "There is no God, and there is no soul. Hence, there are no needs for the props of traditional religion. With dogma and creed excluded, then immutable truth is also dead and buried. There is no room for fixed, natural law or moral absolutes." No wonder our schools are in the sorry state they are in today.

According to those who have researched our current public education system, too many American History books now used in public schools omit important people and events and include an amazing amount of misinformation, disinformation, trivia, and other "politically-correct" nonsense.

E. Merrill Root, in describing leftwing history revisionists who he called "destroyers of history," delivered this withering denunciation:

> *They are always seeking to deflect truth and to shock men, to reverse and pull apart, to destroy by "debunking." They are not content with the truth. They seek fame by destroying fame. In the twentieth century, such men began to multiply in the land, raising and training a guerrilla army of smilers with the knife, hero-mockers, vivisectors of value, haters of life, "debunkers," pint-sized Vandals of the mind, termites in the timber of culture who, having no greatness, resented all greatness...who, since they could not create, lusted to destroy. Like the fungus of decay, like the rust that eats pure metal, like the moths that devour the lustrous fabric, mere bellies with gray wings! They lusted to devour and destroy and corrode and tarnish. They sought to shout a huge NO to life and goodness and to love and greatness. They were and are the devil's army. They act as they do because they are little, and know it; because they are sick and they know they are sick...They cannot endure that there should be*

greatness, because they are not great; they cannot endure that there should be goodness for they are not good. They cannot revere a master, for they are not even artists...If they could see George Washington as he is in truth, they could not bear to see themselves as they are; therefore, they hate him because he shames them." (4)

I wish I had said that. I'm happy that there are men like Professor Root who use their command of the English language, and their contempt for "political correctness," to forcefully point out the truth about the "termites in the timber of culture."

In her informative and disquieting book entitled *The Rewriting of America's History*, Catherine Millard sounds this alarm: "Rewriting a nation's history is frequently one of the first strategies taken by a conquering nation. Why? Because a people who do not know from where they came also do not know where they are going. Thus, they become easy prey for a conquering nation." Millard goes on to say, "While this phenomenon has occurred repeatedly throughout history and throughout the world, today it is happening to our beloved United States!" (5)

It's happening, she says, "through the rewriting and/or reinterpretation of American Historical records; in our national parks, monuments, memorials, landmarks, shrines and churches. In some cases, changes are subtle, and others blatant. It's done through removal of key historic pieces that do not support the current ungodly bias. And it's also done through emphasis and de-emphasis of historical periods according to what fits a mode. In fact, the history of our founding period has been eroded and eliminated, almost to the point of oblivion. A nationwide phenomenon has occurred whereby there is an emphasis upon history from the Civil War onwards, or even as recent as the early 1900s, to the deliberate exclusion of the founding period, which in itself, is an incredible testimony to the hand of Almighty God upon this land, and His intricate involvement in the affairs of our nation, from its earliest beginnings," Millard points out. (6)

Millard and Root aren't alone is their indictment of the subversiveness, whether intended or otherwise, of public school presentations of early American history. In *The Conspiracy of Ignorance*, Martin L. Gross had this to say: "From the American history quizzes, it is apparent that youngsters are not properly taught the story of their nation. Two out of three seventeen-year-olds, most ready to go on to college, did not know the meaning of Abraham Lincoln's Emancipation Proclamation. Less than half the 16,000 high school seniors tested recognized Patrick Henry's defiant challenge, 'Give me liberty or give me death'." (7)

Many other respected observers of the public school system have commented on its demise. Ronald H. Nash, editor of *Liberation Theology*, recently wrote, "Under the phony canopy of what is deceptively described as value-free education, public school students are being…indoctrinated in all kinds of value-charged ideas. The only thing we know for certain is that only one set of values is deemed out of bounds in this process, and that is the values of the Christian worldview."

In *From Dawn to Decadence*, Jacques Barzun offered this stinging evaluation of today's public education: "The once proud and efficient public school system of the United States has turned into a wasteland where violence and vice share the time with ignorance and idleness."

"American education," wrote Charles Morasch, "should always first be about teaching love of the truth. Whether this nation and our freedoms survive through difficult times, may well depend on our children's free, uncensored, and unrestrained access to the words, ideas and beliefs of the Founding Fathers." History revisionists are strangers to the idea of "love of truth." They specialize in half truths which are at least half lies.

It wasn't always so in the public schools. For most of the 19th Century, the McGuffey readers, while used primarily in teaching students to read, also, as a byproduct, taught Biblical morality. In his introduction for a reissue of *McGuffey's Fifth Reader*, Henry Steel Commager, Jr., said: "What is most impressive in the McGuffey Readers is the morality. From the First Reader through the Sixth, the morality is pervasive and insistent, there is rarely a page but addresses itself to some moral problem, points up some moral lesson – industry, sobriety, thrift, propriety, modesty, punctuality – there were essential virtues and those who practiced them were sure of success...The world of the *McGuffey's* was a world where no one questioned the truths of the Bible, or their relevance to everyday conduct." (9)

Secular humanists want nothing of the kind taught in public schools today which goes a long way towards explaining the rise in popularity of private education. Thomas Sowell sounded like a prophet when he said, "If every parent in America knew what was really going on in the public schools, there would be a revolution." The public school system is a major battleground in the culture war. Can any serious observer of what goes only daily in many public schools doubt that the reintroduction of Bible-based morality in those schools would change things for the better?

Valuable prophetic advice more parents would do well to heed today comes from Martin Luther over 400 years ago: "I am much afraid that schools will prove to be great gates of hell unless they diligently labor in explaining the Holy Scriptures, engraving them in the hearts of youth. I advise no one to place his child where the Scriptures do not remain paramount. Every institution in which men are not increasingly occupied with the word of God must become corrupt."

"Rewritten history," says Robert Bork, "has always been a weapon in the struggle for control of the present and the future."

Another warning from a man known for his love of country, General Douglas MacArthur, deserves the attention of all who would enlist in the culture war on the correct side: "History fails to record a single precedent in which nations subject to moral decay have not passed into political and economic decline. There has been either a spiritual awakening to overcome the moral lapse, or a progressive deterioration leading to ultimate national disaster." (10)

Brad Bright, in his book entitled *God is the Issue*, succinctly described the crux of the matter: ". . . as we begin the new millennium we are confronted with a society that is shamelessly attempting to shake off all remaining vestiges of decency and morality.

"Society has removed God from His place at the center of everything and given Him a seat on the sidelines."

In researching people and events influencing the Founding Fathers collective thinking, in a general way as gleaned from their writings, John Eidsmoe presented an impressive bibliography including the works of Baron Charles Montesquieu, Sir William Blackstone, John Locke, Hugo Grotius, Samuel de Pufendorf, Emmerich de Vattel, Adam Smith, Algernon Sidney, Sir Edward Coke, and John Milton, all of whom would have been familiar to the Founders, as they were to all educated men of that time. Eidsmoe put together a list of fifteen principles "which underlie the thinking of the founding fathers":

1. *A belief in God and his providence, by which he guides and controls the universe and the affairs of mankind.*
2. *A belief in and respect for revealed religion—that is, recognition that God has revealed his truth through the Holy Scriptures.*
3. *A belief in the God-given power of human reason to apprehend truth. While reason does not supercede revelation, it serves as an aid in the search for truth where the Scriptures are silent.*
4. *A belief that man is not a perfect or perfectible being and that governmental theories must take that fact into account.*
5. *A belief that God has ordained human government to restrain the sinful nature of man.*
6. *A belief that God has established certain physical laws for the operation of the universe, as well as certain moral laws for the governance of mankind*
7. *A belief that God has revealed his moral laws to man through the Scriptures (revealed or divine law) and through the law of nature, which is discoverable through human reason and the human conscience.*
8. *A belief that human law must correspond to the divine law and the law of nature. Human laws which contradict the higher law are invalid, nonbinding, and are to be resisted.*
9. *A belief that the revealed law and law of nature form the basis for the law of nations (international law) and that this law of nations includes the right of a nation to defend itself against aggressors (just warfare).*

10. *A belief that the revealed law and the law of nature include natural, God-given unalienable human rights which include life, liberty, and property.*
11. *A belief that governments are formed by covenant or compact of the people in order to safeguard human rights.*
12. *A belief that governments have only such powers as are delegated to them by the people in the said covenants or compacts, and that when governments attempt to usurp powers not so delegated, they become illegitimate and are to be resisted.*
13. *A belief that, human nature being what it is, rulers tend to usurp more and more power if given the opportunity.*
14. *A belief that the best way to prevent governments from usurping power is to separate their powers and functions into legislative, executive and judicial branches.*
15. *A belief that, human nature being what it is, a free enterprise economy is the best way to give people an incentive to produce and develop national prosperity.*(11)

After having studied personal letters from many of the Founding Fathers written to his grandfather, founder Richard Henry Lee, President of the Continental Congress and the man who officially introduced in Congress the call for America's independence, wrote these words: "The wise and great men of those days were not ashamed publicly to confess the name of our blessed Lord and Savior Jesus Christ! In behalf of the people, as their representatives and rulers, they acknowledged the sublime doctrine of his mediation!" (12)

Intellectual dishonesty wilts under the illuminating light of truth. Revisionist history, an especially egregious form of intellectual dishonesty, will be consigned to its proper place, the ash heap of history, when people understand the truth.

Chapter Two

In The Beginning:
The early settlements

There is no country in the whole world in which
the Christian religion retains a greater influence
over the souls of men than in America
and there can be no greater proof of its utility,
and of it's conformity to human nature,
than that its influence is most powerfully felt
over the most enlightened and free nation on earth.
-- **Alexis de Tocqueville**

Measured by the standards of men of their time,
[the pilgrims] *were the humble of the earth.*
Measured by later accomplishments, they were the mighty.
In appearance weak and persecuted they came –
rejected, despised – an insignificant band; in reality strong
and independent, a mighty host of whom
the world was not worthy, destined to free mankind.
-- **Calvin Coolidge**

Apparently, almost everyone still agrees that Christopher Columbus officially discovered "the new world" in 1492, a fact that is difficult to rewrite, although some still try. That he was a devout Catholic is clear from his own words as recorded in his many writings. From that point on, there is a recently promulgated portrayal of the explorer as having been motivated by greed and that he was a merciless killer of Native Americans. This new version of history attempts to blame Columbus and other early European explorers for the death of nearly every Native American that occurred during those times, including those caused by disease and intertribal wars. Those accounts are based on wildly inflated estimates or, more accurately, guestimates, of pre-Columbus native populations living near the eastern seaboard. Their numbers and the causes of death were undoubtedly influenced by the point they were trying to make.

The view of Columbus as mass murder is obviously at odds with what was written about him in the past and it does not square in the slightest with what he wrote in his own journals and correspondence. The recorded writings of Queen Isabella and other contemporaries of Columbus support what was written earlier about him and refute the revisionists' attempts to make him out to be one of history's villains.

Just one example of the slanderous attacks on one of American history's heroes appeared on *Columbus Day* in 1990: "…Columbus liked the Indians. But when he saw that their jewelry was made of gold, he began making evil plans. He decided that the Indians should be the slaves of the Europeans who would settle in this region. The Indians would mine gold for the Europeans and do their other work. Columbus also hoped the Indians would become Christians. He felt they would gain more from Christianity than they would lose by becoming slaves. Before leaving the island, Columbus kidnapped a few Indians. He wanted them to guide him to other islands. And he wanted to show them off back in Spain." (1)

According to Catherine Millard in *The Rewriting of America's History*, of ten modern Columbus biographies she reviewed, "none makes mention of Christopher Columbus' faith in Christ and no mention of his motivation for the furtherance of the gospel. This phenomenon conforms to the style and content of the vast majority of history books, textbooks, dramatic presentations and exhibitions promoted throughout America on the life and adventures of Christopher Columbus ..."

As have many doers of great deeds before and since, Columbus was convinced that God was calling him to an important task, as recorded in his own words in, among other sources, his *Libro de las profecias* (Book of Prophecies):

> *At a very early age I began to sail upon the ocean. For more than forty years, I have sailed everywhere that people go. I prayed to the most merciful Lord about my heart's desire, and He gave me the spirit and the intelligence for the task: seafaring, astronomy, geometry, arithmetic, skill in drafting spherical maps and placing correctly the cities, rivers, mountains, and ports. I also studied cosmology, history, chronology and philosophy.*
>
> *It was the Lord who put into my mind (I could feel His hand upon me) the fact that it would be possible to sail from here to the Indies. All who heard of my project rejected it with laughter, ridiculing me. There is no question that the inspiration was from the Holy Spirit, because he comforted me with rays of marvelous illumination from the Holy Scriptures, a strong and clear testimony from the 44 books of the Old Testament, from the four Gospels, and from the 23 Epistles of the blessed Apostles, encouraging me continually to press forward, and without ceasing for a moment they now encourage to make haste.*

Later in the same document, Columbus wrote:

> *For the execution of the journey to the Indies I did not make use of intelligence, mathematics or maps. It is simply the fulfillment of what Isaiah had prophesied. All this is what I desire to write down for you in this book. No one should fear to undertake any task in the name of our Savior if it is just and if the intention is purely for His holy service. The working out of all things has been assigned to each person*

by our Lord, but it all happens according to His sovereign will even though He gives advice.

He lacks nothing that is in the power of men to give him. Oh what a gracious Lord, who desires that people should perform for Him those things for He holds Himself responsible! Day and night moment by moment, everyone should express to Him their most devoted gratitude.

I said that some of the prophecies remained yet to be fulfilled. These are great and wonderful things for the earth, and the signs are that the Lord is hastening the end. The fact that the gospel must still be preached in so many lands in such a short time, this is what convinces me. (1)

When Columbus landed on what is now known as San Salvador, meaning "Holy Savior," he had his crew erect, as he did on each island upon which they landed, a large wooden cross. Here he offered this recorded prayer: "O Lord, Almighty and everlasting God, by Thy holy Word Thou has created the heaven, and the earth, and the sea; blessed and glorified be Thy Name, and praised be Thy Majesty, which hath deigned to use us, Thy humble servants, that Thy holy Name maybe proclaimed in this second part of the earth." (2)

The ongoing concern of Columbus regarding the spiritual condition of the natives is obvious in his *Testament of Founding Hereditary Family Estate* dated February 22, 1498: "Also I order to said Don Diego, my son, or to him who will inherit said mayorazgo, that he shall help to maintain and sustain on the island Espanola four good teachers of the holy theology with the intention to convert to our holy religion all those people in the Indias, and when it pleases God that the income of the mayorazgo will increase, that then also be increased the number of such devoted persons who will help all these people to become Christians. And may he not worry about the money that it will be necessary to spend for the purpose..." (3)

The faux historians and wild-guessers who have attempted to present the man and his mission as less than honorable may have heavily and disproportionably relied on an incident that occurred in January of 1493 when a landing party was attacked by Indians they believed to be cannibals. Columbus wrote in his journal dated January 13, 1493:

> *Seeing them [the Caribs] running towards them the Christians...gave an Indian a great slash on the buttocks, and wounded another in the breast with an arrow. Seeing that they could gain little although the Christians were not more than seven, the [Caribs] 50 and more, began to flee, until not one remained, one leaving his arrows here, and another his bow there. The Christians would have killed many of them, it is said, if the pilot who went with them as their captain had not prevented it. The Christians returned to the caravel with their boat, and when the Admiral knew of it he said that on the one hand he was sorry and on the other not, since they would have fear of the Christians, because without doubt, says he, the folk there are bad actors (as one says), and he believed that they were Caribs, and ate men... (4)*

The writings of Christopher Columbus, of which there are many readily available to anyone interested in understanding the truth about the man, are laced with so many references to his devout Christian beliefs, that it is difficult to believe there could have been such a huge discrepancy between his words and his alleged actions.

So goes revisionist history from the beginning through the formative years of what was to become the nation first referred to during its early history as "a city on a hill." Nothing infuriates secular humanists like references to the overwhelming record of Christian influence in the foundational documents of this nation which unquestionably was founded upon Biblical principles. The agenda-driven revisionists are determined to debunk the evidence and many appear to be willing to forego the truth in order to accomplish their goals.

It is undoubtedly true that not everyone who came to America between 1492 and 1776 was a Christian or that they came primarily to seek religious liberty. Many did, indeed, arrive on these shores seeking instead fortune and adventure; some may have been just a few steps ahead of the long arm of the law. But it is abundantly clear that those who were instrumental in establishing the foundation of law, education, ethics, traditions, and personal responsibility relied on God and the Bible for guidance. They also believed unequivocally in the need for God's providential care in the miraculous survival of America as a free and sovereign nation.

Examples of the Godly heritage of America abound in records from the earliest colonies beginning at Jamestown in 1607 which was under the First Charter of Virginia (1606). Here's part of that charter:

> *We, greatly commending, and graciously accepting of, their desires for the furtherance of so noble a work, which may, by the providence of Almighty God, hereafter tend to the glory of His Divine Majesty, in propagating of the Christian religion to such people as yet live in darkness and miserable ignorance of the true knowledge and worship of God, and may in time bring the infidels and savages living in those parts to human civility and to a settled and quiet government, do, by these Our letters patent, graciously accept of, and agree to, their humble and well-intended desires. (7)*

It would be difficult to produce a more evangelically-inspired mission statement than that.

A few years later, the Pilgrims, who were supposed to settle in Northern Virginia, arrived in the Cape Cod area of Massachusetts after having been blown off course during their ocean voyage from Leyden, Holland. Eleven years before departing Leyden, they had departed from Scrooby, England in search of a society founded on Biblical principles. While they were well-received in Leyden, they were not satisfied that they had found their true destination and, after much prayer and debate, decided to send a delegation to America.

That group of Pilgrims, who would later produce the *Mayflower Compact*, received this sendoff from their Pastor, John Robinson, prior to setting sail from Leyden to the new world:

> *I charge you before God and his blessed angels, that you follow me no further than you have seen me follow the Lord Jesus Christ. The Lord has more truth yet to break forth out*

of his holy word. I cannot sufficiently bewail the condition of the reformed churches, who are come to a period in religion, and will go at present no further than the instruments of their reformation.—Luther and Calvin were great and shining lights in their times, yet they penetrated not into the whole counsel of God. – I beseech you, remember it, -- 'tis an article of your church covenant, -- that you be ready to receive whatever truth shall be made known to you from the written word of God. (8)

When the Pilgrims arrived on the Mayflower in 1620, they produced, prior to disembarking from the ship, the *Mayflower Compact*, which many consider the birth certificate of America. It reads, in its original form:

<u>In the Name of God, Amen.</u> We, whose names are underwritten,<u> the loyal subjects</u> <u>of our dread sovereign Lord King James, by the grace of God, of Great Britain, France and Ireland King, defender of the faith, etc.</u>, having <u>undertaken for the glory of God, and advancement of the Christian faith, and honor of our kind and</u> <u>country</u>, a voyage to plant the first colony in the northern parts of Virginia, do, <u>by these presents</u>, solemnly and mutually, in the presence of God and one of another, covenant and combine ourselves together into a civil body politic, for our better ordering and preservation, and furtherance of the ends aforesaid; and by virtue hereof to enact, constitute and frame such just and equal laws, ordinances, acts, constitutions, and offices, from time to time, as shall be thought most meet and convenient for the general good of the colony; unto which we promise all due submission and obedience. In witness whereof we have hereunder subscribed our names at Cape Cod the 11 of November, in the year of the reign of our sovereign lord, King James of England, France, and Ireland and the eighteenth, and of Scotland the fifty-forth, Anno Dom. 1620.

Public school students using the 1986 high school history text *Triumph of the American Nation*, were not informed that the words underlined above had been omitted, according to Gary DeMar in *America's Christian History: The Untold Story*. If you read the Compact again omitting those words, you lose the full impact of its religious nature. That kind of censorship has no place in the education of children, but it appears to be widespread.

The Mayflower Pilgrim's settled in Plymouth, Massachusetts and formed Plymouth Plantation which "was first a religious society, secondly an economic enterprise, and, last, a political commonwealth governed by biblical standards. The religious convictions of the Pilgrims were early expressed in the drafting of the Mayflower Compact." (9) The underlying mission of Plymouth Plantation, according to William Bradford's *History of Plymouth Plantation*, was motivated by evangelism:

> *Last and not least, they cherished a great hope and inward zeal of laying good foundations, or at least of making some way towards it, for the propagation and advance of the gospel of the kingdom of Christ in the remote parts of the world, even though they should be but stepping stones to others in the performance of so great a work. (10)*

The settlement of Salem, Massachusetts, in 1630 by Pilgrims arriving on the *Arabella*, resulted in the following covenant being established by Governor John Winthrop:

> *It is of the nature and essence of every society to be knot together by some covenant, either expressed or implied...*
>
> *For the work we have in mind, it is by mutual consent, through a special over-ruling providence and a more than ordinary approbation of the churches of Christ, to seek out a place of cohabitation and consortship, under a due form of government both civil and ecclesiastical...*
>
> *Therefore we must not content ourselves with usual ordinary means. Whatsoever we did or ought to have done*

when we lived in England, the same we must do, and more also where we go...

Neither must we think that the Lord will bear such failings at our hands as He doth from those among whom we have lived...

Thus stands the cause between God and us: we are entered into a covenant with Him for this work; we have taken out a commission, the Lord hath given us leave to draw our own articles...

We shall find that the God of Israel is among us, when ten of us shall be able to resist a thousand of our enemies, when He shall make us a praise and glory, that men of succeeding plantations shall say, The Lord make it like that of New England. For we must consider that we shall be as a city upon a hill, the eyes of all people are upon us; so that if we shall deal falsely with our God in this work we have undertaken and so cause him to withdraw his present help from us, we shall be made a story and a by-word through the world, we shall open the mouths of enemies to speak evil of the ways of God and all professors for God's sake; we shall shame the faces of many of God's worthy servants, and cause their prayers to be turned into curses upon us till we be consumed out of the good land whether we are going... (11)

Regarded by some as the world's first written constitution, the Fundamental Orders of Connecticut, adopted January 14, 1639, contained this statement connecting God and the Bible with government:

Forasmuch as it has pleased Almighty God by the wise disposition of His Divine Providence so to order and dispose of things that we the inhabitants and residents of Windsor, Hartford and Wethersfield and now cohabiting and dwelling in and upon the river Conectecotte [Connecticut] and the lands thereunto adjoining; and well knowing where a people are gathered together the Word of God requires that to maintain the peace and union of such a people there should be an orderly and decent government established according to God, to order and dispose of the affairs of all the people at all seasons as occasions shall require; do therefore associate and conjoin ourselves to be as one public State or Commonwealth, and do, for ourselves and our successors and such as shall be adjoined to us at any time hereafter, enter into combination and confederation together, so to maintain and preserve the liberty and purity of the Gospel of our Lord Jesus which we now profess, as also the discipline of the churches, which according to the truth of the said Gospel is now practiced among us. (12)

Included in the New England Federation (1643) text was this declaration:

We all came into these parts of America with one and the same end and aim, namely, to advance the Kingdom of our Lord Jesus Christ and to enjoy the liberties of the Gospel in purity with peace...The said United Colonies, for themselves and their posterities, do jointly and severally hereby enter into a firm and perpetual league of friendship and amity for offense and defense, mutual advice and succor upon all just occasions, both for preserving and propagating the truth and liberties of the Gospel and for their own mutual safety and welfare. (13)

When New Hampshire became a separate province after separating from the colony of Massachusetts in 1679, the following statement was included in their Commission:

And, above all things we do by these presents, will, require, and command our said Council, to take all possible care for the discountenancing of vice, and encouraging of virtue and good living; and that by such examples, the infidel may be incited and desire to partake of the Christian religion; and for the greater ease and satisfaction of the said loving subjects in matters of religion, we do hereby require and command that liberty of conscience shall be allowed unto all Protestants. (14)

Similar statements of dedication to the Bible as a source of America's laws, ethics, and traditions are plentiful in written documents produced during the Colonial period including the pre-revolution state constitutions of Delaware, New Jersey, Georgia, Maryland, Massachusetts, New Hampshire, North Carolina, South Carolina, and Pennsylvania.

John F. Kennedy stated the case well: "For more than three centuries, moral values have been the life-support system of this country. The men and women who planted their stand on these shores in the year 1607 vowed to build here a nation founded on virtue and moral integrity. And during all those years their promises and plan held true. The American people brought forth on this continent a nation dedicated to liberty and justice. The founders were committed to strong moral principles based on individual liberty and personal responsibility."

Unquestionably, those "strong moral principles" were based on Biblical principles. Documented proof of the inclusion of Biblical Christian concepts are readily available to anyone interested in reading for themselves the words of those who laid the foundation for the revolution that was to come, words and Christian concepts established by our earliest ancestors that were most certainly adopted by the Founding Fathers and placed in our foundational documents. That those Bible-based concepts were unambiguously adopted by our Founders is unmistakably demonstrated "in their own words."

Chapter Three

George Washington

Washington, the brave, the wise, the good,
supreme in war, in council, and in peace.
Valiant without ambition, discreet without fear,
confident without presumption.
In disaster, calm, in success, moderate; in all, himself.
The hero, the patriot, the Christian.
The father of nations, the friend of mankind, who,
when he had won all, renounced all,
and sought in the bosom of his family and of nature,
retirement, and in the hope of religion, immortality.
-- **Mount Vernon Inscription**

First in war, first in peace, first in the hearts of his countrymen.
-- **Richard Henry Lee's tribute to George Washington**

Similarities between George Washington and David, ancient King of Israel, are striking among people familiar with The Holy Bible and early U. S. history. David, directed and protected by God, led the forces that secured Israel as a sovereign nation. George

Washington, first as military leader and later as statesman/political leader, was instrumental in securing nationhood for the United States of America.

It doesn't take much imagination to visualize the contest between Colonial America and Great Britain as a battle between little David and gigantic Goliath although on a much larger scale. Eye witness accounts of Washington's seemingly miraculous deliverance in battle, have lead many to believe he was the beneficiary of supernatural protection as was King David, according to the Bible. David was convinced that God would intervene in his and Israel's behalf; George Washington was convinced that God would intervene on his and America's behalf. No one who has read much about Washington can deny that he, like David, was devoted to his God and that he, as did David, spent much time in prayer. George Washington and David were "men after God's own heart."

George Washington was born into a Christian family February 22, 1732, at Wakefield Plantation in Westmoreland County, Virginia. Washington's father, who died in 1743, was described as "a man of monumental proportions, a figure of great energy, and an established member of the Virginia gentry," which opened some doors for his sons.(1) As a youth, Washington was on friendly terms with many prominent and influential people of North Virginia which led to opportunities in public service. While still a teenager, Washington was appointed county surveyor in his home country of Culpeper and soon was doing survey work in frontier areas of Virginia and West Virginia where he learned much about life in and development problems of the West, knowledge that was to serve him well later in life. He had more first hand knowledge of the western frontier than any of the other Founding Fathers. At the age of 21, Washington gained military experience serving in Virginia's militia. Among other assignments, Washington was appointed emissary to French posts on the Ohio frontier, serving with distinction. Later, as a Colonel, Washington was an aide to British General Edward Braddock during the French and Indian War and in that position spent three years involved in the rigors of frontier military problems. Eventually, Washington was given authority over the forces responsible for defending Virginia's frontier.

An event in the life of Washington that seemed to confirm his destiny occurred during the battle of Monongahela when General Braddock's forces "were being annihilated" according to an account that appeared in American textbooks until 1934. During the engagement, "Washington rode back and forth across the battle delivering General Braddock's orders. As the battle raged, every officer on horseback, except Washington, was shot down, until even General Braddock was killed, at which point the troops fled in confusion." (2)

A few days after the battle, Washington confirmed his belief in his supernatural protection in a letter to his brother when he wrote: "But by the all-powerful dispensations of Providence, I have been protected beyond all human probability or expectation; for I had four bullets through my coat, and two horses shot under me, yet escaped unhurt, although death was leveling my companions on every side of me." (3)

Washington wasn't the only one who, as a result of that incident, believed in the special supernatural protection extended to him. Hear the words of an Indian chief who was on the other side of that battle, upon meeting Washington 15 years later:

> *I am a chief and ruler over my tribes. My influence extends to the waters of the great lakes and to the far blue mountains.*
>
> *I have traveled a long and weary path that I might see the young warrior of the great battle. It was on the day when the white man's blood mixed with the streams of our forests that I first beheld this chief [Washington].*
>
> *I called to my young men and said, mark yon tall and daring warrior? He is of the red-coat tribe – he hath an Indian's wisdom, and his warriors fight as we do – himself alone exposed.*
>
> *Quick, let your aim be certain, and he dies. Our rifles were leveled, rifles which, but for you, knew not how to miss – "twas all in vain, a power mightier far than we, shielded you.*
>
> *Seeing you were under the special guardianship of the Great Spirit, we immediately ceased to fire at you. I am old and*

soon shall be gathered to the great council fire of my fathers in the land of shades, but ere I go, there is something bids me speak in the voice of prophecy: Listen! The Great Spirit protects that man [pointing to Washington], and guides his destinies – he will become the chief of nations, and a people yet unborn will hail him as the founder of a mighty empire. I am come to pay homage to the man who is the particular favorite of Heaven, and who can never die in battle." (4)

Another participant in that battle, fighting on the side of the Indians, said, "Washington was never born to be killed by a bullet! I had seventeen fair fires at him with my rifle, and after all could not bring him to the ground." (5)

After resigning from the militia in 1759, Washington acquired insight into legislative procedures and practices in the House of Burgesses. Upon reading biographical details of Washington's early years, it is easy to believe he was providentially prepared, protected, and directed in order to play the role, labeled by many, as that of "the indispensable man" and the "Father of his country."

During the years from 1759 to 1774, the year the royal governor dissolved the Virginia Assembly, Washington, as private citizen, little by little became convinced that independence from Great Britain would become necessary. He then joined the "revolutionary" legislature and became one of Virginia's delegates to the First Continental Congress and a year later to the Second Continental Congress held in Philadelphia.

When it was decided that a Continental army should be formed by bringing various militia and regular regiments together, Washington was selected to be commander of the original American "standing army." His first task was to organize and train the disparate groups from which he was to create a national military force. As a result of his earlier military experiences, he placed great importance and emphasis upon Godly behavior among those placed under his command. He also "believed that (1) good government is a blessing from God; (2) national entities as such should acknowledge, obey, thank, and pray to God; and (3) national entities should seek forgiveness from God for national transgressions as well as individual transgressions." (6)

Washington established what was to become the Chaplain Corps and made attendance at regular worship services mandatory. His first general order read:

> *The General most earnestly requires and expects a due observance of those articles of war established for the government of the army, which forbid profane cursing, swearing, and drunkenness. And in like manner he requires and expects of all officers and soldiers, not engaged in actual duty, a punctual attendance on Divine service, to implore the blessing of Heaven upon the means used for our safety and defense." (7)*

Washington's recorded words are laced with references to the dependence upon God of the young nation-to-be as they prepared for war against what was then the world's most powerful and extensive empire. He knew they could only be victorious with the help of almighty God and he wasn't shy about saying so. Prior to the beginning of official hostilities, he gave his troops this exhortation: "The time is now near at hand which must probably determine whether Americans are to be freemen or slaves; whether they are to have any property they can call their own; whether their houses and farms are to be pillaged and destroyed, and themselves consigned to a state of wretchedness from which no human efforts will deliver them. The fate of unborn millions will now depend, under God, on the courage of this army. Our cruel and unrelenting enemy leaves us only the choice of brave resistance, or the most abject submission. We have, therefore to resolve to conquer or die."

His recorded words also make frequent references to the providence of God in events leading to America's status as an independent nation. While addressing his troops at Valley Forge May 2, 1778, Washington said, "The instances of Providential goodness which we have experienced and which have now almost crowned our labors with complete success demand from us in a peculiar manner the warmest returns of gratitude and piety to the Supreme Author of all good."(8) Later that year, in a letter to General Thomas Nelson,

Washington wrote, "The hand of providence has been so conspicuous in all this [the course of the war] that he must be worse than an infidel that lacks faith, and more wicked that has not gratitude to acknowledge his obligations; but it will be time enough for me to turn Preacher when my present appointment ceases."(9)

When the Treaty of Paris was signed in 1783, officially ending the Revolutionary War, Washington resigned his military commission and returned to private life as a farmer on his Mount Vernon estate where he reportedly was initially content but soon became concerned about inherent weakness in the Articles of Confederation as a document capable of meeting the governing needs of the new nation. He came to believe in a strong central government, especially where national defense issues might be involved, a feeling he shared with many other influential citizens. Governing a nation through thirteen sovereign states, it was becoming obvious, could not work in the long run.

National defense issues along with other potentially destructive matters, including a variety of squabbles between adjacent states soon led to the convening of what was initially referred to as the "Grand" or "Federal" convention, the stated purpose of which was to revise the Articles of Confederation, not to write a new constitution. Gathering for the purpose of replacing the Articles with a new Federal Constitution would have, according to many historians, kept at least half of the delegates from attending. They were concerned about maintaining the rights of "sovereign" states under a more centralized government.

Under the Articles of Confederation, there were no provisions for national defense nor were there any mechanisms through which taxes could be assessed or collected, a potentially disastrous condition, especially during times of national emergency. As commander in chief during the War, Washington had become especially sensitive to monetary problems since his troops consistently, due to lack of money and any way to generate it, were without adequate supplies, clothing, food, weapons, and medicine.

Soon after the opening of the Convention May 25, 1787, Washington was selected by unanimous vote to be its president. Because he was so well known and universally respected,

Washington was probably the one individual who could hold the convention together with all the vitally important and emotionally charged issues, including slavery, that would be put forward by the various delegations.

"Washington showed himself firm, courteous, inflexible. When he approved a measure, delegates reported that his face showed it. Yet it was hard to tell what the General was thinking and impossible to inquire. In his silence lay his strength. His presence kept the Federal Convention together, kept it going, just as his presence had kept a straggling, ill-conditioned army together throughout the terrible years of war," according to Catherine Drinker Bowen.(10) "Be assured," said James Monroe, "his influence carried the government."

An anecdote by George Read, delegate from Delaware, recorded in *Farrand's Records of the Federal Convention* is illustrative of the aura connected with Washington:

> *When the Convention to form a Constitution was sitting in Philadelphia in 1787, of which General Washington was president, he had stated evenings to receive the calls of his friends. At an interview between Hamilton, the Morrises, and others, the former remarked that Washington was reserved and aristocratic even to his intimate friends, and allowed no one to be familiar with him. Gouverneur Morris said that was a mere fancy and he could be as familiar with Washington as with any of his other friends. Hamilton replied, "If you will, at the next reception evening, gently slap him on the shoulder and say, 'My dear General, how happy I am to see you look so well!' a supper and wine shall be provided for you and a dozen of your friends." The challenge was accepted. On the evening appointed, a large number attended; and at an early hour Gouverneur Morris entered, bowed, shook hands, laid his left hand of Washington's shoulder, and said, "My dear General, I am very happy to see you look so well!" Washington withdrew his hand, stepped suddenly back, fixed his eye on Morris for several minutes with an angry frown, until the latter retreated abashed, and sought refuge in the*

crowd. The company looked on in silence. At the supper, which was provided by Hamilton, Morris said, "I have won the bet, but I paid dearly for it, and nothing could induce me to repeat it."

By September, 1787, the assembled delegates had, under the quiet but firm leadership, produced, with but few changes, the Constitution we live under today. Seven months later, George Washington, by action of the Electoral College, was inaugurated as the first President of the United States of America.

Prior to the Inauguration ceremony, a newspaper announcement providing information regarding the event said, "On the morning of the day on which our illustrious President will be invested with his office, the bells will ring at nine o'clock, when the people may go up and in a solemn manner commit the new Government, with its important train of consequences, to the holy protection and blessings of the Most High. An early hour is prudently fixed for this peculiar act of devotion, and it is designed wholly for prayer."(11)

Also prior to the first-ever presidential inauguration, both the Senate and the House of Representatives passed a resolution: "Resolved, That after the oath shall have been administered to the President, he, attended by the Vice President, and the members of the Senate, and House of Representatives, proceed to St. Paul's Chapel, to hear divine service, to be performed by the Chaplain of Congress already appointed." So much for separation of church *from* state as disingenuously promoted by the ACLU and other suspect organizations promoting their mistaken and destructive agendas.

Once again pointing out his belief in God's hand in establishing the United States of America, Washington, in his Inaugural Address said:

Such being the impressions under which I have, in obedience to the public summons, repaired to the present station, it would be peculiarly improper to omit, in this first official act, my fervent supplications to that Almighty Being who rules over the universe, who presides in the councils of nations and whose providential aids can supply every human defect.

That His benediction may consecrate to the liberties and happiness of the people of the United States a Government instituted by themselves for these essential purposes; and may enable every instrument employed in its administration to execute with success, the functions allotted to his charge.

In tendering this homage to the Great Author of every public and private good, I assure myself that it expresses your sentiments not less than my own; nor those of my fellow-citizens at large, less than either.

No people can be bound to acknowledge and adore the Invisible Hand which conducts the affairs of men more than the people of the United States.

Every step by which they have advanced to the character of an independent nation seems to have been distinguished by some token of providential agency;

And in the important revolution just accomplished in the system of their United government, the tranquil deliberations and voluntary consent of so many distinct communities, from which the event has resulted can not be compared with the means by which most governments have been established, without some return of pious gratitude, along with an humble anticipation of the future blessings which the past seem to presage.

These reflections, arising out of the present crisis, have forced themselves too strongly on my mind to be suppressed. You will join with me I trust in thinking that there are none under the influence of which the proceedings of a new and free Government can more auspiciously commence.

We ought to be no less persuaded that the propitious smiles of Heaven can never be expected on a nation that disregards the eternal rules of order and right which Heaven itself has ordained; and since the preservation of the sacred fire of liberty and the destiny of the republican model of government are justly considered as deeply, perhaps finally, staked of the experiment...

I shall take my present leave; but not without resorting once more to the Benign Parent of the Human Race, in humble supplication that, since He has been pleased to favor the American people with opportunities for deliberating in perfect tranquility, and dispositions for deciding with unparalleled unanimity on a form of government for the security of their union and the advancement of their happiness, so His divine blessings may be equally conspicuous in the enlarged views, the temperate consultations and the wise measures on which the success of this Government must depend. (12)

Upon assuming the presidency, Washington said, "I walk on untrodden ground. There is scarcely any part of my conduct that may not hereafter be drawn into precedent." He essentially "invented" the office of president during his first term. During his second term, he dealt much more with foreign policy and, although with much distaste, partisan politics. By the end of his second term, he was more than ready to step out of the spotlight. In his famous *Farewell Address*, Washington took advantage of one more opportunity to remind the nation of the importance of religion and morality and its link with national security, domestic tranquility, and the rights of individuals. He said:

Of all the dispositions and habits which lead to political prosperity, Religion and Morality are indispensable supports. In vain would that man claim the tribute of Patriotism, who should labor to subvert these great pillars of human happiness, these firmest props of the duties of Men and Citizens. The mere Politician, equally with the pious man, ought to respect and cherish them. A volume could not trace all their connections with private and public felicity. Let it simply be asked, where is the security for property, for reputation, for life, if the sense of religious obligation desert the oaths which are the instrument of investigation in Courts of Justice? And let us with caution indulge the supposition that morality can be maintained without religion. Whatever may be conceded to the influence of refined education on minds of peculiar structure, reason and experience both forbid us to expect that national morality can prevail in exclusion of religious principle.

It is substantially true that virtue or morality is a necessary spring of popular government. The rule, indeed, extends with more or less force to every species of free government. Who, that is a sincere friend to it, can look with indifference upon attempts to shake the foundation of the fabric? (13)

Many re-writers of history have maintained that George Washington was not a church member and a deist rather than a Christian. Biographical materials available on the religious beliefs and practices of our first president abound including *Washington's Prayer for the United States of America* which appears on a plaque in St. Paul's Chapel in New York City as well as at Pohick Church, Fairfax County, Virginia, where Washington was a vestryman from 1762 to 1784:

Almighty God; We make our earnest prayer that Thou wilt keep the United States in Thy Holy protection; and Thou wilt incline the hearts of the Citizens to cultivate a spirit of subordination and obedience to Government; and entertain a brotherly affection and love for one another and for their fellow Citizens of the United States at large, and particularly for their brethren who have served in the Field.

And finally that Thou wilt most graciously be pleased to dispose us all to do justice, to love mercy, and to demean ourselves with that Charity, humility, and pacific temper of mind which were the Characteristics of the Divine Author of our blessed Religion, and without a humble imitation of whose example in these things we can never hope to be a happy nation. Grant our supplication, we beseech Thee, through Jesus Christ our Lord. Amen. (14)

George Washington was a God-fearing, Bible-believing man and we can know that with certainty by what he repeatedly said including the following quotations contained in *America's God and Country* compiled by William J. Federer:

"It is impossible to govern rightly without God and the Bible."

"Reason and experience both forbid us to expect that national morality can prevail in exclusion of religious principle."

"It is the duty of all nations to acknowledge the Providence of Almighty God, to obey His will, to be grateful for His benefits, and to humbly implore His protection and favor."

As part of a Thanksgiving proclamation dated Jan. 1, 1795, Washington wrote:

"...I, George Washington, President of the United States, so recommend to all religious societies and denominations, and to all persons whomsoever, within the United States, to set apart and observe Thursday, the 19th day of February next, as a day of public thanksgiving and prayer, and on that day to meet together and render sincere and hearty thanks to the great Ruler of nations for the manifold and signal mercies which distinguish our lot as a nation..."

Washington often used the words *God, Providence, the Almighty, Almighty Ruler of the Universe, Almighty Father, Lord, the Great Governor of the Universe*, etc., in his writings and in his speeches. When he used the word *religion*, he was always referring to his Christian religion. While speaking to Indian chiefs in 1779 that had brought some of their children to be trained in the American schools, Washington said, "...You do well to wish to learn our arts and ways of life, and above all, the religion of Jesus Christ. These will make you a greater and happier people than you are. Congress will do everything they can to assist you in this wise intention."

In a prayer during the Revolutionary War Washington is quoted as saying: "And now, Almighty Father, if it is Thy holy will that we shall obtain a place and name among the nations of the earth, grant that we may be enabled to show our gratitude for Thy goodness by our endeavors to fear and obey Thee. Bless us with Thy wisdom in our counsels, success in battle, and let all our victories be tempered with humanity. Endow, also our enemies with enlightened minds, that they become sensible of their injustice, and will to restore our liberty and peace. Grant the petition of Thy servant, for the sake of

Him whom Thou hast called Thy beloved Son; nevertheless, not my will, but Thine be done."

On another occasion, Washington offered this prayer: "Pardon, I beseech thee, my sins, remove them from thy presence, as far as the east is from the west and accept me for the merits of thy son Jesus Christ. I have called on Thee for pardon and forgiveness of sins, but so coldly and carelessly that my prayers are become my sin and stand in need of pardon. I have heard thy holy word, but with such deadness of spirit that I have been an unprofitable and forgetful hearer. Cover [my sins] with the absolute obedience of Thy dear Son, that those sacrifices which I have offered may be accepted by Thee, in and for the sacrifice of Jesus Christ offered upon the cross for me."

Best-selling author Tim LaHaye included in his well-researched book entitled *Faith of Our Founding Fathers* excerpts from Washington's personal prayer book with this lead-in: "That President George Washington was a devout believer in Jesus Christ and had accepted Him as His Lord and Savior is easily demonstrated by a reading of his personal prayer book (written in his own handwriting), which was discovered in 1891 among a collection of his papers. To date no historian has questioned its authenticity. It consists of twenty-four pages of his morning and evening prayers, revealing many of his theological beliefs about God, Jesus Christ, sin, salvation, eternal life, and himself as a humble servant of Christ."

It is clear not only from Washington's own words but also in the words of many who knew him best that he was very much a Christian. John Marshall, Chief Justice of the Supreme Court who had also served with Washington at Valley Forge, said, "Without making ostentatious professions of religion, he was a sincere believer in the Christian faith, and a truly devout man." (15)

Henry Muhlenberg, one of the founders of the Lutheran Church in America and pastor of the Lutheran church near Valley Forge made this statement regarding Washington:

I heard a fine example today, namely, that His Excellency General Washington rode around among his army yesterday and admonished each and every one to fear God, to put away the wickedness that has set in and become so general, and to practice the Christian virtues. From all appearances, this gentleman does not belong to the so-called world of society, for he respects God's Word, believes in the atonement through Christ, and bears himself in humility and gentleness. Therefore, the Lord God has also singularly, yea, marvelously, preserved him from harm in the midst of countless perils, ambuscades, fatigues, etc., and has hitherto graciously held him in His hand as a chosen vessel."(16)

Richard Henry Lee delivered the official Washington eulogy December 26, 1799:

First in war, first in peace, and first in the hearts of his countrymen, he was second to none in humble and enduring scenes of private life. Pious, just, humane, temperate, and sincere; dignified, and commanding; his example was as edifying to all around him as were the effects of that example lasting....Correct throughout, vice shuddered in his presence and virtue always felt his fostering hand. The purity of his private character gave effulgence to his public virtues."

Another tribute to the character and reputation of Washington was delivered after the death of our first president by Rev. J. T. Kirkland: "The virtues of our departed friend were crowned by piety. He is known to have been habitually devout. To Christian institutions he gave the countenance of his example; and no one could express, more fully, his sense of the Providence of God, and the dependence of man."(17)

Perhaps one of the most important testimonials to the other-worldly qualities of Washington came from an unlikely source, an enemy during the Revolutionary War. The Duke of Wellington, a British general, described Washington as having "the purest and noblest character of modern time – possibly of all time."

Washington's colleague, Thomas Jefferson presented this tribute:

He was incapable of fear, meeting personal dangers with the calmest unconcern. Perhaps the strongest feature in his character was prudence, never acting until every circumstance, every consideration, was maturely weighed; refraining if he saw a doubt, but, when once decided, going through with his purpose, whatever obstacles opposed. His integrity was most pure, his justice the most flexible I have ever known, no motive of interest or consanguinity, or friendship or hatred being able to bias his decision. He was in every sense of the words, a wise, a good and a great man. (18)

William White, author of *Washington's Writings*, gives us this insight into the personal habits of George Washington:

It seems proper to subjoin to this letter what was told to me by Mr. Robert Lewis at Fredricksburg, in the year 1827. Being a nephew of Washington and his private secretary during the first part of his presidency, Mr. Lewis lived with him on terms of intimacy, and had the best opportunity for observing his habits.

Mr. Lewis said that he had accidentally witnessed his private devotions in his library both morning and evening; that on those occasions he had seen him in a kneeling posture with a Bible open before him, and that he believed such to have been his daily practice.

Jared Sparks, whose twelve-volume collection of Washington's writings published from 1834 to 1837, summarized Washington's character with these words.

A Christian in faith and practice, he was habitually devout. His reverence for religion is seen in his example, his public communications, and his private writings. He uniformly ascribed his successes to the beneficent agency of the Supreme Being. Charitable and humane, he was liberal to the poor and kind to those in distress. As a husband, son, and brother, he was tender and affectionate...'

If a man spoke, wrote, and acted as a Christian through a long life, who gave numerous proofs of his believing himself to be such, and who was never known to say, write or do a thing contrary to his professions, if such a man is not to be ranked among the believers of Christianity, it would be impossible to establish the point by any grain of reasoning. (19)

George Washington was a practicing Christian, a man of prayer, and one who walked humbly before his God. He was a Christian patriot with a strong sense of calling and purpose to which he responded courageously. He was the right man at the right place at the right time. He had no use for the creed of secular humanists and their elevation of man over God. "That man," Washington said, "who refuses to see the hand of God in human events is worse than an infidel."

His sense of propriety would have put him at loggerheads with those who routinely use the First Amendment to allow the spread of pornography and who have perverted that wonderful Amendment to the point that it has been used to protect those unbelievably misguided American citizens who burn the American flag and call it merely an "expression." To mention the burning of an American flag in the same sentence with the name of George Washington is a sacrilege to clear-thinking people.

In his *Farewell Address*, Washington said, "The name of American, which belongs to you, in our national capacity, must always exalt the just pride of Patriotism, more than any appellation derived from local discriminations."

Patriot is not a word he would have connected in any way with American citizens who would in any way dishonor the American flag.

"Citizens by birth or choice, of a common country, that country has a right to concentrate your affections," he said. "The name of American, which belongs to you, in your national capacity, must always exalt the just pride of patriotism."

Today's devotees to the flawed and fading theory of evolution may want to study these words of our first president: "It is impossible to account for the creation of the universe, without the agency of a Supreme Being. It is impossible to govern the universe without the aid of a Supreme Being. It is impossible to reason without arriving at a Supreme Being.

If the spirit of George Washington with his sense of propriety, decency and morality were to reappear on the political scene today, changes would have to be made; changes for the better.

Chapter Four

John Witherspoon

The Ten Commandments are the sum of the moral law.
– John Witherspoon

A true son of liberty. So he was. But first, he was a son of the cross
**-- John Adams tribute upon of learning
of Witherspoon's death.**

John Witherspoon was a Christian theist, known pejoratively today as a fundamentalist. He believed, wrote, sermonized, and taught that, unequivocally, eternal salvation was possible *only* through the sacrificial, substitutionary death on the cross of Jesus Christ. He believed that there *are* absolutes. As do today's "fundamentalist" Christians, he believed that God blesses and protects those individuals and nations who honor Him and that ignoring God and His precepts is a recipe for individual and national disaster. He shared these beliefs with his fellow founders, most of whom are on record as having made similar statements. Differing, no doubt, in the intensity of their devoutness, most were, none the less, Christians.

Witherspoon was the only member of the clergy to sign the Declaration of Independence. Serious students of early American history believe he was the originator of the phrase "with a firm Reliance on the protection of Divine Providence" as part of the last sentence in the Declaration. An impressive number of those stalwart, God-fearing, Bible-believing men who were to become prominent in the American Revolution were mentored by Witherspoon. As a teacher and preacher, his mission was to imprint upon the minds of his students an extensive knowledge and love of Holy Scripture. He was firm in his belief that "civil liberty cannot be long preserved without virtue."

Born in 1723 into a Presbyterian family in Edinburgh, Scotland, Witherspoon aligned himself, as had his father before him, with the orthodox or fundamentalist branch of the church, known as the Popularists. Witherspoon's mother was a lineal descendant of church reformer John Knox whose Puritanical traditions they carried on. Not one to avoid conflict, he found himself in frequent and intense confrontations with Presbyterian liberals, who like today's theological liberals of all denominations, referred to themselves as the "Moderate" wing of the denomination. Witherspoon disdained the "Moderates" ridiculing them in sermons and writings including a sixty-page pamphlet entitled *Ecclesiastical Characteristics*, an excellent piece of satire in which he especially lampoons what he saw as their tendency to claim intellectual superiority. His pamphlet was reprinted and widely distributed in America and throughout Europe. He frequently found himself involved in verbal duals and legal battles with lawyers and judges many of whom, even during that time, tended to be political liberals who aligned themselves with the "Moderate" Presbyterians.

Witherspoon, who became a doctor of theology at the young age of twenty, earned the title "pastor, politician, and patriot," words used by Martha Lou Lemmon Stohlman in the title of her biographical book about one of our least-known Founding Fathers. By reputation, Witherspoon was an oratorical powerhouse. Stohlman also referred to him as "a firebrand of the Revolution" and "the Big Bertha of the Popularist artillery." As a powerful and formidable preacher, teacher, debater, and writer, Witherspoon influenced the thinking of thousands of his fellow citizens, including those former students who would play leading roles in the campaign for independence and the governing of the newly formed republic.

After coming to the Colonies in 1768 to become President of the College of New Jersey (now known as Princeton University), Witherspoon was active in events and organizations that were instrumental in confirming and reinforcing the foundational morality of his adopted country. He was a member of both the First and Second Continental Congress, a signer of the Declaration of Independence, and a delegate to the New Jersey convention of 1787 that ratified the U.S. Constitution. He is also credited with playing a major role in producing a Bible thought to be America's first Family Bible in 1791. His reprinted sermons and political essays were widely distributed.

Witherspoon's most important contribution to the formulation of our system of government, our moral codes, and ethical standards was to help shape the men who shaped America through his position as the College of New Jersey's chief lecturer where he touched the lives of nearly 500 graduates. Eleven percent of those graduates became presidents of colleges. Nearly one-sixth of the 56 participants in the national Constitutional Convention of 1787 were Princeton graduates.

James Madison who would later become known as the "Father of the Constitution" and the fourth president of the United States was Witherspoon's most notable student. In addition to Madison, he taught a vice president, 21 senators, 29 representatives, 56 state legislators, and 33 judges, three of whom became members of the United States Supreme Court." (1) According to Richard B. Morris, Witherspoon was "most influential" in shaping Madison's world view. He called Witherspoon "a leading empiricist of his day...whose expositions of the doctrines of resistance and liberty quickly established him throughout the Continent as an imposing intellectual."

By many students of early American history, Witherspoon has been included among such notables as Samuel Rutherford, John Locke, and William Blackstone as the most powerful and influential minds that inordinately influenced the writing of the Constitution. All of them were strong believers in limited government and the rights of individuals, especially in the area of personal religious beliefs. Witherspoon's direct influence upon the formulation of the Constitution was also felt through sixteen members of the Constitutional Convention of 1787 who had studied under Witherspoon at Princeton.

Witherspoon and his fellow Popularists were inspired by John Calvin's affirmation of law and its relationship to Biblical precepts. Believing there was theological authority for participation in the political arena, orthodox Presbyterians, who were closely aligned in their thinking with the Puritans and the Westminster Confession of 1646, were nearly unanimous in supporting the American Revolution. Calvin's ideas regarding government, with which Witherspoon certainly agreed, are also credited with playing a role in shaping the American political structure, notably the establishment of checks and balances through separate and equal branches of government.

Many historians give Calvinism's influence on the principles and precepts that went into the eventual formation of the U. S. Constitution credit for keeping the American Revolution from turning into the kind of bloody fiasco that became known as the French Revolution a few years later. Calvinists understood it was important to balance the desire for freedom with an appreciation for the necessity of public orderliness. At the risk of over-simplification, it seems accurate to characterize the French Revolution as a civil war among an assortment of secular humanist factions over mostly materialistic issues. Religious issues, of which there were few, didn't seem to be the primary motivation of any of the disparate French revolutionary groups. There is little evidence of Biblical thinking among any of the competing ideologies in France which is in stark contrast with the factual history of the American Revolution.

Contrary to modern day history revisionists, there is overwhelming evidence that fundamentalist Christian teaching and preaching was the rule rather than the exception during the times preceding the beginning of the Revolutionary War and the ensuing period when the final form of our government was in its formative stages. In his well-researched and documented book entitled *They Preached Liberty*, Franklin P. Cole demolishes the proposition put forth by agenda-driven secular humanist revisionists who would have us believe the Bible and Christian precepts had nothing to do with our foundational beliefs.

In his preface, he points out that "The New England ministers are the forgotten heroes of the American Revolution. If they are pictured at all in the distorted imagination of the average citizen, they appear as witch hunters, or long winded exponents of an archaic theology, or as vigilantes snooping into the private lives of their parishioners – a divinely ordained Colonial Gestapo."

He goes on to say, "Their sermons and writings, their devotion to education and good government, their patriotic activities during the Revolution – all testify to the fact that 'there were giants in those days.' ... The Church today is vitally concerned with liberty. Whence does it originate? Is it a divine gift or an outmoded theory of human rationalism? What are the obligations of liberty, its types and results? The New England ministers answered these questions so wisely that their answers have contemporary significance. They preached when liberty was under fire, as is it today. While they cannot solve our problems for us, they can afford us insight and inspiration, perhaps even formulas and programs." (2)

Cole presents 170 pages of convincing proof, using direct quotes from sermons by the most prominent clergymen of that time who believed in a direct relationship between Christianity and personal freedom. Fundamentalist Christian thoughts and attitudes prevailed among the population in general.

"Witherspoon and most American political thinkers," wrote John Willson, "believed that society was antecedent to government; that is, social institutions, rooted in the family, village life, and voluntary associations, existed prior to government and took precedent over it. In practical terms, this meant that the commanding position of Christianity in American Society would allow religion to flourish as long as the civil government did nothing to interfere with it. That Americans were a Protestant Christian people was taken for granted by Witherspoon and most of his generation." (3)

Contrast that with the campaign today to marginalize Christianity through the use of one of the three branches of government, the judicial branch, by well-financed organizations such as the American Civil Liberties Union and others with similar goals. The government today *is indeed* interfering with the freedom to display symbols of the Christian religion and, to some extent, the freedom of speech of

Christians in general and Christian pastors in particular, especially with the help of the Internal Revenue Service thanks to some ill-advised and self-serving legislation sneaked through by President Lyndon B. Johnson.

Another area of major concern to Witherspoon was theatre, the primary source of entertainment available at that time. In his *Serious Enquiry into the Nature and Effects of the Stage*, Witherspoon said "The truth is, the need of amusement is much less than most people commonly apprehend, and where it is not necessary, it must be sinful." He didn't think the expense involved to both the promoters and the public were worth it in relation to any positive effect, if any, it might have. He questioned its educational value by asking why anything needs to be known unless it leads to our spiritual improvement. Today, a vast majority of responsible people could certainly agree with his statement that "no woman...who has been ten times in a playhouse durst repeat in company all that she has heard there," especially where movies and television "entertainment" are concerned. (4) It would be interesting to hear what Witherspoon would have to say about today's entertainment industry leaders and their total lack of corporate responsibility, not to mention an unbelievable deficit in common sense and decency.

Princeton under the leadership of Witherspoon was recognized as being more directed toward a Biblical attitude regarding liberty, while recognizing the need for personal responsibility, than were other prominent colleges of that time period. Under the Witherspoon presidency, a number of rules regarding worship were promulgated for the edification of the Princeton study body including: "Every student shall attend worship in the college hall morning and evening at the hours appointed and shall behave with gravity and reverence during the whole service. Every student shall attend public worship on the Sabbath."

Princeton is said to have had its origins in the revival of 1740's known as the Great Awakening, generally recognized as America's greatest spiritual revival. Many prominent pastors with connections to Princeton were active in the Great Awakening including Jonathan Dickinson, Aaron Burr, Sr., Jonathan Edwards, Samuel Davies and Samuel Finley. (5) Dickinson, Princeton's first president, was quoted as saying, "Cursed be all that learning that is contrary to the cross of Christ."

In a sermon delivered just prior to his election to the First Continental Congress, Witherspoon completed his remarks with this admonition:

> *Upon the whole, I beseech you to make a wise improve-ment of the present threatening aspect of public affairs, and to remember that your duty to God, to our country, to your families, and to yourselves, is the same. True religion is nothing else but an inward temper and outward conduct suited to your state and circumstances in providence at any time. And as peace with God and conformity to him, adds to him, adds to the sweetness of created comforts while we possess them, so in times of difficulty and trial, it is in the man of piety and inward principle, that we may expect to find the uncorrupted patriot, the useful citizen, and the invincible soldier. God grant that in America true religion and civil liberty may be inseparable, and that the unjust attempts to destroy the one, may in the issue tend to the support and establishment of both. (6)*

Did Reverend John Witherspoon believe in the separation of church and state? Yes, in the sense that he was absolutely opposed to the establishment of a state controlled church. He was just as absolutely opposed to the idea that the church had no business in the political arena. Nor would he have accepted the idea that symbols of Christianity should be hidden from public view. The fairly recently discovered right "not to be offended" wouldn't have survived the laugh test with Witherspoon. That some citizens of his adopted country would someday be offended by the public display of any of the symbols of Christianity would have been unthinkable to him and to every one of the Founding Fathers.

He believed freedom and religion depended upon each other and said so in many of his widely reproduced sermons including this one: "There is not a single instance in history, in which civil liberty was lost, and religious liberty preserved entire." As he knew from his study of history, and as confirmed by a study of more recent world events, loss of freedom, i.e. becoming subject to a foreign power such as the colonies faced in relation to the mother country had they succumbed, always results in the loss of religious freedom and he couldn't stand by idly and let that happen to his adopted country.

When he spoke of religion, he was referring to Christianity in particular since it has been estimated that 99% of the people living in the colonies at that time professed to be Christians. He also said "civil liberty cannot be long preserved without virtue." It is clear from his writings that the virtues he was talking about were those defined and illustrated in the Judeo-Christian Bible.

"Whoever is an avowed enemy of God," Witherspoon said, "I scruple not to call him an enemy of his country." Should we consider people and organizations who want to take God out of our schools, out of politics, out of our legal system, and out of public view "avowed enemies of God?" As Americans concerned for the future of our country, that is a question we need to ask ourselves. Judging from the actions and belief systems of modern day humanists, what else should we consider them? From their own words, we know the Founding Fathers would have answered that question in the affirmative.

Witherspoon also said, "A republic once equally poised [independently established] must either preserve its virtue or lose its liberty." Those who want to marginalize God in today's America see no connection between virtue and liberty. They want God out of their way; the idea of having to answer to a higher power gets in the way of their preferred lifestyles which would have been anathema to Witherspoon and the other founders.

Prior to commencement of armed conflict in the war for independence, Witherspoon, as part of a group of like-minded ministers, encouraged those who would become directly involved in hostilities with these words: "[T]here is no soldier so undaunted as the pious man, no army so formidable as those who are superior to the fear of death. There is nothing more awful to think of than that those whose trade is war should be despisers of the name of the Lord of hosts and that they should expose themselves to the imminent danger of being immediately sent from cursing and cruelty on earth to the blaspheming rage and despairing horror of the infernal pit. Let therefore everyone who...offers himself as a champion in his country's cause be persuaded to reverence the name and walk in the fear of the Prince of the kings of the earth; and then he may with the most unshaken firmness expect the issue [God's protection] either in victory or death." (7)

Regarding the importance of electing men or women of character to public office, Witherspoon made this often disregarded piece of advice in today's elections: "Those who wish well to the State ought to choose to places of trust men of inward principle, justified by exemplary conversation. Is it reasonable to expect wisdom from the ignorant? [F]idelity from the profligate? [A]ssiduity and application to public business from one living a dissipated life? Is it reasonable to commit the management of public revenue to one who hath wasted his own patrimony? Those, therefore, who pay no regard to religion and sobriety in the persons whom they send to the legislature of any State are guilty of the greatest absurdity and will soon pay dear for their folly."

"He is the best friend to American liberty who is most sincere and active in promoting true and undefiled religion, and who set himself with the greatest firmness to bear down profanity and immorality of every kind," Witherspoon said. Those who are campaigning to marginalize Christianity are doing everything in their power to undercut the teaching of John Witherspoon and most of the other Founding Fathers; the secular humanists' mission is to do anything *but* promote true and undefiled religion.

Witherspoon would be aghast at the routine incivility and coarseness of today's post-Christian society. "Nothing is more certain," Witherspoon said, "than that a general profligacy and corruption of manners make a people ripe for destruction. A good form of government may hold the rotten materials together for some time, but beyond a certain pitch, even the best constitution will be ineffectual, and slavery must ensue."

Historian B. J. Lossing ended his essay on the life of Witherspoon with this fitting description: "As a theological writer, Doctor Witherspoon had few superiors, and as a statesman he held the first rank. In him were centered the social elements of an upright citizen, a fond parent, a just tutor, and humble Christian; and when, on the tenth of November, 1794, at the age of nearly seventy-three years, his useful life closed, it was widely felt that a 'great man had fallen in Israel'."

It is clear from the study of founder John Witherspoon's own words that he would be calling for revival in America today, not a diminishing Christian influence and certainly not a diminishing of the instillation of Christian principles in our education system. Rather than allowing the Bible to be hidden behind church doors, Witherspoon would be demanding that the Bible be restored to its rightful place of honor and authority in our society.

Chapter Five

John Adams

*The man to whom the country is most indebted for
the great measure of independence is Mr. John Adams
… I call him the Atlas of American independence.
He it was who sustained the debate,
and by force of his reasoning demonstrated
not only the justice, but the expediency of the measure.*
**-- Richard Stockton,
delegate to the Second Continental Congress**

*And now, O Lord, my God,
Thou hast made Thy servant (John Adams)
ruler over the people. Give unto him an understanding heart,
that he may know how to go out and come in before this great
people; that he may discern between good and bad.
For who is able to judge this Thy so great a people.*
(Based on 1 Kings: 3:7-9)
**-- Abigail Adams' prayer in a letter to
her husband dated February 8, 1779**

It was with more than adequate reason that Richard Stockton referred to John Adams, who was to become the second president of the United States (1797-1801), as "the Atlas of American Independence." Adams did indeed bear a heavy burden as one of the Titans shaping and supporting the world-shaking events that led to freedom and independence for the world's first decolonized country.

Recognized by his colleagues as a man of extraordinary integrity, Adams was one of five men chosen to draft *The Declaration of Independence* along with Thomas Jefferson, Benjamin Franklin, Roger Sherman, and Robert R. Livingston. It was Adams who insisted that Jefferson produce the original draft after the committee members narrowed it down to the two of them. After Jefferson wrote the declaration, Adams became its articulate and passionate presenter when it was unveiled to the assembled members of the Second Continental Congress.

It was also Adams who nominated George Washington to be Commander in Chief of the Continental Army, one of the most, if not *the* most, important decisions of the movement for independence.

Add to the superlatives applied to Adams the word *colossus*, a word selected by his friend Thomas Jefferson to describe him following a particularly moving and effective speech delivered by Adams on the floor of the Second Continental Congress in support of independence. Adams said in that speech:

> *The second day of July, 1776, will be the most memorable epoch in the history of America, to be celebrated by succeeding generations as the great anniversary festival, commemorated as the day of deliverance by solemn acts of devotion to God Almighty from one end of the Continent to the other, from this time forward forevermore. You will think me transported with enthusiasm, but I am not. I am well aware of the toil, the blood, and treasure that it will cost us to maintain this Declaration and support and defend these states; yet, through all the gloom, I can see the rays of light and glory; that the end is worth all the means; that posterity will triumph in that day's transaction, even though we shall rue it, which I trust in God we shall not." (1)*

The *Declaration of Independence* was proclaimed that day although it wasn't signed until July 4, a day which he said in a letter to his wife "will be celebrated by succeeding generations, as the great anniversary festival. It ought to be commemorated as the day of deliverance...with pomp and parade, with... guns, bells, bonfires, and illuminations, from one end of this continent to the other..."

Adams was named by Congress to be chairman of the Board of War and Ordnance, the committee responsible for conducting the Revolutionary War.

Renowned for the power of his intellect and the quality of his writing, Adams has been labeled by some as *the mind* of the Revolution. Summing up the important role Adams played in the formation of our republic, Bradley Thompson wrote, "Adams witnessed the American Revolution from beginning to end: In 1761 he assisted James Otis in defending Boston merchants against enforcement of Britain's Sugar Act. Gradually, Adams became a key leader of the radical political movement in Boston and one of the earliest and most principled voices for independence at the Continental Congress. Likewise, as a public intellectual, he wrote some of the most important and influential essays, constitutions, and treatises of the Revolutionary period movement. John Adams exemplifies the *mind* of the American Revolution." (2)

Adams was born October 19, 1735 in Quincy (formerly Braintree), Massachusetts, where he received his primary and secondary schooling. Entering Harvard at the age of 16, he graduated in 1755 at which time, he became a teacher while continuing to study law. Originally intending to enter the clergy, Adams began his law practice in Braintree before moving on to Boston where he became acquainted with men of standing and influence with whom he would later be heavily engaged in the movement leading to independence. During those years leading up to the Revolutionary War, Adams had established himself as one of the Colonies most respected constitutional scholars.

His marriage to Abigail Smith in 1764 produced five children, one of whom, John Quincy Adams, was to become our sixth president. During their 54 year marriage, Abigail was a strong source of support for her husband's activities in service to his country as evinced by many of her writings that have also become historical documents that shed much light on the times and circumstances in which they lived. Between 1774 and 1784, they exchanged more than 300 letters. The daughter of a minister, Abigail's writings reflected her strong belief's in the God of Israel to which she often referred as in this letter to her husband dated June 18, 1775:

> *The race is not to the swift, nor the battle to the strong; but the God of Israel is He that giveth strength and power unto His people. Trust in Him at all times, ye people, pour out your hearts before Him; God is a refuge for us. (3)*

In a letter to her husband dated June 20, 1776, she wrote:

> *I feel no anxiety at the large armament designed against us. The remarkable interpositions of heaven in our favor cannot be too gratefully acknowledged. He who fed the Israelites in the wilderness, who clothes the lilies of the field and who feeds the young ravens when they cry, will not forsake a people engaged in so right a cause, if we remember His loving kindness. (4)*

Her knowledge of the Bible and her devotion to it were a source of confidence and mental strength to her husband during these trying times. Adams letters to his wife make it clear they shared a devotion to God's word as illustrated in this letter to Abigail:

> *We went to meeting at Wells and had the pleasure of hearing my friend upon "Be not partakers in other men's sins. Keep yourselves pure." Mr. Hemmenway came and kindly invited us to dine, but we had engaged a dinner at Littlefield's, so we returned there, dined, and took our horses to the meeting in the afternoon and heard the minister again upon "Seek first the kingdom of God and his righteousness, and all these things shall be added unto you." There is great pleasure in hearing sermons so serious, so clear, so sensible and instructive as these. (5)*

John and Abigail were members of the Congregational Church at Brattle Square in Boston. When in Philadelphia, Adams, along with Benjamin Rush, regularly attended worship services at the Old Pine Presbyterian Church where they enjoyed the Biblical sermons of Reverend George Duffield who openly supported the American Revolution. In 1776, Rev. Duffield was named Chaplain to the Continental Congress.

While Adams supported the growing resistance to the British government in the early 1770s, he generally was in favor of reconciliation with Britain. That changed irrevocably in December 1773 following the Boston Tea Party. From that point on, Adams was staunchly committed to the cause of American independence. By 1774, Adams urged his fellow Americans to adopt "revolution principles," a resolve to do what had to be done in order to guarantee American rights and liberties.

As a member of the Second Continental Congress that convened in May 1775 in Philadelphia, Adams and others advocated for mobilizing for war and to establish an official confederation of colonies. The New England militiamen would become the basis for an army. The Continental Army was established by the Congress and George Washington was chosen to be its commanding general. Later, Adams was able to get a resolution passed by Congress directing the colonies to form their own independent governments. (6)

After serving nearly two years as a member of the diplomatic mission to France in 1777, Adams returned to his home in Massachusetts where, in 1779, he played a leading role in the state constitutional convention that produced the Massachusetts Constitution, a document which became a model for a number of other states constitutions and was influential in shaping the thinking of those who produced the Federal Constitution of 1787. He, along with Benjamin Franklin and John Jay, drafted the final peace treaty with England. Adams is also recognized as the father of the U. S. Navy; the Department of the Navy was created by Congress at his urging in 1798.

Adams was first elected Vice President of the United States in 1789 by members of the Electoral College, finishing second to George Washington in total number of votes cast. According to the system in place at that time, the person receiving the most votes became President and the person receiving the next highest number of votes became Vice President. Adams served two terms as Vice President under Washington. As originally conceived, the office of Vice President was intended primarily as a means of providing a successor in the event of the President's death or incapacitation. The industrious Adams called the vice presidency "the most insignificant office that ever the invention of man contrived."

When Washington decided not to run for a third term in 1796, Adams, Thomas Jefferson, Aaron Burr, and Thomas Pinckney each declared their candidacy. Adams and Pinckney were Federalists while Jefferson and Burr were Republicans, a party which was later to become known as the Democratic-Republican Party. They were also known as anti-Federalists because of their opposition to what they considered to be too much centralization of power in a national government. The election of 1796 was, for all practical purposes, the beginning of our two party political system, an approach opposed by Washington who didn't like the idea of dividing the country into partisan groups.

As winner of the largest number of electoral votes, Adams became the second President of the United States. Jefferson, recipient of the second largest number, became Vice President, the only time in our history when we have had a president and vice president from opposing political parties.

Adams was the first president to reside in the White House although it wasn't officially known by that name until 1901 when Theodore Roosevelt made it official. Adams was inaugurated March 4, 1797, in Philadelphia before the nation's capital was moved to Washington, D.C. in November, 1800, even though work on the White House was not yet completed. The day after his arrival at the White House, Adams wrote a letter to Abigail in which he included the following prayer: "I Pray Heaven to bestow THE BEST OF BLESSINGS ON This House and All that shall hereafter Inhabit it, May no one but Honest and Wise Men ever rule under This Roof." This prayer can still be seen engraved upon the mantel of the White House State Dining Room.

After Adams lost the election of 1800 to Jefferson, the two Founding Fathers became fierce rivals until their reconciliation in 1812 when they began a correspondence that has been recognized as one that is "unquestionably the most impressive in the history of American letters." (7) Both men died July 4, 1826, within hours of each other.

The writings of John Adams attest to his devotion to principle, integrity, and self control. Weakness of character was anathema to him and he placed great demands on himself to conform to his high ideals. Self improvement was an important goal from early in life as illustrated by this entry in his journal: "I resolve to rise with the Sun and to study the Scriptures, on Thursday, Fryday, Saturday, and Sunday mornings, and to study some Latin author the other 3 morning. Noons and Nights I intend to read English Authors. This is my fixt Determination, and I will set down every neglect and every compliance with this Resolution. May I blush whenever I suffer one hour to pass unimproved." (8)

Evidence of John Adams' strong belief in the importance of the Christian religion and Biblical principles as the foundation upon which the United States of America rests appears over and over again in his writings. For example, an entry in his *Diary* dated July 26, 1796, said, "The Christian religion is, above all the Religions that ever prevailed or existed in ancient or modern Times, the Religion of Wisdom, Virtue, Equity, and humanity, let the Blackguard [Thomas] Payne say what he will; it is Resignation to God, it is Goodness itself to Man." (9)

On another occasion, Adams said, "Suppose a nation in some distant region should take the Bible for their only law book and every member should regulate his conduct by the precepts there exhibited...What a Eutopia, what a Paradise would this region be." (10)

Again, regarding the Bible, he said, "I have examined all [religions]...and the result is that the Bible is the best Book in the world. It contains more of my little philosophy than all the libraries I have seen." (11)

"The general principles on which the fathers achieved independence were...the general principles of Christianity," Adams said. "I will avow that I then believed, and now believe, that those general principles of Christianity are as eternal and immutable as the existence and attributes of God; and that those principles of liberty are as unalterable as human nature," (12)

In a letter to Abigail dated December 15, 1777, Adams expressed his belief in God's protective care for America: "I have had many opportunities in the course of this journey to observe how deeply rooted our righteous cause is in the minds of the people...One evening as I sat in one room, I overheard a company of the common sort of people in another [room] conversing upon serious subjects... At length I heard these words: 'It appears to me the eternal Son of God is operating powerfully against the British nation for their treating lightly serious things'." (13)

Reflecting his concurrence with that generally held belief, Adams said, "As the safety and prosperity of nations ultimately and essentially depend on the protection and the blessing of Almighty God, and on the national acknowledgment of this truth is not only an indispensable duty which the people owe to Him...I have therefore thought fit to recommend...a day of solemn humiliation, fasting, and prayer that the citizens of these [United] States...offer their devout addresses to the Father of Mercies." (14)

Evidence of the Founders' belief in God and His divinely-inspired Judeo-Christian Bible is to be found in thousands and thousands of pages of eye witness history available in libraries throughout the land. Secular humanists wear themselves out rewriting early American history in a misguided effort to convince the unsuspecting and the ill-informed that the United States of America has no Christian roots. In a letter written to Abigail dated 16 September, 1774, Adams recounted this experience:

When the Congress first met, Mr. Cushing made a motion that it should be opened with prayer. It was opposed by Mr. Jay, of New York, and Mr. Rutledge of South Carolina, because we were so divided in religious sentiments, some Episcopalians, some Quakers, some Anabaptists, some Presbyterians, and some Congregationalists, that we could not join the same act of worship. Mr. Samuel Adams arose and said he was no bigot, and could hear a prayer from a gentleman of piety and virtue, who was at the same time a friend to his country. He was a stranger in Philadelphia, but had heard that Mr. Duche (Dushay they pronounce it) deserved that character, and therefore he moved that Mr. Duche, an Episcopal clergyman, might be desired to read prayers to the Congress, tomorrow morning. The motion was seconded and passed in the affirmative. Mr. Randolph, our president waited on Mr. Duche, and received for an answer that if his health would permit he certainly would. Accordingly, next morning he appeared with his clerk and in his pontificals, and read several prayers in the established form; and then read the Collect for the seventh day of September, which was the thirty-fifth Psalm. You must remember this was the next morning after we heard the horrible rumor of the cannonade of Boston. I never saw a greater effect upon an audience. It seemed as if Heaven had ordained that Psalm to be read on that morning.

After this Mr. Duche, unexpected to everybody, struck out into an extemporary prayer, which filled the bosom of every man present. I must confess I never heard a better prayer, or one so well pronounced. Episcopalian as he is, Dr. Cooper himself (Dr. Samuel Cooper, well known as a zealous patriot and pastor of the church in Brattle Square, Boston) never prayed with such fervor, such earnestness and pathos, and in language so elegant and sublime – for America, for Congress, for the Province of Massachusetts Bay, and especially the town of Boston. It has had an excellent effect upon everybody here. I must beg you to read that Psalm. If there was any faith In the Sortes Biblicae, it would be thought providential.

It will amuse your friends to read this letter and the thirty-fifth Psalm to them. Read it to your father and Mr. Wibird. I wonder what our Braintree Churchmen will think of this! Mr. Duche is one of the most ingenious men, and best characters, and greatest orators in the Episcopal order, upon this continent. Yet a zealous friend of Liberty and his country. (15)

Psalm 35, thought by those who heard it used as a prayer during the critical period of time leading up to the Revolutionary War, was timely, indeed. Read it again with their circumstances in mind:

Contend, O Lord, with those who contend with me;
Fight against those who fight against me.
Take hold of buckler and shield,
And rise up for my help.
Draw also the spear and the battle-axe to meet those who
    pursue me;
Say to my soul, "I am your salvation."
Let those be ashamed and dishonored who seek my life;
Let those be turned back and humiliated who devise evil
    against me.
Let them be like chaff before the wind,
With the angel of the Lord driving them on.
Let their way be dark and slippery,
With the angel of the Lord pursuing them.
For without cause they hid their net for me;
Without cause they dug a pit for my soul.
Let destruction come upon him, unawares;
And let the net which he hid catch himself;
Into that very destruction let him fall.
And my soul shall rejoice in the Lord;
It shall exult in His salvation.
All my bones will say,
"Lord, who is like Thee,
Who delivers the afflicted from him who is too strong for
    him,
And the afflicted and the needy from him who robs him?"
Malicious witnesses rise up:
They ask me of things I do not know.
They repay me evil for good,
To the bereavement of my soul.
But as for me, when they were sick, my clothing was
    sackcloth;
I humbled my soul with fasting;

And my prayer kept returning to by bosom.
I went about as though it were my friend or brother;
I bowed down mourning, as one who sorrows for a mother.
But at my stumbling they rejoiced, and gathered themselves
*   together;*
The smiters whom I did know gathered together against me.
They slandered me without ceasing.
Like godless jesters at a feast,
They gnashed at me with their teeth.
Lord, how long wilt Thou look on?
Rescue my soul from their ravages,
My only life from the lions.
I will give Thee thanks in the great congregation;
I will praise Thee among a mighty throng.
Do not let those who are wrongfully my enemies rejoice over
*   me;*
Neither let those who hate me without cause wink
*   maliciously.*
For they do not speak peace,
But they devise deceitful words against those who are quiet
*   in the land.*
And they opened their mouth wide against me;
They said, "Aha, aha, our eyes have seen it!"
Thou hast seen it, O Lord, do not keep silent;
O Lord, do not be far from me.
Stir up Thyself, and awake to my right,
And to my cause, my God and my Lord.
Judge me, O Lord my God, according to Thy righteousness;
And do not let them rejoice over me.
Do not let them say in their heart, "Aha, our desire!"
Do not let them say, "We have swallowed him up!"
Let those be ashamed and humiliated altogether who rejoice
*   at my distress;*
Let those be clothed with shame and dishonor who magnify
*   themselves over me.*
Let them shout for joy and rejoice, who favor my
*   vindication;*

And let them say continually, "The Lord be magnified,
Who delights in the prosperity of His servant."
And my tongue shall declare Thy righteousness
And Thy praise all day long."

As was true, according to their own recorded words, of the vast majority of those known as Founding Fathers, John Adams left no doubt of his Christian beliefs. In a letter to Thomas Jefferson after the death of Abigail, he said, "That you and I shall meet in a better world I have no doubt than we now exist on the same globe; if my reason did not convince me of this, Cicero's Dream of Scipio, and his Essay on Friendship and Old Age would have been sufficient for that purpose. But Jesus taught us that a future state is a social state, when He promised to prepare places in His Father's house of many mansions, for His disciples." (16)

John Adams unquestionably considered himself one of Jesus' disciples.

Chapter Six

Thomas Jefferson

*My views…are the result of a life of inquiry and reflection,
and very different from the anti-Christian system
imputed to me by those who know nothing of my opinions.
To the corruptions of Christianity I am, indeed opposed;
but not to the genuine precepts of Jesus himself.
I am a Christian in the only sense
in which he wished any one to be; sincerely attached
to his doctrines in preference to all others.* (1)
-- Thomas Jefferson

Thomas Jefferson's own words, as shown above and in many other direct quotations, fly in the face of secular humanists' insistence that their favorite Founding Father was a deist rather than a Christian. The history revisionists who would separate us from our Christian roots have targeted the Founding Fathers, especially Thomas Jefferson, as a strategy in advancing their dishonest, agenda-driven campaign. "No great American," says historian Clyde N. Wilson, "has been put to so many contradictory uses by later generations of enemies and apologists, and therefore none has undergone so much distortion. In fact, most of what has been asserted about Jefferson in the last hundred years – and even more of what has been implied or assumed about him – is so lacking in context and proportion as to be essentially false. What we commonly see is not Jefferson. It is a strange amalgam or composite in which the misconceptions of each succeeding generation have been combined until the original is no longer discernible."

It makes much more sense to base our understanding of Jefferson's religious and political beliefs on what he said about himself rather than what others of questionable motives would have us believe. Convincing evidence of his Christian beliefs and his lifestyle based on those beliefs can be found in many of his public utterances. For instance, Jefferson, in a National Prayer for Peace delivered March 4, 1805, said:

> *Almighty God, Who has given us this good land for our heritage; We humbly beseech Thee that we may always prove ourselves a people mindful of Thy favor and glad to do Thy will. Bless our land with honorable ministry, sound learning, and pure manners.*
>
> *Save us from violence, discord, and confusion, from pride and arrogance, and from every evil way. Defend our liberties, and fashion into one united people the multitude brought hither out of many kindreds and tongues.*
>
> *Endow with Thy spirit of wisdom those to whom in Thy Name we entrust the authority of government, that there may be justice and peace at home, and through obedience to Thy Law, we may show forth Thy praise among the nations of the earth.*
>
> *In time of prosperity fill our hearts with thankfulness, and in the day of trouble, suffer not our trust in Thee to fail; all of which we ask through Jesus Christ our Lord, Amen. (2)*

In the first paragraph of the Declaration of Independence, Jefferson wrote: "WHEN in the Course of human Events, it becomes necessary for one People to dissolve the Political Bonds which have connected them with another, and to assume among the Powers of the Earth, the separate and equal Station to which the Laws of Nature and of Nature's God entitle them…"

Notice, he didn't say *the Great Spirit*. He didn't say *the force*. He didn't say *the man upstairs*. He said *Nature's God*. The people of his day, especially his fellow Founders, knew he was referring to the Judeo-Christian God of the Bible. At the time of the Revolutionary War, the people of the United States were said to be 99% Christian. The anti-Christian history revisionists of recent vintage also understand to whom Jefferson was referring, but they would rather stick a fork in their eye than admit it.

On many other occasions, Jefferson mentioned an engaged God in his speeches and correspondence including this testimony: "There is a God who presides above the destinies of nations." Deists believe no such thing. According to the dictionary definition, a deist is one who denies the involvement of the Creator with the operation of His creation. If Jefferson were a deist, why would he refer to "a God who *presides* above the nations"? He obviously believed that God took an interest in His creation and that He influenced the outcome of history. He believed in a presiding God who could be called upon and who controlled "the destinies of nations."

At times during his life, Jefferson was quoted as saying he doubted the doctrine of the Triune God which puts him in the company of many Christians who have sometimes questioned the Trinity and other basic Christian doctrine. Secular humanists who use those occasional statements as proof that Jefferson was not a Christian ignore this straight forward statement: "A more beautiful or precious morsel of ethics [the Bible] I have never seen; it is a document in proof that I am a real Christian; that is to say, a disciple of the doctrines of Jesus." (3)

Throughout his presidency, Jefferson signed all official documents "In the year of our Lord." A deist couldn't say that. Many biographers have mentioned the fact that Jefferson made it a daily practice to pray and read his Bible, activities not usually associated with deists who would find such activities a waste of time. Later in his life, he served on the vestry of the Anglican Church, a position similar to that of an Elder in many modern day denominations. It was Jefferson who recommended that the Great Seal of the United States depict a Bible story and include the word "God" in the national motto.(4)

Those quotations, and many more, from the mouth of Thomas Jefferson represent a strange choice of words for anyone but a Christian and would definitely separate him from the definition of a deist. Those who continually label Jefferson a deist, in my opinion, don't know the definition of the term they so loosely toss around.

Secular humanists, who try to back up their self-serving assertions by labeling Jefferson an atheist, an infidel, a skeptic, and an infrequent church attendee, ignore evidence to the contrary including the factual history of his documented regular attendance of worship services his entire life, having been born into a devout Anglican family. Many of the Christian church services he attended while in Washington were held in courthouses, the chambers of the U. S. House of Representatives, and the Capitol Rotunda, with music often supplied, at Jefferson's request, by the U. S. Marine Corps Band. He approved money out of the Federal Treasury for the support of a Christian missionary program to the Indians and for the construction of a Christian church in which they could worship. A common statement made about Jefferson was that he cut accounts of Jesus' miracles out of his Bible, but an accurate reading of history shows that Jefferson, who had a considerable concern for the Indians, used clippings from a Bible to create a book on the ethics and morals of Jesus as a teaching tool to be used to help civilize and educate them.

In his *American Government Supplemental Mini-Course*, Charley Morasch pointed out that Jefferson, as President of the United State and head of the Washington D.C. public school system, had mandated only two books for the classroom ... the Bible and a hymnbook." He described the Bible as "the cornerstone of liberty," and as "the rock on which our republic rests." No intellectually honest person can believe that Jefferson, regardless of his misinterpreted "separation of church and state" remark, would side today with those who want the Bible to disappear from public view or discount its' influence in public policy. That letter, it is instructive to understand, was written in 1802, thirteen years after Congress passed the First Amendment to the Constitution.

Evidence of Jefferson's true intentions regarding the now famous "separation of church and state" phrase, which first appeared in a letter the purpose of which was to assure a Baptist congregation that there would be no state sponsored denomination, can be found throughout his writings. Along with the other Founders involved in producing the First Amendment, he clearly intended for the government to be *completely* neutral where religious issues were concerned. Evidence is incontrovertible that Jefferson never imagined a time when the church would not be looked to for moral and ethical leadership.

Justice Joseph Story, who is recognized as an authority on the Constitution and the framers, wrote, in his *Commentaries on the Constitution of the United States,* "The real object of the First Amendment was not to countenance, much less advance, Mohammedanism, or Judaism, or infidelity, by prostrating Christianity; but to exclude all rivalry among Christian sects, and to prevent any national ecclesiastical establishment which should give to a hierarchy the exclusive patronage of the national government. It thus cut off the means of religious persecution (the vice and pest of former ages), and the subversion of the rights of conscience in matters of religion which had been trampled upon almost from the days of the Apostles to the present age…" (5)

Incongruous with assertions of secular humanist propagandists, the words "separation of church and state" are not now and never were part of the US Constitution or the First Amendment. They do, however, appear in the constitution of the former USSR from which many American Civil Liberties Union supporters seem to receive their inspiration. That unfortunate phrase may have had its roots in a letter written years earlier by Roger Williams who wrote: "… (W)hen they have opened a gap in the hedge or *wall of separation* between the garden of the church and the wilderness of the world, God hath ever broke down the wall itself, removed the candlestick, and made his garden a wilderness, as at this day. And that therefore if He will ever please to restore His garden and paradise again, it must of necessity be walled in peculiarly unto Himself from the world." (6) In other words, the church must not allow the world to corrupt its' holiness which is what is happening today. Liberal theology, as championed by the ACLU, is corrupting the church and tragically misleading millions of confused and uninformed people.

Those who continually attempt to reverse the meaning of the First Amendment in order to promote their own nefarious agenda ignore this lesser known unambiguous statement by Jefferson: "I consider the government of the United States as interdicted by the Constitution from intermeddling with religious institutions, their doctrines, discipline, or exercises. This results not only from the provision that no law shall be made respecting the establishment or free exercise of religion, but from that also which reserves to the states the powers not delegated to the United States. Clearly, no power to prescribe any religious exercise, or to assume authority in religious discipline, has been delegated to the general government." How much more clearly can Jefferson's true feelings about religious freedom be stated? (7)

His writings contain so many references to the rightful place of religion, especially the Judeo-Christian religion, in government that the secularists have nothing to stand on except their perverted version of the First Amendment. "Religion, Jefferson said, "deemed in other countries incompatible with good government proved by our experience to be its best support." On another occasion, he said, "It yet remains a problem to be solved in human affairs, whether any free government can be permanent, where the public worship of God, and the support of religion, constitutes no part of the policy or duty of the state in any assignable shape."

"God" he said, "who gave us life gave us liberty. And can the liberties of a nation be thought secure when we have removed their only firm basis, a conviction in the minds of the people that these liberties are the gift of God? That they are not to be violated but with His wrath? Indeed, I tremble for my country when I reflect that God is just; that His justice cannot sleep forever."

So much for Jefferson's alleged devotion to the phony issue of separation of church as preached today by the ACLU and other radical anti-Christian organizations. These organizations have had some success in convincing many unenlightened and gullible people that the First Amendment means freedom *from* religion rather than freedom *of* religion. Jefferson and the other Founders wouldn't agree with the ACLU; they clearly intended the First Amendment to guarantee freedom to worship, to speak freely about their beliefs, and to publicly display symbols of their religion.

"When secularists talk about separation of church and state today, they are always talking about what churches can't do, what ministers can't do, what Christians can't do, what religious people can't do. They've completely turned it around, so instead of protecting the people from the government, now it's protecting the government from any religious people which is a total reversal of the meaning of the first Amendment," Dr. D. James Kennedy wrote in a pamphlet entitled "Returning to Our Roots."

Backing up Dr. Kennedy's accurate observation is this statement by President Ronald Reagan, "To those who cite the First Amendment as reason for excluding God from more and more of our institutions every day, I say: The First Amendment of the Constitution was not written to protect the people of this country from religious values; it was written to protect religious values from government tyranny."

In commenting on the *Wallace vs. Jaffree* case in 1985, then Supreme Court Justice William Rehnquist stated his opinion on the true purpose of the First Amendment: "The Framers intended the Establishment Clause to prohibit the designation of any church as a 'national' one." Elsewhere in his remarks, Rehnquist said, "There is simply no historical foundation for the proposition that the framers intended to build a wall of separation [between church and state]... The recent court decisions are in no way based on either the language or intent of the framers."

The campaign currently conducted by the ACLU clearly has as its purpose the marginalizing of Christianity because Christianity stands imposingly in the way of their secular humanist, that is to say "Godless" agenda for the United States of America. Separating Jefferson and the other Founding Fathers from their Christian approach to life and to government is part of their strategy.

Born in 1743, Jefferson began his formal education at the age of 5, studied Latin, Greek, and French under Reverend William Douglas at the age of 9, studied classical literature and other languages under Reverend James Maury at the age of 14, and entered the College of William and Mary, a Christian college, at the age of 16. After graduating from W&M at the age of 19, he entered into a five-year study of the law under George Wythe.

First elected to public office at the age of 25, Jefferson represented Albemarle County in the Virginia House of Burgesses. Seven years later, he was selected as a delegate to the Second Continental Congress. One year later, at the age of 33, he authored the Declaration of Independence.

Jefferson was elected Governor of Virginia at the age of 36. Four years later, he was elected to Congress where he served for two years before succeeding Benjamin Franklin as American minister to France. He was appointed by George Washington as the first Secretary of State in 1789 at the age of 46 where he served for four years before returning to his Virginia home. He was elected Vice President of the United States in 1797 and third President of the United States in 1801 where he served two terms. During his first term, he oversaw the Louisiana Purchase which more than doubled the U. S. land area. At the age of 81, Jefferson served as the first president of the University of Virginia of which he has been recognized as the primary force in its founding. Quite a resume.

Throughout his life, Jefferson was considered by those who knew him best to be a man of the highest moral character. Excerpts from a letter, written by Thomas Jefferson Randolph, his grandson, to biographer Henry S. Randall, provide eye witness glimpses into the personal life and character of Thomas Jefferson:

Dear Sir: In compliance with your request, I have committed to paper my reminiscences of Mr. Jefferson as they, still green and fresh in my memory, have occurred to me.

I was thirty-four years old when he died. My mother was his oldest and, for the last twenty-two years of his life, his only child. She lived with him from her birth to his death, except in his absence on public service at Philadelphia and Washington. Having lost her mother at ten years [of age], she was his inseparable companion until her marriage; he had sought to supply her loss with all the watchful solicitude of a mother's tenderness. Her children were to him as the younger members of his family, having lived with him from their infancy. . .

I was more intimate with him than with any man I have ever known. His character invited such intimacy – soft and feminine in his affections to his family, he entered into and sympathized with all their feelings, winning them to paths of virtue by the soothing gentleness of his manner.

His private apartments were open to me at all times; I saw him under all circumstances. While he lived, and since, I have reviewed with severe scrutiny those interviews, and I must say that I never heard from him the expression of one thought, feeling, or sentiment inconsistent with the highest moral standard, or the purest Christian charity in its most enlarged sense. His moral character was of the highest order, founded upon the purest and sternest models of antiquity, [but] softened, chastened, and developed by the influences of the all pervading benevolence of the doctrines of Christ – which he had intensely and admiringly studied.

As proof of this, he left two codifications of the morals of Jesus – one for himself, and another for the Indians. The first of [these] I now possess, [namely] a blank volume, red morocco gilt, [and] lettered on the back, "The Morals of Jesus," into which he pasted extracts in Greek, Latin, French, and English, taken textually from the four Gospels, and so arranged that he could run his eye over the readings of the same verse in four languages.

The boldness and self-confidence of his mind was the best guaranty of his truthfulness. He never uttered an untruth himself, or used duplicity, and he condemned it in others. No end, with him, could sanctify falsehood.

In his contemplative moments his mind turned to religion, which he studied thoroughly. He had seen and read much of the abuses and perversions of Christianity; he abhorred those abuses and their authors, and denounced them without reserve. He was regular in his attendance [at] church, taking his prayer book with him. . . A gentleman of some distinction calling on him and expressing his disbelief in the truths of the Bible, his reply was, "Then, sir, you have studied it to little purpose."

He was guilty of no profanity himself, and did not tolerate it in others. He detested impiety, and his favorite quotation for his young friends, as a basis for their morals, was the 15th psalm of David...

His family, by whom he was surrounded, and who saw him in all the unguarded privacy of private life, believed him to be the purest of men. His precepts were those of truth and virtue. "Be just, be true, love your neighbor as yourself, and your country more than yourself" were among his favorite maxims, and they recognized in him a truthful exemplar of the precepts he taught. (8)

Jefferson's favorite Psalm seems to well describe the way he lived:

Lord, who may abide in your tabernacle?
Who may dwell in Your holy hill?
He who walks uprightly, and works righteousness,
And speaks the truth in his heart;
He who does not backbite with his tongue,
Nor does evil to his neighbor,
Nor does he take up a reproach against his friend;
In whose eyes a vile person is despised,
But he honors those who fear the Lord;
He who swears to his own hurt and does not change;
`He who does not put out his money at usury,
Nor does he take a bribe against the innocent.
He who does these things shall never be moved.

Like all holders of high office in America, Thomas Jefferson had his political enemies. As a Republican, he was the subject of on-going vilification by the Federalist press, most of which was originated by Thomson Callender, a man pardoned by Jefferson as a victim of the Sedition Act. After being rejected in an effort to secure an appointive position in the government, Callender was hired as a journalist by a Federalist newspaper in Richmond. Callender and his tactics have been described as follows:

> *True to his style, [Callender] fabricated a series of scandalous stories about Jefferson's personal life, the ugliest of which charged him with having fathered several children by a mulatto slave at Monticello, a young woman named Sally Hemings. Although Callender had never gone near Jefferson's estate, he alleged that this was common knowledge in the neighboring area. He included many lurid details of this supposed illicit relationship among the "entertaining facts" he created for his readers, even inventing the names of children whom "Dusky Sally" had never borne.*
>
> *Other Federalist editors took up these accusations with glee, and Callender's stories spread like wildfire from one end of the country to the other – sometimes expanded and embellished by subsequent writers. The President was charged with other evils as well; the torrent of slander never seemed to let up. As one biographer has written, "He suffered open personal attacks which in severity and obscenity have rarely if ever been matched in presidential history in the United States." (9)*

Responding to the spurious, politically-inspired Sally Hemings allegations, Professor Dumas Malone, whose six-volume biography of Jefferson won a Pulitzer Prize in 1975, said such allegations would be "virtually unthinkable in a man of Jefferson's moral standards and habitual conduct."

> *To say this is not to claim that he was a plaster saint and incapable of moral lapses. But his major weaknesses were not of this sort....It is virtually inconceivable that this fastidious gentleman whose devotion to his dead wife's memory and to the happiness of his daughters and grandchildren bordered on the excessive could have carried on through a period of years a vulgar liaison which his own family could not have failed to detect. It would be as absurd as to charge*

this consistently temperate man with being, through a long period, a secret drunkard." (10)

Randolph, when asked about the Hemings allegations, responded by revealing that Hemings was the mistress of Peter Carr, Jefferson's nephew, pointing out "their connection...was perfectly notorious at Monticello." Randolph shed additional light on the grandeur of his grandfather when describing the manner in which Jefferson reacted to the fraudulent attacks upon his character: "In speaking of the calumnies which his enemies had uttered against his public and private character with such unmitigated and untiring bitterness, he said that he had not considered them as abusing him; they had never known *him.* They had created an imaginary being clothed with odious attributes, to whom they had given his name; and it was against that creature of their imaginations they had leveled their anathemas." (11)

Thomas Jefferson's character is perhaps best described in his own words: "Whenever you are to do a thing, though it can never be known but to yourself, ask yourself how you would act were all the world looking at you, and act accordingly."

Chapter Seven

James Madison

We have staked the whole future of American civilization,
not upon the power of government, far from it.
We have staked the future upon the capacity of each
and all of us to govern ourselves, to sustain ourselves,
according to the Ten Commandments of God.
– James Madison

Menaced by the collectivist trends,
we must seek revival of our strength in the spiritual foundations
which are the bedrock of our republic. Democracy is the outgrowth
of the religious convictions of the sacredness of every human life.
On the religious side, its' highest embodiment is the Bible;
on the political side, the Constitution.
– Herbert Hoover

Often referred to as the Father of the Constitution, James Madison, fourth president of the United States, has been acclaimed by biographers for his energy, his determination, his character, and his deep-seated devotion to the principle of religious freedom and the individual liberties associated with it. His extensive involvement in producing our Constitution was a providential opportunity for him to exercise his considerable writing and speaking abilities as well as his understanding of governance.   Already at the young age of 23, he was committed to separation of the American colonies from Great Britain and to the formation of a republican form of government. He had a strong desire to be part of these world-shaking events which led to a 40-year political career that started with his pre-war work for independence.

As a member of the Constitutional Convention of 1787, Madison played a major role in what is often called "The Miracle of Philadelphia." He reportedly spoke more than 160 times helping to keep the often-times contentious proceedings from getting hopelessly bogged down. He is said to have been the best prepared delegate, arriving in Philadelphia well ahead of its scheduled opening date and armed with ideas gleaned from his studies on confederacies as well as experience gained from his previous eleven years involvement in colonial government. According to William Pierce, delegate from Georgia, Madison possessed "the most correct knowledge [of]…the affairs of the United States" to be found among the political leaders of his generation. (1)

Described as "an indefatigable reporter," Madison is credited with keeping the most detailed and reliable records of the convention's proceedings. "I chose a seat in front of the presiding member, with the other members on my right and left hand," Madison later wrote. "In this favorable position for hearing all that passed, I noted in terms legible and in abbreviations and marks intelligible to myself what was read from the Chair or spoken by the members; and losing not a moment unnecessarily between the adjournment and reassembling of the Convention I was enabled to write out my daily notes during the session or within a few finishing days after its close in the extent and form preserved in my own hand on my files…I was not absent a single day, nor more than a fraction of an hour in any day, so that I could not have lost a single speech unless a very short one," he said. (2)

While not necessarily known for being outspoken regarding his Christianity, Madison made the motion that Benjamin Franklin's appeal for prayer be accepted by the delegates at the Convention. That motion was seconded by Roger Sherman who was pastored by Jonathan Edwards, the younger, in the Congregational Church of which he was a member.. Later, he did acknowledge his conviction that God had directed the outcome of the Convention: "It is impossible for the man of pious reflection not to perceive in [the Constitutional Convention] a finger of that Almighty hand," he said.

In reference to Madison's convention journal, Thomas Jefferson stated in a letter to John Adams in 1815, "Do you know that there exists in manuscript the ablest work of this kind ever yet executed, of the debates of the constitutional convention of Philadelphia? The whole of everything said and done there was taken down by Mr. Madison, with a labor and exactness beyond comprehension." (3) Without Madison's journal, many of the interesting and informative details of the proceedings leading to the writing of our Constitution would be left to conjecture and mystery. We have the privilege of knowing much more about the character and intelligence of many of the Founding Fathers than we could possibly know had it not been for Madison's diligence.

Many historians have highlighted his role as the Founder most responsible for passage of the Bill of Rights, although early on he didn't see the need for such a bill. He eventually presented it to the House in 1789. As early as 1776, Madison, as a delegate to the Virginia constitutional convention, served on the committee that had prepared a declaration of rights. He worked closely in the Virginia House with Thomas Jefferson establishing grounds for religious freedom for Virginians. Madison's having written the provision that asserted the right "to the free exercise of religion, according to the dictates of conscience" was a foreshadowing of his later efforts to have a Bill of Rights in the new U. S. Constitution, especially the religious freedom provision of the First Amendment.

Eventually that Bill of Rights, after much debate and several changes, became part of the Constitution in the form of the first Ten Amendments. Madison is credited with putting this specific clause into the U. S. Constitution: "Congress shall make no law respecting an establishment of religion, **or prohibiting the free exercise thereof;"** which is the real meaning of the phrase "separation of church and state." There would be no favored or official national church in the United States of America but public morality was expected to be influenced by biblical concepts. "Religion [is] the basis and Foundation of Government," Madison said.

Getting the Bill of Rights included wasn't an easy task since a majority of delegates to the Constitutional Convention of 1787 at first concluded a list of individual rights wasn't necessary because of the limited nature of the proposed federal government. The Federalists' position was that the people retained all powers not specifically delegated to the federal government by the proposed Constitution. The anti-Federalists rejected this logic as wishful thinking. Little by little, they made their case. It soon became obvious that without a bill of rights, ratification of the Constitution would face stiff opposition. Rhode Island and North Carolina refused to ratify the Constitution specifically because it didn't include a bill of rights. Other states held back their support for that and other reasons.

Madison, who had lost a seat in the new Senate, primarily due to opposition by anti-Federalist Patrick Henry, a strong supporter of a bill of rights, easily won election to the House of Representatives in 1789 where he kept the idea of guaranteed freedom of religion alive based in large part on his campaign pledge to fight for it. He was supported in his election campaign by groups concerned about the absence in the Constitution of specific religious rights. He was also supported by other loosely organized groups who were worried about possible restrictions on the press, government searches, and other general individual rights that had routinely been trampled upon by England prior to the Revolutionary War.

Upon taking his seat in the new Congress, Madison soon found that few members saw a pressing need for prompt action on what he considered to be a fundamental issue. In order to attract support, he agreed to consider all reasonable suggestions for the new bill of rights which helped over time to carry the day. Thomas Jefferson lent his moral support: "No just government," he wrote, "should refuse, or rest on inference." Speaking a little more bluntly, Madison was quoted as saying, "All men having power ought to be distrusted."

Along with Alexander Hamilton and John Jay, Madison authored a series of 85 articles known as *The Federalist* in support of ratification of the Constitution. Madison is believed to have been the author of 26 of the articles which were printed by a number of newspapers, many under the signature of *Publius*. He is believed to have collaborated with Alexander Hamilton on an additional three articles.

"What is government itself but the greatest of all reflections on human nature?" Madison had written in Federalist No. 51. His opinion of human nature led him to agree with Jefferson regarding the need for written and ratified Constitutional assurances of basic human rights, human nature being what both Founders had observed it to be.

As a delegate to the Virginia ratification convention in 1788, Madison was instrumental in winning his home state's approval of the U. S. Constitution in that important and influential state, emerging victorious over anti-ratification forces led by Patrick Henry, James Monroe, and George Mason.

Although a Federalist at heart, Madison consistently supported measures, at both the state and national levels of government, designed to safeguard individual rights. His Federalist convictions originated in his belief in the need for a strong national defense, a coherent national foreign policy and issues connected with international trade. Tax collection and payment of public debt could best be enforced, he believed, through the vehicle of federal government. "The powers delegated by the proposed Constitution to the federal government," Madison said, "are few and defined [and] will be exercised principally on external objects, as war, peace, negotiation and foreign commerce."

Madison also advocated the development of uniform rules and regulations among the states to govern trade and interstate commercial relations and he was convinced that only a federal government, albeit with divided and balanced powers, would be able to effectively enforce such regulations. He argued that "the people would not be less free as members of one great Republic than as members of thirteen small ones." Although convinced of the need for a stronger federal government, Madison, because of his dedication to individual freedom, always had an anti-Federalist side to his thinking.

"In framing a government which is to be administered by men over men, the great difficulty lies in this: you must first enable the government to control the governed; and in the next place oblige it to control itself," Madison wrote. In other words, government must be powerful, but not too powerful. Power must be divided into separate but equal branches which he believed would provide some checks on the power wielded by a federal government. Some historians have described Madison's form of federalism as "a mild" form. Many of his writings in *The Federalist* emphasized that the Constitution "leaves to the several States a residuary and inviolable sovereignty over all other objects," referring to the fact that the new Federal government had superior authority over "certain enumerated objects only." More and more over time, he began to move toward the thinking of the anti-Federalists, or Democratic-Republican Party which led to his storied friendship with Thomas Jefferson.

Madison and Jefferson, both of whom have been referred to as "champions of religious freedom," first met in 1776 when each was a member of the Virginia legislature, but it wasn't until 1782 that their political kinship began to flower. By 1792 when the first presidential election was held, Madison had shifted his allegiance to Thomas Jefferson and the anti-Federalists. The friendly relations he had enjoyed with President George Washington during his first years in Congress, along with his relationship with Hamilton, also had cooled, even though the president formerly had often consulted with Madison on basic policies. By the end of his second term in Congress, the two party system had begun to take shape with Madison as a leader of the anti-Federalists.

When Jefferson was elected president in 1801, he appointed Madison Secretary of State. In his capacity as Secretary of State, and as a result of his growing friendship with Jefferson, Madison became the president's most trusted advisor. In 1803, Madison played a major role in completing the Louisiana Purchase which resulted in the addition of more than 800,000 square miles of land area west of the Mississippi River extending to the Rocky Mountains and beyond. Upon Jefferson's retirement at the end of his second term as president, Madison was elected the fourth president winning over Federalist candidate Charles Cotesworth Pinckney of South

Carolina. He was sworn into office March 4, 1809, by fellow founder and Chief Justice John Marshall.

The seminal event of his presidency was the war of 1812 which was, for the most part, an unpopular war for which he was criticized by some because of our involvement and by others because he didn't pursue it aggressively enough, in their view. But fighting the war did establish a heightened awareness of the United States as a respectable participant in world events, a force to be reckoned with in the international arena. Later, Madison received accolades for his leadership through this trying and defining moment in history.

Madison was born March 16, 1751, in Port Conway, Virginia where he was raised by devout Episcopalian parents. At that time, the Episcopal/Anglican Church was the state-sanctioned church of Virginia. Activities of the church in dealing with dissidents, many of which he considered excessive and abusive, greatly influenced his attitude regarding religious freedom.

The plantation on which he grew up provided the family with an upscale lifestyle. Madison was educated at home by his mother, grandmother, and tutors who assisted in his education and from whom he received a classical and spiritually-based preparatory education prior to his enrolling in the College of New Jersey, soon to become Princeton University. Originally a divinity student, Madison came under the influence of Reverend John Witherspoon, a prominent theologian and legal scholar as well as president of the university. His advanced education under Christian patriot Witherspoon provided Madison with a lifelong theological orientation and understanding of history and law that helped to motivate him in his drive to protect individual rights, especially religious freedom, as the hallmark of his legislative activities.

At the age of 43, Madison married Dolley Payne Todd, a widow and committed Christian who reportedly shared his knowledge of Scripture. According to many accounts, the Madison's, although of somewhat different temperaments – she was reputedly the more outgoing and socially involved while he has been described as having a more reserved nature – enjoyed a close relationship and loving marriage. They had no children.

Many history revisionists have tried to portray Madison as being adamant regarding the issue of separation of church and state, a term that doesn't appear in any of his writings although passages from his *Memorial and Remonstrance,* written in 1785, have been used by latter day anti-Christian liberals to support their thesis that the Christian religion should be suppressed and barricaded behind church doors. This excerpt from *The Rewriting of America's History* is helpful in understanding Madison's thinking versus the more recent "interpretation" of his writing:

James Madison's Memorial and Remonstrance has been quoted at length because of the recent anti-Christian onslaught upon our society with the now popular phrase: "Separation of Church and State." In the past score of years in America, the coined phrase: Separation of Church and State" has been proclaimed and heralded by the media. The interpretation given is that the state or government of our nation and the Christian religion are two separate and distinct entities, totally disconnected and disassociated one from the other. Armed with this reasoning, the State has encroached more and more upon the education of America's youth, thus gaining control of their minds. Examples are given, such as removing prayer and the Ten Commandments from the public school classrooms. The Christian church has now been targeted, new laws dictating more and more as to what it can and cannot do. The term "Separation of Church and State," however, was never used by Madison, the father of the U. S. Constitution. Neither was it ever employed by George Washington or John Adams; but only once used in a letter written by Thomas Jefferson to a Baptist group, never in any public or political writing.

The truth of the matter is that Madison's famous document extols the values of Christianity and the light of the gospel. It has been singled out as the great document which under girds the "Religious Freedom Clause" in our United States Constitution. The message is crystal clear, as with Thomas Jefferson's statute for Religious Freedom in Virginia:

Freedom of worship under the banner of Christianity. Both of these founding fathers spoke abut the Christian religion when dealing with freedom of religion. They were referring to the different and varying types of Christian worship: Quakers, Mennonites, Baptists, Episcopalians, Methodists and so forth – not to anything outside mainline Christianity. This is apparent in all their writing. The founding fathers were indisputably Christian and biblical in their thinking and approach to drafting a unique form of government. Madison's writings, as also those of Jefferson, clearly outline what the issue, which led to our first Amendment Clause, really was: Separation of Church from interference by the State in its mission, goals and outreach for Christ. In other words, it is the guaranteeing of liberty of worship of different denominational groups within the Christian community outside the civil jurisdiction and interference of the State. (4)

Joseph Story, nominated by Madison to be associate justice of the Supreme Court, saw the issue the same way: "The real object of the First Amendment was not to countenance, much less to advance Mohammedanism, or Judaism, or infidelity, by prostrating Christianity, but to exclude all rivalry among Christian sects [denominations] and to prevent any national ecclesiastical establishment which would give to an hierarchy the exclusive patronage of the national government," he wrote.

That Madison was a devout Christian and that he believed in God's involvement in the founding of America cannot be denied although some have tried. "No people," he said, "ought to feel greater obligations to celebrate the goodness of the Great Disposer of Events and of the Destiny of Nations than the people of the United States...And to the same Divine Author of every good and perfect gift we are indebted for all those privileges and advantages, religious as well as civil, which are so richly enjoyed in this favored land."

That "Divine Author," his contemporaries knew, was the Judeo-Christian God to whom all men are accountable. "Before any man can be considered as a member of civil society," Madison pointed out, "he must be considered as a subject of the Governor of the Universe."

"The belief in a God All Powerful wise and good, is so essential to the moral order of the world and to the happiness of man, that arguments which enforce it cannot be drawn from too many sources nor adapted with too much solicitude to the different characters and capacities impressed with it," Madison said.

It is clear from Madison's own words and the words of the other Founders that they never intended for the Christian religion to be marginalized. They also never intended for judges to usurp the legislative process as has become so commonplace today with judges routinely ruling legislation as well as the outcome of local and state elections to be "unconstitutional."

Here's James Madison on the subject: "As the courts are generally the last in making the decision [on laws], it results to them, by refusing or not refusing to execute a law, to stamp it with its final character. This makes the Judiciary dept paramount in fact to the Legislature, which was never intended, and can never be proper." Speaking to that subject on another occasion, he made this point: "The members of the legislative department are numerous. They are distributed and dwell among the people at large. Their connections of blood, or friendship, and of acquaintance embrace a great proportion of the most influential part of the society...they are more immediately the confidential guardians of the rights and liberties of the people."

The Father of the Constitution also said, "[Some contend] that wherever [the Constitution] meaning is doubtful, you must leave it to take its course, until the judiciary is called upon to declare its meaning...But I beg to know upon what principle it can be contended that any one department draws from the Constitution greater powers than another.... I do not see that any one of these independent departments has more right than another to declare their sentiments on that point."

And again from the pen of Madison: "In republican government, the legislative authority necessarily predominates," Obviously, James Madison would take strong exception to today's activist judges and the legislators who allow them to get away with the unconstitutional power-grab. Judges who want to legislate from the bench would have been anathema to Madison. Those judges seem to have forgotten that the judicial branch was created only to interpret existing laws, not to create and impose new ones. The framers clearly expected judges to respect the law as written and to stay within their constitutional authority.

Sir William Blackstone, author of *Commentaries on the Laws of England*, and the legal scholar most often quoted by the Founding Fathers where the judiciary was concerned, wrote: "If [the legislature] will positively enact a thing to be done, the judges are not at liberty to reject it, for that were to set the judicial power above that of the legislature, which would be subversive of all government." His *Commentaries* provided the foundation of legal education in America.

Thomas Jefferson, the liberals favorite Founding Father, made a number of statements warning of the dangers inherent in an out-of-control judiciary branch including this one contained in a letter to William Jarvis: "You seem ... to consider the judges as the ultimate arbiters of all constitutional questions; a very dangerous doctrine indeed, and one which would place us under the despotism of an oligarchy. Our judges are as honest as other men and not more so ... and their power (is) the more dangerous, as they are in office for life and not responsible, as the other functionaries are, to elective control. The Constitution has erected no such single tribunal, knowing that to whatever hands confided, with corruptions of time and party, its members would become despots."

Again, he warned, "Nothing in the Constitution has given to them a right to decide for the Executive, more than to the Executive to decide for them...[T]he opinion which gives to the judges the right to decide what laws are constitutional, and what not....for the legislature and the executive...would make the judiciary a despotic branch."

Perhaps anticipating the "living document" nonsense promoted today by those who use the courts to make political gains they can't make elsewhere, John Adams observed, "The Constitution...is a mere thing of wax in the hands of the judiciary which they may twist and shape into any form they please."

We'll give Samuel Adams the last word on the subject: "Laws they are not, which the public approbation hath not made so." Judges do not determine "public approbation; that's the legislature's job."

Small in stature, James Madison was a giant in the events that led to creating the U. S. Constitution, a unique document in the history of the world. He died July 4, 1836, outliving all the other Founding Fathers.

Chapter Eight

Benjamin Franklin

Venerated for benevolence, admired for talents;
esteemed for patriotism; beloved for philanthropy.
Franklin eulogy by George Washington

A Bible and a newspaper in every house,
a good school in every district – all studied and appreciated as
they merit – are the principal support of virtue,
morality and civil liberty.
Benjamin Franklin

B enjamin Franklin extolling the Bible? Gadzooks! Do history revisionists and their friends at the ACLU know about this?

Well, yes, they do, as a matter of fact, but they don't want anyone else, especially our children, to know about it. That's why they have devoted so much energy and wealth during the recent past to removing the Bible and any mention of it from public view.

That campaign is a bald-faced attempt to separate the Founding Fathers association with Christianity in general and the Bible in particular in the minds of the populace. When the Bible is restored to its rightful place of honor and authority in our society, and when the public rediscovers their Christian heritage, the history revisionists will have to crawl back into their dank, dark holes. Although they deny it with a torrent of weasel words, their agenda is to create a society in which no one is accountable for anything to anyone. The Bible and Evangelical Christians are standing in their way.

Those who are working day and night to convince their fellow citizens that America was never "a Christian nation," recognizing the importance of Franklin as one of our most important founders, claim that Franklin was a deist rather than a Christian. That claim is made most often about Franklin and George Washington because, one could conclude, they have long been recognized by historians as the two most acclaimed of the Founding Fathers. Benjamin Franklin was the only one of the Founding Fathers who signed all four of the major founding documents including the Declaration of Independence, the Treaty of Alliance with France, the Treaty of Paris officially ending the Revolutionary War, and the U. S. Constitution. He was one of only six signers of the Declaration of Independence who also signed the Constitution. Upon signing the Declaration, he made the famous statement, "We must all hang together, or assuredly we shall all hang separately," exhibiting his talent for packing a great deal of meaning and wisdom into a few words.

Because of his prominence and importance as a Founding Father, Franklin's references to Christianity and the foundational role of the Bible *must* be ignored or discredited by those who would revise history to better promote their atheistic agenda.

Where their "Franklin was a deist" claim originated is anyone's guess. Some claim Franklin labeled himself a deist which, I suppose, he could have done at some point in his life; many of us have gone through "searching" phases in our lives before finally getting it right. There is a preponderance of evidence that Franklin did in deed "get it right" among his prodigious writings. At one time, before I got around to studying the Bible, I thought I believed in reincarnation.

Or, perhaps the "Franklin was a deist" claim is based on the assertion of Bishop Paul O'Brien, a "bishop" in something called the Universal Life Church, who reportedly said, "The United States was started by men we today would call pagans. They wrote a Constitution without one word about God or Jesus in it. And in the amendments they said there would be no laws respecting the establishment of religion. This too is excluding God. Jefferson, Madison, Washington, John Adams, John Quincy Adams, Paine, Patrick Henry and most of our Founding Fathers were deists. They believed: If there were a God who made the world, he is beyond some star and cares nothing about what mankind does." (1)

According to The New Oxford American Dictionary, 2001, a deist is: "a person who believes in the existence of a supreme being, specifically of a creator who does not intervene in the universe. The term is used chiefly of an intellectual movement of the 17th and 18th centuries that accepted the existence of a creator on the basis of reason but rejected belief in a supernatural deity who interacts with human-kind." J. Gresham Machen, author of *Liberalism and Christianity*, lays it out for us: "According to the deistic view, God set the world going like a machine and then left it independent of Himself. Such a view is inconsistent with the actuality of the supernatural; the mira-cles of the Bible presuppose a God who is constantly watching over and guiding the course of this world. The miracles of the Bible are not arbitrary intrusions of a Power that is without relation to the world, but are evidently intended to accomplish results within the order of nature. Indeed the natural and the supernatural are blended, in the miracles of the Bible, in a way entirely incongruous with the deistic conception of God. In the feeding of the five thousand, for example, who shall say what part the five loaves and two fishes had in the event; who shall say where the natural left off and the super-natural began? Yet that event, if any, surely transcended the order of nature. The miracles of the Bible, then, are not the work of a God who has no part in the course of nature; they are the work of a God who through His works of providence is 'preserving and governing all His creatures and all their actions'."

Did Benjamin Franklin and the other founders believe in an uninvolved God? Would a deist have called for prayer at the Constitutional Convention as Franklin did when he asked, "How has it happened that we have not hitherto once thought of humbly applying to the Father of lights to illuminate our understanding!

In the beginning of the contest with Great Britain, when we were sensible of danger, we had daily prayer in this room for the Divine protection. – Our prayers, Sir, were heard and they were graciously answered. All who were engaged in the struggle must have observed frequent instances of a superintending Providence in our favor. To that kind Providence, we owe this happy opportunity of consulting in peace on the means of establishing our future national felicity. And have we now forgotten this powerful Friend? Or do we imagine we no longer need His assistance?"

He could hardly have made this follow-up-statement: "I have lived, Sir, a long time, and the longer I live, the more convincing proofs I see of this truth – that God governs in the affairs of men. And if a sparrow cannot fall to the ground without His notice, is it probable that an empire can rise without His aid? We have been assured in the Sacred Writings that except the Lord build the house, they labor in vain that build it. I firmly believe this. I also believe that, without His concurring aid, we shall succeed in this political building no better than the builders of Babel."

When his friend Thomas Paine asked Franklin for his thoughts, prior to publication of Paine's controversial book entitled *Age of Reason*, he was advised in no uncertain terms to abandon the idea because of its anti-religion tone. In response, Franklin said, "I have read your manuscript with some attention. By the argument it contains against a particular Providence, though you allow a general Providence, you strike at the foundations of all religion. *For without the belief of a Providence that takes cognizance of, guards, and guides, and may favor particular persons, there is no motive to worship a Deity, to fear his displeasure, or to pray for his protection.* I will not enter into any discussion of your principles though you seem to desire it. At present I shall only give you my opinion that….the consequence of printing this piece will be a great deal of odium [hate] drawn upon yourself, mischief to you and no benefit to others. He that spits into the wind, spits in his own face. But were you to succeed, do not imagine any good would be done by it?….[T]hink how great a portion of mankind consists of weak and ignorant men and women and of inexperienced, inconsiderate youth of both sexes who have need of the motives of religion to restrain them from vice, to support their virtue....I would advise you, therefore, not to attempt unchaining the tiger, but to burn this piece before it is seen by any other person....*If men are so wicked with religion, what would they be if without it.* I intend this letter itself as a proof of my friendship." (Italics added.) (2)

Franklin's own words make it clear that the ersatz bishop and other re-shapers of early American history don't have much of a clue about Franklin's religious beliefs nor of those of the other founders O'Brien attempted to tar with the same brush. Why would a deist pray to a God he believed "is beyond some star and cares nothing about what mankind does"? The short answer is that a deist wouldn't, but a Bible-believing Christian would.

In his writings, Franklin often made it clear he knew his Bible and used Bible passages to illustrate his belief in an involved God. "We hear," Franklin said, "of the conversion of water into wine at the marriage in Cana as of a miracle. But this conversion is, through the goodness of God, made every day before our eyes. Behold the rain which descends from heaven upon our vineyards; there it enters the roots of the vines, to be changed into wine; a constant proof that God loves us, and loves to see us happy. The miracle in question was only performed to hasten the operation, under circumstances of present necessity, which required it."

Further explaining his deep-seated beliefs concerning God, Franklin said, "Next to His wisdom, I believe He is pleased and delights in the happiness of those He has created; and since without virtue man can have no happiness in this world, I firmly believe He delights to see me virtuous, because He is pleased when He sees me happy....I love Him therefore for His Goodness, and I adore Him for His Wisdom."

No, Franklin bears no resemblance to a deist. Either the history revisionists are going to have to find a different label for Franklin and the other founders so labeled or the definition of the word *deist* will have to be changed.

The Franklin family, staunch Calvinists by reputation, had their own designated pew in Philadelphia's Christ Church on the grounds of which the bodies of Franklin and seven other signers of the Declaration of Independence are interred. A plaque on that pew records the following historical fact: "Here worshipped Benjamin Franklin, philosopher and patriot....Member of the Committee which erected the Spire of the Church. Interred according to the terms of his will in this churchyard." (2)

Especially during colonial times, most churches required, as a condition of membership, belief in the Bible as God's revealed word and belief in Jesus Christ as the Son of God. Anyone holding deist beliefs while belonging to Christian churches would have been swearing falsely in the presence of God. Judging from their own words, none of the Founding Fathers would have likely been guilty of swearing falsely in the presence of God.

In his *Articles of Belief and Acts of Religion,* Franklin wrote this prayer:

> *O Creator, O Father, I believe that Thou are Good, and Thou art pleas'd with the pleasure of Thy children.*
> *Praised be Thy Name forever.*
> *By Thy Power hast thou made the glorious Sun, with his attending worlds; from the energy of Thy mighty Will they first received their prodigious motion, and by Thy Wisdom hast Thou prescribed the wondrous laws by which they move.*
> *Praised be Thy Name forever.*
> *Thy Wisdom, Thy Power, and Thy GOODNESS are every where clearly seen; in the air and in the water, in the heavens and on the earth; Thou providest for the various winged fowl, and the innumerable inhabitants of the water; Thou givest cold and heat, rain and sunshine in their season, and to the fruits of the earth increase.*
> *Praised be Thy Name forever.*
> *I believe Thou hast given life to Thy creatures that they might live, and art not delighted with violent death and bloody sacrifices.*
> *Praised be Thy Name forever.*
> *Thou abhorrest in Thy creatures treachery and deceit, malice, revenge, intemperance and every other hurtful Vice; but Thou art a Lover of justice and sincerity, of friendship,*

*benevolence and every virtue. Thou art my Friend, my
Father, and my Benefactor.
Praised be Thy Name, O God, forever. Amen. (4)*

That prayer could proudly be delivered today by Bible-believing, Evangelical preachers from coast to coast, none of whom could be described as deists.

For all practical purposes, Benjamin Franklin, born January 17, 1706, the fifteenth of seventeen children was self-educated due to limitations on the family finances that were only able to provide formal education for a couple of years of grammar school. Even with his abbreviated formal education, he eventually became known as an intellectual in both Europe and America, as well as a literary genius and American statesman. He became known later in life for his many philanthropies.

Along the way, he is also said to have taught himself five languages. Among the many honors bestowed up him, Franklin received honorary degrees from Yale, Harvard, William & Mary, Oxford, and St. Andrews. Because of his many important inventions and scientific discoveries, he was often labeled "the Newton of his age."

In his *Patriot's Handbook*, George Grant gave us this succinct description of the public life of one of our most outstanding founders:

Patriot, inventor, scientist, philosopher, musician, editor, printer, and diplomat, Benjamin Franklin brought the prestige of his unparalleled achievements to the public service that consumed over half of his life. He was a living example of the richness of life that man can achieve with the freedom – and the will – to do so. In many senses he was the first American, and he was a Founding Father of the first rank. His rise from apprentice to man of affairs was paralleled by an ever-widening circle of interests. His curiosity led him from subject to subject: He mastered printing, learned French, invented a stove, discovered electrical principles, organized a postal service, and helped discover the Gulf

Stream. Though a free-thinker – an oddity among his over-whelmingly devout Christian peers – he was the close friend and publisher of George Whitefield, the great evangelist. As his country's representative in England in the 1760s, he defended America's position before hostile, arrogant officials; he helped win repeal of the Stamp Act and pleaded for American representation in Parliament. In the 1770s he continued trying to reason with British officials, but they were inflexible, and he returned to America ready to support the cause of independence. In the Continental Congress Franklin headed the committee that organized the American postal system, helped draft the Articles of Confederation, and began negotiations with the French for aid. He also helped draft and signed the Declaration of Independence. Franklin was the colonies' best choice as commissioner to France; well known as a scientist and philosopher, he was warmly welcomed in Paris, and his position as a world figure, coupled with his diplomatic skill, helped him negotiate the 1778 alliance with France that brought America desperately needed military support. Soon after, he began negotiating with the British for peace, but only after the French fleet had joined with Washington to defeat Cornwallis at Yorktown would the British consider granting independence. Franklin signed the peace treaty September 3, 1783. After he returned to America, Franklin had one more vital role to play: At the Constitutional Convention his very presence gave weight and authority to the proceedings, and he used his influence to moderate conflicts. On the final day he appealed to the delegates: "I confess that there are several parts of this Constitution which I do not at present approve, but I am not sure I shall never approve them. For having lived long, I have experienced many instances of being obliged by better information, or fuller consideration, to change opinions even on important subjects, which I once thought right, but found to be otherwise. I cannot help expressing a wish that every member of the Convention who may still have objections to it, would with me, on this occasion, doubt a little of his own infallibility, and to make manifest our unanimity, put his name of this instrument." A few minutes later all but three delegates signed the Constitution. (5)

This impressive resume had its beginnings when Franklin was a 12-year-old , printer's apprentice under his brother James, owner of the *New England Courant.* During his five years there, he began to write under the byline "Silence Dogood." His best-known and most enduring writing began in 1732 with the advent of his *Poor Richard's Almanack* much of which is still in print today. A kind of secular book of proverbs, the *Almanack,* described by Franklin as "the wisdom of many ages and nations," eventually became second only to The Bible in popularity.

In his voluminous writings, Franklin emphasized moral living, personal responsibility, and the need for self-improvement. While his writings were infrequently couched in biblical terminology, his principles usually had a biblical root which only those who know the Bible would recognize as such. For instance, this exhortation from *Poor Richards Almanack* which deals with slothfulness, a human trait disparaged in the Bible, was stated thusly: "He that riseth late, must trot all day, and shall scarce overtake his business at night." And, on the same subject, Franklin said, "At the working man's house hunger looks in, but dares not enter." "Sloth (like Rust)," said Franklin, consumes faster than Labour wears; the used Key is always bright." "Up, sluggard, and waste not life; in the grave will be sleeping enough," he warned.

On the subject of fools, Franklin said, "Half Wits talk much but say little." "Tricks and treachery," Franklin points out, "are the practice of fools that have not wit enough to be honest." Franklin observed an all-too prevalent characteristic of modern man when he said, "Good Sense is a Thing all need, few have, and none think they want." I think he was saying most of us think we already have good sense, a common delusion.

One of the most often mentioned sins in the Bible is the destructive sin of pride. Here's one of Franklin's ways of pointing out the worldly consequences one can expect from prideful living: "As Pride increases, Fortune declines." The other side of that coin is humility which Franklin extols: "None but the well-bred man knows how to confess a fault, or acknowledge himself in an error."

Regarding the biblical principle of forgiveness, Franklin advised, "Doing an Injury puts you below your Enemy; Revenging one makes you but even with him; Forgiving it sets you above him." This warning to youth regarding the wisdom of listening to the advice of their elders and the value of time are common themes in the book of Proverbs: "Ah simple Man! when a boy two precious jewels were given thee, Time and good Advice; one thou has lost, and the other thrown away." He was commenting on the obvious practices of nominal Christians when he said, "How many observe Christ's Birth-day; How few his Precepts! O, 'tis easier to keep Holidays than Commandments." The very human tendency to repeat gossip, a no-no in the Bible, is addressed in these few words: "In a discreet man's mouth a publick thing is private."

This general exhortation can be traced to a large number of verses contained in the Bible: "Be at War with your Vices, at Peace with your Neighbours, and let every New-Year find you a better Man."

From all indications, Franklin tried to practice what he preached. He carried with him a small book in which he listed thirteen virtues upon which he would concentrate, zeroing-in on one specific virtue every day. From his autobiography, we find the following list:

1. *Temperance: Eat not to dullness, drink not to elevation.*
2. *Silence: Speak not but what may benefit others or your-self; avoid trifling conversation.*
3. *Order: Let all your things have their places; let each part of your business have its time.*
4. *Resolution: Resolve to perform what you ought; perform without fail what you resolve.*
5. *Frugality: Make no expense but to do good to others or yourself; i.e. waste nothing.*
6. *Industry: Lose no time; be always employ'd in some-thing useful; cut off all unnecessary actions.*
7. *Sincerity: Use no hurtful deceit; think innocently and justly; and if you speak, speak accordingly*

8. *Justice: Wrong none by doing injuries, or omitting the benefits that are your duty.*
9. *Moderation: Avoid extremes; forbear resenting injuries to much as you think they deserve.*
10. *Cleanliness: Tolerate no uncleanliness in body, cloaths, or habitations.*
11. *Tranquility: Be not disturbed at trifles, or at accidents common or unavoidable.*
12. *Chastity: Rarely use venery but for health or offspring, never to dullness, weakness, or the injury of your own or another's peace of reputation.*
13. *Humility: Imitate Jesus.*

This observation from his *Maxim's and Morals*, an extensive list of worthy goals that Franklin believed would lead to happy and contented lives for those who practice them in their everyday lives, seems to summarize Benjamin Franklin's basic approach to life and his advice to future generations: "Virtue alone is sufficient to make a man great, glorious and happy."

Chapter 9

Samuel Adams

*It is but natural that the first paragraph of
the Declaration of Independence should open with a reference
to nature's God and should close in the final paragraphs with an
appeal to the supreme judge of the world and an assertion of a firm
reliance on divine providence. Coming from these sources, having
as it did this background, it is no wonder that Samuel Adams would
say, 'The people seem to recognize this resolution as though it
were a decree promulgated from heaven.'*
-- **Calvin Coolidge**

*I could say a thousand things to you, if I had leisure.
I could dwell on the importance of piety and religion,
of industry and frugality, of prudence, economy, regularity and
even Government, all of which are essential to the well being of a
family. But I have not time. I cannot however help repeating piety,
because I think it indispensable. Religion in a family is at once its
brightest ornament and its best security.*
-- *Samuel* **Adams**

Samuel Adams was a royal pain in the neck; the neck, that is, of British Royalty who knew him well as one of the most effective of the Founding Fathers in building support for the revolution and in generating opposition to every political or military provocation. Those activities earned Adams the title "Father of the American Revolution" and "the spirit of the independence movement," a designation he shared with fellow founder Patrick Henry.

Population-wise, the prospect of war against the British looked like a David vs. Goliath situation, and there was much to support that characterization. Like David, the founders had faith that their cause was just and that God would give them the victory over a much stronger adversary. Many of them, including Samuel Adams, could have been described, as David was, as men after God's own heart. By 1770, the population of the colonies totaled approximately 2,500,000, 20% of whom were black slaves; the combined population of the British Isles totaled approximately 9,000,000. Adams didn't see that as an insurmountable problem. "It does not take a majority to prevail," he was quoted as saying, "but rather an irate, tireless minority, keen on setting brushfires of freedom in the minds of men." Samuel Adams was an irate and tireless setter of brushfires that eventually brought freedom to his beloved country.

The dynamic role he played in the independence movement was understood by British leaders to the point that General Thomas Gage, in an effort to end hostilities with the Colonists before they began, offered pardons to all rebels except for Adams and John Hancock "whose offenses are of too flagitious nature to admit of any other consideration than that of condign punishment." (1)

On another occasion, in response to a British pardon initiative, Adams said, "I am told that Lord Howe has lately issued a Proclamation offering a general pardon with the Exception of only four Persons viz Dr. Franklin Coll, Richard Henry Lee, Mr. John Adams, and my self. I am not certain of the Truth of this Report. If it be a Fact I am greatly obliged of his Lordship for the flattering opinion he has given me of my self as being a Person obnoxious to those who are desolating a once happy Country for the sake of extinguishing the remaining Lamp of Liberty, and for the singular Honor he does me in ranking me with Men so eminently patriotick." (2)

General Gage also tried bribery as a method of silencing Adams, offering him "great gifts and advancement" if he would stop agitating the Colonists which Adams indignantly refused. That incident was recorded as follows in *The Signers of the Declaration of Independence*: "When the governor was asked why Mr. Adams had not been silenced by office, he replied, that 'such obstinacy and inflexible disposition of the man, that he can never be conciliated by any office or gift whatever.' And when, in 1774, Governor Gage, by authority of ministers, sent Colonel Fenton to offer Adams a magnificent consideration if he would cease his hostility to government, or menace him with all the evils of attainder, that inflexible patriot gave this remarkable answer to Fenton: 'I trust I have long since made my peace with the King of kings. No personal consideration shall induce me to abandon the righteous cause of my country. Tell Governor Gage, it is the advice of Samuel Adams to him, no longer to insult the feelings of an exasperated people'."

He first began to attract the attention of those in charge of governing the colonies in 1764 when he took a strong public stand against strict enforcement of the Sugar and Molasses Acts which imposed shipment restrictions and high taxes on those commodities imported into the English colonies. Those taxes were one of the first economic incitements to talk of independence.

Adding fuel to the fire in 1765, the British Parliament passed the Stamp Act which required a tax stamp on all legal documents, newspapers, pamphlets, and even playing cards. This tax placed on the Colonists by the British Parliament was denounced as "taxation without representation," an effective rallying cry that influenced many to join the movement for independence. Formed to oppose the Stamp Act in 1765, the Sons of Liberty, a patriotic society, made it difficult if not impossible, through a campaign of physical violence, to distribute the stamps. The Boston Chapter of the Sons of Liberty was headed up by Adams and Paul Revere. Adams was also the motivator behind formation of the Stamp Act Congress held in New York to formulate a plan of resistance to the stamp tax. Although the Stamp Act was repealed in 1766, it is still considered to have been one of the major causes of the American Revolution.

The Sons of Liberty were also successful in organizing colonial merchants in opposition to the importing of merchandise in British ships which resulted in a substantial reduction in the importation of British goods. Parliament had managed to stir up a hornets nest with a series of ill-conceived pieces of anti-Colonial legislation and Samuel Adams was one of the more vexatious hornets.

From the Sons of Liberty sprang new Committees of Correspondence, in which, again, Adams emerged as a prominent participant leading the Boston chapter. Committees located through the Colonies had been established years earlier as a way for Colonial legislatures to communicate with each other, but now they became essential tools for shaping public opinion and for generating opposition to British rule throughout the colonies. The original committee in Boston, led by Adams, had a three-fold goal: (1) to delineate the rights the Colonists had as men, as Christians, and as subjects of the crown, (2) to detail how these rights had been violated, and (3) to publicize throughout the Colonies the first two items. (3)

The committees became instrumental in beginning to create a sense of interdependence and identity throughout the colonies. For the first time, the revolutionary-minded colonists using the Committees of Correspondence were able to begin to develop a unified, embryonic though it was, policy of resistance. Adams extensive writings made him one of the best known of the persistent promoters of the call to revolution. "If ye love wealth better than liberty," Adams wrote, "the tranquility of servitude than the animating contest of freedom, go from us in peace. We ask not your counsels or arms. Crouch down and lick the hands which feed you. May your chains sit lightly upon you, and may posterity forget that ye were our countrymen!" Thomas Paine's *Common Sense*, published January 10, 1776, is credited by many historians as providing the argument that swung public opinion in favor of independence.

Most of his prolific revolutionary writings appeared originally in *The Boston Gazette*, a large circulation newspaper for its time, and in his *The Rights of the Colonists* which was circulated in 1772 in which he expressed this tenet of the revolution: "The right to freedom being the gift of the Almighty...The rights of colonists as Christians...may be best understood by reading and carefully studying the institution of The Great Law Giver and Head of the Christian Church, which are to be found clearly written and promulgated in the New Testament." (4) "The natural liberty of man," said Adams, "is to be free from any superior power on earth, and not to be under the will or legislative authority of man, but only to have the law of nature for his rule." The "law of nature," also called "the laws of the Creator" by Adams, the founders knew, referred to the law of God as presented in the Bible. They were to be subject to the law of God, not the laws of the British Empire.

Adams led opposition to the Townshend Acts that taxed imports of a number of commodities, including tea, and, on December 16, 1773, instigated the event the world knows today as *The Boston Tea Party*. Recognized for his leadership role in opposing British oppression, and as acknowledgment of his diligent work behind the scenes in generating support for establishment of a general congress, Adams was elected a delegate to the First Continental Congress convened September 5, 1774, which, for all practical purposes, became the de facto American revolutionary government. It had recently become obvious that a more highly developed national consciousness leading to an effective means of organized resistance was becoming a necessity. British provocations demanded a united opposition if the Colonies were to successfully counter British attempts at further subjugation. One large united entity would have a greater opportunity to succeed than 13 small, separate entities, each with its own government, could achieve. The First Continental Congress was a step in that direction.

Although many Christian denominations with differing doctrines were represented among the congressional delegates, Adams proposed that the days' business be opened with prayer. It was unseemly, Adams said, for "Christian men, who had come together for solemn deliberation in the hour of their extremity, to say there was so wide a difference in their religious belief that they could not, as one man, bow the knee in prayer to the Almighty, whose advice and assistance they hoped to obtain." Adams knew his fellow delegates; he knew them to be Christians, regardless of the minor doctrinal differences that might have existed among them.

Passage by the British Parliament of four laws designed as punishment for the Boston Tea Party, known by the Colonists as the "Intolerable Acts," provided the impetus for convening the congress. The four punitive acts were (1) the Boston Port Act which closed Boston to trade; (2) the Massachusetts Government Act which revoked the Colony's charter; (3) the Quartering act which required Colonists to provide quartering for British soldiers; and (4) the Impartial Administration of Justice Act which removed British officials from the jurisdiction of Massachusetts courts. In conjunction with these four acts, Parliament passed the Quebec Act which expanded the territory of Quebec and did not allow for representative government in that Colony. (5)

Adams, who some historians have labeled a radical, led the faction calling for the use of force in resisting the heavy-handed British provocations, a position not yet shared by a majority of his counterparts. That Adams was a driving force for independence as a member of the congress was supported by B. J. Lossing: "The journals of Congress during that time show his name upon almost every important committee of that body. And probably no man did more toward bringing about the American Revolution, and in effecting the independence of the Colonies, than Samuel Adams. He was the first to assert boldly those political truths upon which rested the whole superstructure of our confederacy – he was the first to act in support of those truths – and when, in the General Council of States, independence was proposed, and the timid faltered, and the over-prudent hesitated, the voice of Samuel Adams was ever loudest in denunciations of a temporizing policy, and also in the utterance of strong encouragement to the fainthearted. 'I should advise,' he said, on one occasion, 'persisting in our struggle for liberty, though it were revealed from Heaven that nine hundred and ninety-nine were to perish, and only one of a thousand were to survive and retain his liberty! One such freeman must possess more virtue, and enjoy more happiness, than a thousand slaves; and let him propagate his like, and transmit to them what he hath so nobly preserved'." (6)

Prior to adjournment of the First Continental Congress, the delegates called for a second congress to be convened May 10, 1775, if the British persisted in their "Coercive Acts," another popular name for the Parliamentary measures they considered to be intolerable. Prior to that date, the die had been cast by a number of events including the intransigence of Parliament and the April 19, 1775 battles of Lexington and Concord involving British soldiers and American "minutemen," the name given to the Colonial militia who pledged to fight "at a minute's notice."

Facing a growing crisis, the Second Continental Congress was convened as scheduled with Adams again serving as a delegate from Massachusetts. The primary responsibilities of the congress were threefold: (1) to formulate and oversee the conduct of the war, (2) to advance and preserve the newly formed "union" of the 13 colonies, and (3) to develop a constitution of sorts to guide the emerging independent country. The means of accomplishing any of these objectives were not clear-cut, to say the least. Virginia delegate George Washington was commissioned to organize and command a continental army. Committees were established to generate plans for the conduct of international trade, develop fiscal policies, and to find ways to seek much-needed military and financial assistance overseas.

Developing a constitution proved to be tedious and contentious work with agreement on the Articles of Confederation finally being achieved November 15, 1777. It took more than three years from the time it was approved by the congressional delegates for the colonies to officially ratify it. In the meantime, the Second Continental Congress approved the Declaration of Independence July 2, 1776 and formerly adopted it on the Fourth of July. At the signing of the Declaration, Adams said, "We have this day restored the Sovereign to Whom all men ought to be obedient. He reigns in heaven and from the rising to the setting of the sun, let His kingdom come." Also in reference to the Declaration, Adams said, "The people seem to recognize this as though it were a decree promulgated from heaven."

In 1788, Adams played a major role in the ratification of the U.S. Constitution by the state of Massachusetts. In 1789 he was elected lieutenant governor of Massachusetts, and governor in 1794. He died October 2, 1803.

The early life of Adams was capsulized by B. J. Lossing:

This distinguished patriot of the Revolution, was born in Boston, Massachusetts, on the twenty-second of September 1782. He was of pilgrim ancestors, and had been taught the principles of Freedom, from his infancy. His father was a man of considerable wealth, and was for a long series of years a member of the Massachusetts Assembly, under the Colonial Government. He resolved to give Samuel a liberal education. After a preparatory course of study, he entered him at Harvard College, Cambridge, where, in 1740 at the age of eighteen years, he took his degree of A.B. He was uncommonly sedate, and very assiduous in the pursuit of knowledge, while a pupil.

His father destined him for the profession of the law, but this design was relinquished, and he was placed as an apprentice with Thomas Cushing, a distinguished merchant of Boston, and afterward an active patriot. His mind, however, seemed fixed on political subjects, and the mercantile profession presented few charms for him. His father furnished him with ample capital to commence business as a merchant, but his distaste for the profession, and the diversion of his mind from its demands, by politics, soon caused him serious embarrassments, and he became almost a bankrupt.

When Samuel was twenty-five years old, his father died, and the cares of the family and estate devolved on him as the oldest son. Yet his mind was constantly active in watching the movements of the British government, and he spent a great deal of his time in talking and writing in favor of the resistance of the Colonies to the oppressions of the crown and its ministers. He took a firm and decided stand against the Stamp Act and its antecedent kindred schemes to tax the Colonies. As early as 1763, he boldly expressed his sentiments relative to the rights and privileges of the Colonists; and in some instructions which he drew up for the guidance of the Boston members of the General Assembly, in that year, he denied the right of Parliament to tax the Colonies without their consent – denied the supremacy of Parliament, and suggested a union of all the Colonies, as necessary for their protection against British aggressions. It is asserted that this was the first public expression of such sentiments in America, and that they were the spark that kindled the flame upon the altar of Freedom here. (7)

That he was a man of character, steadfast in his Christian faith, is clear from the life he lived and many of the memorable words he said, especially on the importance of public morality, words we need to take to heart today: "A general dissolution of principles and manners will more surely overthrow the liberties of American than the whole force of the common enemy. While the people are virtuous they cannot be subdued; but when once they lose their virtue they will be ready to surrender their liberties to the first external or internal invader...If virtue and knowledge are diffused among the people, they will never be enslaved. This will be their great security."

That we are today experiencing an unprecedented assault on morality, often said to have constitutional authority, is indisputable and diametrically opposed to the original intent of the Founding Fathers as evinced over and over in their own words. Every one of the founders would look in utter disbelief upon many of the judgments recently handed down by our courts and often supported by publicly elected officials. Adams would have had this advice for them: "He therefore is the truest friend to the liberty of his country who tries most to promote its virtue, and who, so far as his power and influence extend, will not suffer a man to be chosen into any office of power and trust who is not a wise and virtuous man....The sum of all is, if we would most truly enjoy this gift of Heaven, let us become a virtuous people." (8)

To those who want God to be removed from the public schools, Adams would say, "Let divines and philosophers, statesmen and patriots, unite their endeavors to renovate the age, by impressing the minds of men with the importance of educating their little boys and girls, of inculcating in the minds of youth the fear and love of the Deity and universal philanthropy, and, in subordination to these great principles, the love of their country; of instructing them in the art of self-government without which they never can act a wise part in the government of societies, great or small; in short, of leading them in the study and practice of the exalted virtues of the Christian system."

History's rewriters have, for the most part, ignored Samuel Adams because it would be difficult indeed to twist these words that were included in his will: "Principally, and first of all, I resign my soul to the Almighty Being who gave it, and my body I commit to the dust, relying on the merits of Jesus Christ for the pardon of my sins." Some radical revisionists have referred to the founders most outspoken about protecting religious freedom, including Adams, as being "radical" as a way of attempting to create the impression that people who today are concerned about religious freedom and traditional Christian beliefs are on the fringe. To some of his contemporaries, he was known as "the last Puritan." *Puritan* has become a pejorative term in the lexicon of twentieth and twenty-first century liberals who either don't know or who would mislead their fellow citizens regarding the rich Christian heritage of the United States of America. Whichever it is, they should be ashamed of themselves. But, they have no shame.

Chapter Ten

Patrick Henry

*The individual activity of one man with backbone will do more
than a thousand men with a mere wishbone.*
-- **William J. H. Boetcker**

*The cries of [Henry's] suffering countrymen pierced his heart,
and he nobly resolved to hazard all in their defence.
Prostrating himself before the altar of his country, he placed
upon it the rich oblation of an honest heart…We might enquire,
if the meekness of the Christian, and the fire of the patriot had not
been so happily blended in him what might have been the result
of the union of vice with the untamed majesty of his spirit-stirring
eloquence? Such is the beauty and the force of virtue.*
-- **William R. Drinkard**

On **March 23, 1775,** just 27 days before "the shot heard round the world" was fired, Patrick Henry delivered a speech that ended with the words that have become synonymous with his name: "Give me liberty or give me death!" The first battles of the

Revolutionary War, which took place April 19, 1775 at Lexington and Concord, were immortalized by Ralph Waldo Emerson in his famous poem entitled *Concord Hymn:*

By the rude bridge that arched the flood,
Their flag to April's breeze unfurled,
Here once the embattled farmers stood,
And fired the shot heard round the world.

The foe long since in silence slept,
Alike the conqueror silent sleeps.
And Time the ruined bridge has swept
Down the dark stream which seaward creeps.
On this green bank, by this soft stream,
We set to-day a votive stone;
That memory may their deed redeem,
When, like our sires, our sons are gone.
Spirit that made those heroes dare
To die, and leave their children free,
Bid Time and Nature gently spare
The shaft we raise to them and thee.

The "spirit that made those heroes dare" existed in abundance among the men known as the Founding Fathers, but two of them, Patrick Henry and Samuel Adams, have been honored with the special label "spirit of the independence movement." Both men were outspoken Christians who reflected the scriptural principle written in Second Corinthians, 3:17: *Where the Spirit of the Lord is, there is liberty.* Both men lived by the admonition in Galatians 5:1: *Stand fast therefore in the liberty wherewith Christ hath made us free.* Both men made frequent references to their belief that independence was God-ordained and that He would give them victory over a much stronger opponent. Early on, that conviction was not shared by a majority of their fellow Colonists.

Although a substantial portion of the population had grave misgivings regarding the matter of independence and permanent separation from the mother country, momentum for such a break had been building during the past ten years as a result of a series of events including passage of the Sugar Act, the Stamp Act, the Townshend Acts, the Boston Massacre, the Boston Port Act, and other punitive measures directed toward the Colonies by Parliament. Much had been written and spoken in favor of independence during the recent past but Henry's passionate oration, in which he forcefully made the point that the colonies must now choose between freedom and slavery, has been generally recognized by historians as the event that soon kindled the spark of revolution into blazing action. Here is the entire speech which was recorded within the proceedings of the March 23, 1775, Virginia Convention:

Mr. President: No man thinks more highly than I do of the patriotism, as well as abilities, of the very worthy gentlemen who have just addressed the House. But different men often see the same subject in different lights; and, therefore, I hope that it will not be thought disrespectful to those gentlemen, if entertaining as I do, opinions of a character very opposite to theirs, I shall speak forth my sentiments freely and without reserve. This is no time for ceremony. The question before the House is one of awful moment to this country. For my own part I consider it as nothing less than a question of freedom or slavery; and in proportion to the magnitude of the subject ought to be the freedom of the debate. It is only in this way that we can hope to arrive at truth, and fulfill the great responsibility which we hold to God and our country. Should I keep back my opinions at such a time, through fear of giving offense, I should consider myself guilty of treason toward my country, and of an act of disloyalty toward the majesty of heaven, which I revere above all earthly kings.

Mr. President, it is natural to man to indulge in the illusions of hope. We are apt to shut our eyes against a painful truth, and listen to the song of that siren, till she transforms us into beasts. Is this the part of wise men, engaged in great and arduous struggle for liberty? Are we disposed to be on the number of those who, having eyes, see not, and having ears, hear not, the things which so nearly concern their temporal salvation? For my part, whatever anguish of spirit it may cost, I am willing to know the whole truth; to know the worst and provide for it. I have but one lamp by which my feet are guided; and that is the lamp of experience. I know of no way of judging of the future but by the past. And judging by the past I wish to know what there has been in the conduct of the British ministry for the last ten years to justify those hopes with which gentlemen have been pleased to solace themselves and the House? Is it that insidious smile with which our petition has been lately received? Trust it not, sir; it will prove a snare to your feet. Suffer not yourselves to be betrayed with a kiss. Ask yourselves how this gracious reception of our petition comports with these warlike preparations which cover our waters and darken our land. Are fleets and armies necessary to a work of love and reconciliation? Have we shown ourselves so unwilling to be reconciled, that force must be called in to win back our love? Let us not deceive ourselves, sir. These are the implements of war and subjugation; the last arguments to which kings resort. I ask gentlemen, sir, what means this martial array, if its purpose be not to force us to submission? Can gentlemen assign any other possible motives for it? Has Great Britain any enemy, in this quarter of the world, to call for all this accumulation of navies and armies? No, sir, she has none. They are meant for us; they can be meant for no other. They are sent over to bind and rivet upon us those chains which the British ministry have been so long forging. And what have we to oppose them? Shall we try argument? Sir, we have been trying that for the last ten years. Have we anything new to offer on the subject? Nothing. We have held the subject up in every light of which it is capable; but it has been all in vain. Shall we resort to entreaty and humble supplication? What terms shall we find which have not been already exhausted? Let us not, I beseech you, sir, deceive ourselves longer. Sir, we have done everything that could be done to avert the storm which is now coming on. We have petitioned; we have remonstrated; we have supplicated; we have prostrated ourselves before the throne, and have implored its interposition to arrest the tyrannical hands of the ministry and parliament. Our petitions have been slighted; our remonstrances have produced additional violence and insult; our supplications have been disregarded; and we have been spurned, with contempt, from the foot of the throne. In vain, after these things, may we indulge the fond hope of peace and reconciliation. There is no longer any room for hope. If we wish to be free – if we mean to preserve inviolate those inestimable privileges for which we have been so long contending – if we mean not basely to abandon the noble struggle in which we have been so long engaged, and which we have pledged ourselves never to abandon until the glorious object of our contest shall be obtained, we must fight! I repeat it, sir, we must fight! An appeal to arms and to the God of Hosts is all that is left us!

They tell us, sir, that we are weak; unable to cope with so formidable an adversary. But when shall we be stronger? Will it be the next week, or the next year? Will it be when we are totally disarmed, and when a British guard shall be stationed in every house? Shall we gather strength by irresolution and inaction? Shall we acquire the means of effectual resistance by lying supinely on our backs, and hugging the delusive phantom of hope, until our enemies shall have bound us hand and foot? Sir, we are not weak, if we make a proper use of the means which the God of nature hath placed in our power. Three millions of people, armed in the Holy cause of Liberty, and in such a country as that which we possess, are invincible by any force which our enemy can send against us. Besides, sir, we shall not fight our battles along. There is a just God who presides over the destinies of nations; and who will raise up friends to fight our battles for us. The battle, sir, is not to the strong alone; it is to the vigilant, the active, the brave. Besides, sir, we have no election. If we were base enough to desire it, it is now too late to retire from the contest. There is no retreat but in submission and slavery! Our chains are forged! Their clanking may be heard on the plains of Boston! The war is inevitable – and let it come! I repeat it, sir, let it come!

It is in vain, sire, to extenuate the matter. Gentlemen may cry peace, peace – but there is no peace. The war is actually begun! The next gale that sweeps from the North will bring to our ears the clash of resounding arms! Our brethren are already in the field! Why stand we here idle? What is it that gentlemen wish? What would they have? Is life so dear, or peace so sweet, as to be purchased at the price of chains and slavery? Forbid it, Almighty God! I know not what course others may take; but as for me, give me liberty or give me death!

Most of those in attendance were moved, many shouting "to arms, to arms," at Henry's stirring words including Thomas Jefferson who commented on that speech in his autobiography: "I attended the debate at the door of the lobby of the House of Burgesses, and heard the splendid display of Mr. Henry's talents as a popular orator. They were great indeed; such as I have never heard from any other man. He appeared to speak as Homer wrote."

While it is incontrovertibly true, based on the written and spoken words of Henry, that he was zealous in his quest for liberty, it is also just as certain that he would have been shocked and angered by the perversions of those constitutionally-guaranteed liberties that have become commonplace in the late twentieth and early twenty-first centuries in the United States of America. Along with his fellow founders, Henry would have risen in strong opposition to the use of First Amendment language to justify distribution of pornographic materials, the burning of an American flag by a U. S. citizen, gross degeneracy in public "entertainment" and all the other subversions of the Bill of Rights twisted and used by the American Civil Liberties Union and other like-minded organizations, supported by liberal judges, to undermine public morality in the name of "civil liberties."

Henry's words leave no room for doubt that the campaign to marginalize Christianity would have been anathema to him. "It is when a people forget God," Henry said, "that tyrants forge their chains. A vitiated state of morals, a corrupted public conscience, is incompatible with freedom. No free government, or the blessings of liberty, can be preserved to any people but by a firm adherence to justice, moderation, temperance, frugality, and virtue; and by a frequent recurrence to fundamental principles." The fundamental principles to which he referred are those whose basis is found in the Judeo-Christian Bible. "The Bible," he said, "is a book worth more than all the other books that were ever printed."

"The greatest pillars of all government and social life," Henry stated, "are virtue, morality, and religion. This is the armor my friend, and this alone that renders us invincible...I go on this great republican principle, that the people will have virtue and intelligence to select men of virtue and wisdom...To suppose that any form of government will secure liberty or happiness without any virtue in the people, is a chimerical idea."

Henry's very publicly displayed beliefs regarding true liberty, versus the licentiousness promoted by the American Civil [Licentiousness] Union, coincide perfectly with the following statement by Supreme Court Justice Joseph Story in his *Commentaries on the Constitution*: "Let the American youth never forget, that they possess a noble inheritance, bought by the toils and sufferings and blood of their ancestors; and capacity, if wisely improved, and faithfully guarded, of transmitting to their latest posterity all the substantial blessings of life, the peaceful enjoyment of liberty, property, religion, and independence. The structure has been erected by architects of consummate skill and fidelity; its foundations are solid; its compartments are beautiful, as well as useful; its arrangements are full of wisdom and order; and its defences are impregnable from without. It has been reared for immortality, if the work of man may justly aspire to such a title. It may nevertheless, perish in an hour by the folly, or corruption, or negligence of its only keepers, THE PEOPLE." (1)

History revisionists with few exceptions resort to the issue of slavery in their attempts to prove that the Founding Fathers couldn't have been Christians, or, if they were, they were not very good ones since slavery was not outlawed in the Constitution. Many of the founders, including George Washington and Benjamin Franklin, did make reference to the ignominious character of the generally accepted practice of owning slaves, but they understood there was a higher priority – to draft a constitution that could be ratified. Because of the entrenched position of slave-owners in a number of southern states, the chances of getting the required number of states to ratify a constitution outlawing slavery were understood to be nonexistent. For that reason, they made the practical decision to postpone that objective until the overriding need of establishing a unified nation under an acceptable national constitution was achieved. Article 1, section 9 of the constitution did give Congress power to end the slave trade in 1808 which was the first step in an incremental approach to abolishing slavery in the United States. Speaking for himself but representing the feelings of most of the founders, Henry wrote the following:

> *Is it not amazing that at a time when the rights of humanity are defined and understood with precision, in a country, above all others, fond of liberty, that in such an age and in such a country we find men professing a religion the most humane, mild, gentle and generous, adopting a principle as repugnant to humanity as it is inconsistent with the Bible, and destructive to liberty? Every thinking, honest man rejects it in speculation; how few in practice from conscientious motives!*
>
> *Would anyone believe I am the master of slaves of my own purchase! I am drawn along by the general inconvenience of living here without them. I will not, I cannot justify it. However culpable my conduct, I will so far pay my devoir to virtue as to own the excellence and rectitude of her precepts, and lament my want of conformity to them. I believe a time will come when an opportunity will be offered to abolish this lamentable evil. Everything we do is to improve it, if it happens in our day; if not, let us transmit to our descendants, together with our slaves, a pity for their unhappy lot and an abhorrence of slavery. If we cannot reduce this wished-for reformation to practice, let us treat the unhappy victims with lenity. It is the furthest advance we can make toward justice. It is a debt we owe to the purity of our religion, to show that it is at variance with that law which warrants slavery. I know*

not when to stop. I could say many things on the subject, a
serious view of which gives a gloomy perspective to future
times. (2)

Henry was born May 29, 1736, on a tobacco plantation in
Studley, Hanover County, Virginia. According to John Eidsmoe in
his *Christianity and the Constitution,* "His parents, Colonel John and
Sarah Henry, came from prominent families of Scottish and English
backgrounds. His mother's family was descended from King Alfred
the Great; his father's family traced its ancestry through the Norman
invaders under William the Conqueror. There were many educa-
tors, orators, statesmen and preachers on both sides of his family.
Dr. William Robertson, a first cousin once-removed, was a well-
known Scottish preacher and scholar whose essay on 'Chivalry'
impressed Henry with the principles of honesty, generosity, courage,
and loyalty. [James] Madison's wife Dolley was a first cousin once-
removed of Patrick Henry.

Henry's formal education consisted of a few years at an English
common school where he learned reading, writing, and a little arith-
metic. His father took him out of school when he was about ten
and taught him at home. Patrick Henry loved nature and enjoyed
canoe trips, fishing, hunting, and rambling through the woodlands
and hillsides. But Patrick also acquired knowledge of Greek and
Latin and of the classics as well as the Bible through his father's
diligent efforts. (3)

Soon after receiving his license to practice law in 1760, his name
became well known, especially for his success in handling criminal
cases. His reputation as a defender of Colonial rights was enhanced
by his involvement in the Parsons' Cause, a case in which he prevailed
against King George III, which helped him to become a prominent
political official first in Virginia then on the national scene.

As a member of the House of Burgesses, he, in concert with
Thomas Jefferson and Richard Henry Lee were successful in initi-
ating a committee of correspondence for Virginia. In 1774, he was
elected as a delegate to the First Continental Congress and, in 1775,
he was elected to the Second Continental Congress. Then, in 1776,
he was elected governor of Virginia where he served three terms.

After a short retirement from public office, he ran for and was elected to the Virginia legislature where he served until, once again, he was elected to serve as governor of the state of Virginia. Although his fellow Virginians elected him as a delegate to the 1787 Constitutional Convention in Philadelphia, he refused to attend because he believed a strong federal government would likely diminish many fundamental rights of the states, and therefore the people. Once the Bill of Rights was added to the constitution, he became reconciled to the federal government and, subsequently, was offered appointments as Secretary of State, Chief Justice of the Supreme Court, Minister to Spain, Minister to France, a seat in the U. S. Senate. Primarily due to poor health, Henry declined each of the appointments.

Along with so many of his fellow founders, Patrick Henry was labeled a deist by some who apparently didn't know the man very well and whose words have been used recently in an attempt to separate modern Americans from their Christian roots. Here's his response to that charge: "...I hear it is said by the deists that I am one of their number; and indeed that some good people think I am no Christian. This thought gives me much more pain than the appellation of Tory [being called a traitor], because I think religion of infinitely higher importance than politics... [B]eing a Christian...is a character which I prize far above all this world has or can boast."

To those who say the United States of America was never a Christian nation, founder Patrick Henry's own words take issue: "It cannot be emphasized too strongly or too often that this great nation was founded, not by religionists, but by Christians; not on religions, but on the Gospel of Jesus Christ. For this very reason people of other faiths have been afforded asylum, prosperity, and freedom of worship here."

Further attesting to his deep religious beliefs, he said, in his last will and testament, "This is all the inheritance I can give to my dear family. The religion of Christ can give them one which will make them rich indeed."

Chapter Eleven

Alexander Hamilton

He [Hamilton] *defined and espoused the principles
of federalism, that is, the creation of government
with powers strictly limited in scope but fully adequate
to the needs of the states, which retained sovereignty
and jurisdiction in all other matters.*
—Norman Cousins

*In my opinion, the present constitution
is the standard to which we are to cling.
Under its banner bona fide must we combat our political foes,
rejecting all changes but through the channel itself provided for
amendments. By these general views of the subject
have my reflections been guided.
I now offer you the outline of the plan they have suggested .
Let an association be formed to be denominated "The Christian
Constitutional Society," its object to be first:
The support of the Christian religion; second:
The support of the United States.--*
Alexander Hamilton

Alexander Hamilton's close relationship with George Washington began in 1777 when, as a twenty-year-old artillery captain, he was introduced to Washington by General Nathanael Greene after Hamilton's notably courageous service in the battles of Long Island, White Plains, Trenton, and Princeton. Upon Greene's recommendation, Hamilton was promoted to the rank of lieutenant colonel and appointed Washington's aide-de-camp and personal secretary, a position he held until 1781 when, by his own request, he returned to active military duty and was given command of an infantry brigade by Washington. In the decisive Revolutionary War battle of Yorktown, Hamilton was in command of an infantry regiment. (1)

The relationship between General Washington and Lieutenant Hamilton, based on mutual respect and admiration that began in the early years of the war, carried over through the Constitutional Convention of 1787 in which both men played important roles. When elected as the first President, Washington appointed Hamilton to be his Secretary of the Treasury. Along with Hamilton, Washington's cabinet was made up of Thomas Jefferson, Secretary of State; Henry Knox, Secretary of War, and Edmund Randolph, Attorney General. Although not a cabinet member, John Jay, appointed the first Chief Justice of the Supreme Court, exerted a great deal of influence in the newly formed government.

The renowned speech delivered September 19, 1796, known as Washington's Farewell Address, was prepared with the assistance of Hamilton, testifying to the high esteem with which Washington had always held his younger colleague, especially his rarely equaled writing ability. It is not known which man actually penned the following statement, but it is known that they were in agreement regarding the sentiment expressed: "Of all the dispositions and habits which lead to political prosperity, religion and morality are indispensable supports."

Hamilton's pre-Revolutionary War association with Washington, his staff, and confederates, including the most powerful and influential men in the colonies, had provided Hamilton, at an early age, with contacts that enabled him to take the prominent role that he enjoyed in the Independence movement and in shaping the newly emerging republic, especially in the area of finance and commerce.

His prodigious writing abilities, which he had previously exhibited in 1774 and 1775 as a pamphleteer, were especially useful to Washington who had many demands on his time. The providential circumstances that brought Washington and Hamilton together at this pivotal point in time "began a collaboration which was to last many years and affect the course of American history. Washington, as commander in chief had important messages and papers to write – to Congress, to foreign governments, to leaders in the states. He found in Hamilton a cool, resourceful mind in which historical experience was neatly balanced by insight into the contemporary situation. Hamilton, moreover, had as lucid and persuasive a pen as any man of the period possessed, not excluding Thomas Jefferson or James Madison. Hamilton also had a full view of his ultimate objective and was in an excellent position to help move other men in that direction." (2)

To those of us who tend to see the hand of God in the lives of men and the fortunes of nations, the out-of-the-blue arrival on the scene in pre-Revolutionary War America by an unknown 19-year-old man from the West Indies with a natural talent for writing and political insight seems to have a supernatural aura. Alexander Hamilton was born January 11, 1757, on the Island of Eustatius, or the Island of Neva, depending on which historian you believe, to unmarried parents and "all but an orphan at eleven. Educated privately on St. Croix, in apprenticeship to the island firm of Nicholas Cruger..." (3) Because of Hamilton's demonstrated precocity, Cruger and Hugh Knox, a Presbyterian minister, made arrangements to send the 15-year-old prodigy to America to live with William Livingston, a future signer of the U. S. Constitution. Livingstone sent him to Francis Barber's school in Elizabethtown, New Jersey, and to King's College (now Columbia University) in New York City where he enrolled at the age of 16. Three years later, he left school without a degree and joined the American army. (4) After the war, Hamilton completed the educational requirements for the practice of law. He soon became known as the most brilliant lawyer in New York.

In his *Patriot's Handbook*, George Grant appropriately summarizes Hamilton's role in early American history in these few words: "Washington's most valued assistant in war and peace, Hamilton was probably the most brilliant writer, organizer, and political theorist among the Founding Fathers. Time after time from 1776 to 1795 he brought his great powers of intellect to bear on the most critical problems facing the new nation – from obtaining a truly national constitution to establishing a sound national financial system."

Because of his combination of military experience and his close association with the politics of his time, Hamilton had a practical view of war and its place in international relations. He understood the importance of national defense and how to prepare for it. Mackubin Owens, writing in *The Founders' Almanac*, explained Hamilton's insight with these words: "Hamilton was a soldier-statesman who could be trusted with the sword of his country. Rejecting the utopian vision of Thomas Jefferson and many of his allies, Hamilton understood that war was a fact of international life, and that the survival of the infant Republic depended on developing and maintaining the potential to make war. But Hamilton was not a militaristic statebuilder along the lines of Frederick the Great or Bismarck. He was an advocate of limited government and therefore always understood the necessity of remaining within the legal bounds established by the Constitution. 'Let us not establish a tyranny,' he wrote in 1798. 'Energy is a very different thing from violence.' Hamilton's goal was to establish a republican regime both fit for war and safe for freedom. He was a strategist before the word was coined, and his strategic objectives were to enable the American Republic to avoid war when possible and to wage it effectively when necessary, all the while preserving both political and civil liberty."

He, along with most of his fellow founders, especially George Washington, understood the principle of "peace through strength.

Hamilton's worldly wisdom and insight were governed and reinforced by his belief in the superintendence of an omnipotent, omnipresent, omniscient God, the Judeo-Christian God of the Bible. "The sacred rites of mankind," Hamilton said, "are not to be rummaged for among old parchments or rusty records. They are written, as with a sunbeam, in the whole volume of human nature, by the hand of the Divinity itself, and can never be erased or obscured by mortal power."

By "the Divinity," Hamilton made it clear to whom he was referring when he said, "Two things which make America great: (1)

Christianity and (2) a Constitution formed under Christianity." He also made this statement following the often contentious but eventually successful Constitutional Convention: "For my own part, I sincerely esteem it a system which without the finger of God, never could have been suggested and agreed upon by such a diversity of interests."

Some historians have called Hamilton "the Ratifier of the Constitution" because of his dedication to that purpose. He was one of the first of the Founding fathers to become convinced of the need for and advantages of a strong, united national government. In 1780, he wrote, "The fundamental defect [of the Articles of Confederation] is a want of power in Congress...But the Confederation itself is defective, and requires to be altered. It is neither fit for war nor peace. The idea of an uncontrollable sovereignty in each State over its internal police will defeat the other powers given to Congress, and make our union feeble and precarious..." (5)

As a growing number of colonists began to be convinced of the perceived advantages inherent in his arguments, they began to give thought as to how to alter the Articles of Confederation to fit the objective of a strong national government. Most of the delegates to the Constitutional Convention of 1787 attended with the belief they were to revise the Articles, not scrap them in favor of an entirely new U. S. Constitution. Many historians doubt that the convention could have taken place had the states understood how the basic form of government would be radically changed from their emphasis on the independent rights of individual states to an emphasis on a strong national, or federal, government. Too many colonists had yet to be convinced that was a desirable thing, although they did see merit in some change in that direction.

When the Constitution was submitted to the states for ratification, even many delegates to the convention opposed ratification because of perceived imperfections and various and sundry provisions with which they were not entirely happy. Although he would have preferred even more power centralized in the federal government, Hamilton worked diligently for ratification. "If mankind," he said, "were to resolve to agree in no institution of government, until every part of it had been adjusted to the most exact standard of perfection, society would soon become a general scene of anarchy, and the world a desert." He believed authoritative government was a necessity "because the passions of men will not conform to the dictates of reason and justice without restraint."

Eventually, two-thirds of the states did ratify the document that has been called "the miracle of Philadelphia" but many have speculated that would not have happened without the timely publication of the *Federalist Papers*, a collection of 85 articles written by Hamilton along with John Jay and James Madison. The essays appeared first in New York City newspapers, then in newspapers in other states, under the byline of Publius. Hamilton, historians generally agree, wrote 52 of the 85 essays that George Washington described as having "thrown a new light upon the science of government; they have given the rights of man a full and fair discussion, and explained them in so clear and forcible a manner, as cannot fail to make a lasting impression." Thomas Jefferson portrayed *The Federalist Papers*, which were also soon published in pamphlet and in book form, as "the best commentary on the principles of government which ever was written." (6) It has been said that Hamilton's *Federalist* writings were the most brilliant of his literary efforts. Over the years, the Supreme Court has often used them as an aid in interpreting the original intent of the Constitution.

Once the Constitution went into effect June 21, 1788, then what? Here's how historian and author Clarence B. Carson described the problem: "The most extensive problem ... was to translate the Constitution into a government. The Constitution was, after all, still a 'piece of paper,' as they would say, an important piece of paper, no doubt, a paper on which some of the best minds in America had worked diligently. Would it work as they had tried to foresee? It had many experimental features. It contained a vision, a hope, a dream, if you will or whatever elegant words might be applied to it, but the government which it described was only in the early stages of becoming a reality. Would people obey this government? Would they support it? Would those who came to power in it adhere to the Constitution? These are always vital questions for a government, but they were especially pressing for one that was yet only a plan and a prospect.

"One thing was certain: If the Constitution did give rise to the reality of an effective government, it would be done by men. It would be men who breathed the breath of life into the government, who provided the flesh to the bones of the Constitution, who in their contests with one another held the government in check, and who gave impetus and direction to it.

"L. D. White, who made extensive studies of early administrations, described the problems in this brief paragraph: 'The government of the Confederation had steadily run down until its movements had almost ceased.' Washington 'took over almost nothing from the dying Confederation. There *was*, indeed, a foreign office with John Jay and a couple of clerks to deal with correspondence from John Adams in London and Thomas Jefferson in Paris; there *was* a Treasury Board with an empty treasury; there *was* a 'Secretary at War' with an authorized army of 840 men; there were a dozen clerks whose pay was in arrears, and an unknown but fearful burden of debt, almost no revenue, and a prostrate credit. But one cold hardly perceive ...a government of the Union." (7)

Figuring out how to handle that "burden of debt," including almost $12,000,000 owed to foreign creditors and over $27,000,000 of domestic debt, with interest growing daily, was one of the considerable problems with which Alexander Hamilton, the Secretary of the Treasury, would have to deal. While those numbers don't seem to be imposing today, they were more than imposing to a new government with bad credit. Hamilton, who had been described as a financial genius by his old boss George Washington, was equal to the task.

"His task," wrote Carson, "would have appeared hopeless enough if he had aimed only to get revenue to run the government. Americans were not, after all, known for their enthusiasm for paying taxes, and their politicians had thus far shown considerable willingness to delay as long as possible the necessity for levying taxes. But Hamilton wanted much more than revenue. He wanted to establish the credit of the United States, when bankruptcy or repudiation was the obvious outlet. And, he wanted to do so in a way that would tie men of wealth and position to the government, and make it clear that the general government would take care of national concerns.

"Hamilton's programs were made public in a series of reports to Congress. These reports dealt with the subjects of public credit, a national bank, and manufactures. It should be said that these reports were composed at the request of Congress, that members of Congress were generally glad to have his direction, and that they did not, themselves, constitute executive interference with the affairs of Congress. It is also true, however, that Hamilton did aggressively push his programs through contacts with Representatives and Senators. 'Nothing is done without him,' according to Senator Maclay of Pennsylvania. Indeed, when the funding bill was up for consideration, Maclay wrote in his diary, 'Mr. Hamilton...was here early to wait on the Speaker, and I believe spent most of his time in running from place to place among the members.' Hamilton not only proposed but also disposed, as much as he could." (8)

Hamilton, then, was the individual primarily responsible for providing the creative thinking and energetic force that defined the embryonic national economic policy needed during the early days of the republic. "His financial system for funding the national and state debts, for converting those liabilities into a basis for credit and commercial activity, and for organizing the Bank of the United States have been remembered since his time simply as 'Hamiltonianism'." (9) Once again, he was the right man at the right place at the right time.

Other broad differences of public opinion on important issues began to come to the surface as the battle for Constitutional ratification, which had divided the public into two sharply divided camps, wound down. The two camps had initially become known as the Federalists and the Anti-Federalists. Originally, those known as the Federalists were in favor of the new Constitution because of its provision for a strong federal government; the Anti-Federalists were not in favor of the new Constitution because of its' de-emphasis of states rights and their fearfulness of the possibility of a diminishing of individual rights.

Once the ratification issue was resolved, marked differences began to surface over economic, especially taxing, issues. As time progressed, the group known as the Anti-Federalists evolved into the Republican Party, led by Thomas Jefferson and James Madison, that opposed the Hamilton and John Adams-led Federalist Party which championed more centralization of power, especially in the area of taxation.

Many of the founders, including George Washington, opposed political parties because of a concern they would do damage to the fabric of the republic. Others understood there would be differences of opinion and that the development of political parties was inevitable. Modern day Democrats claim Jefferson as their originator, but Jefferson called himself a Republican. Modern day Democrats have much more in common with the Federalists and their belief in big government and centralization of economic planning. Thus, the two party system evolved. Once again, Hamilton was one of the high profile individuals providing the impetus and the energy.

George Grant summarized Hamilton's vast contributions to the upstart nation with these words: "The Constitution and the Federalist Papers, the national financial system and the American two-party system – in a very real sense these are the legacy of the brilliant man who came to America a penniless youth." (10)

A few history revisionists have suggested that Hamilton, like many of the other Founding Fathers, was not a Christian. To those, Hamilton would, no doubt, point to these words he spoke on that subject: "I have carefully examined the evidences of the Christian religion, and if I was sitting as a juror upon its authenticity I would unhesitatingly give my verdict in its favor. I can prove its truth as clearly as any proposition ever submitted to the mind of man."

"Mortals hastening to the tomb, and once the companions of my pilgrimage," he advised, "take warning, and avoid my errors. Cultivate the virtues I have recommended. Choose the Saviour I have chosen. Live disinterestedly, and would you rescue anything from final dissolution, lay it up in God."

Hamilton died July 12, 1804, at the hand of Aaron Burr, a dedicated political enemy, in a duel the previous day. Hamilton had been instrumental in denying Burr the presidency in 1800 and the New York governorship in 1804 after which Burr forced Hamilton into the fatal duel. Hamilton declined to fire his weapon. While dueling was illegal, Hamilton thought it would be unmanly of him to refuse the challenge. On July 10, he composed one of his last writings, a letter to his wife:

"This letter, my dear Eliza, will not be delivered to you unless I shall first have terminated my earthly career, to begin, as I humbly hope, from redeeming grace and divine mercy, a happy immortality. If it had been possible for me to have avoided the interview, my love for you and my precious children would have been alone a decisive motive. But it was not possible, without sacrifices which would have rendered me unworthy of your esteem. I need not tell you of the pangs I feel from the idea of quitting you, and exposing you to the anguish I know you would feel. Nor could I dwell on the topic, lest it should unman me. The consolations of religion, my beloved, can alone support you; and these you have a right to enjoy. Fly to the bosom of your God, and be comforted. With my last idea I shall cherish the sweet hope of meeting you in a better world. Adieu, best of wives – best of women. Embrace all my darling children for me."

Chapter Twelve

John Dickinson

I do profess faith in God the Father,
and in Jesus Christ His Eternal Son the true God,
and in the Holy Spirit, one God blessed for evermore;
and I do acknowledge the Holy Scriptures of the Old and New
Testaments to be given by Divine inspiration.
-- **John Dickinson**

John Dickinson – one of the great worthies of the Revolution.
— **Thomas Jefferson**

The United States of America had *A* constitution before it had *The* Constitution: It was called *The Articles of Confederation* so named by Benjamin Franklin (some refer to it as the "preconstitution"). The formal title of the document is *Articles of Confederation and Perpetual Union between the States of New Hampshire, Massachusetts Bay, Rhode Island and Providence Plantations, Connecticut, New York, New Jersey, Pennsylvania, Delaware, Maryland, Virginia, North Carolina, South Carolina, and Georgia.*

Historians seem to agree that credit for the Articles' authorship belongs primarily to John Dickinson who prepared the first draft although it was significantly revised, due to a number of disagreements among the various states, before eventually being adopted.

"The style of this Confederacy shall be 'The United States of America,' declared Article One. Article Two addressed the sovereignty of the individual states: "Each State retains its sovereignty, freedom, and independence, and every power, jurisdiction, and right, which is not by the Confederacy expressly delegated to the United States in Congress assembled." Article Three called for mutual assistance: "The said States hereby severally enter into a firm league of friendship with each other, for their common defence, the security of their liberties, and their mutual and general welfare, binding themselves to assist each other against all force offered to, or attacks made upon them, or any of them, on account of religion, sovereignty, trade, or any other pretence whatever."

Articles Four through Thirteen provided detailed information regarding operational matters. In the Epilogue, we find these ringing words: "AND WHEREAS it hath pleased the Great Governor of the world to incline the hearts of the legislatures we respectfully represent in Congress to approve of and to authorize us to ratify the said Articles of Confederation and perpetual Union, Know Ye, That we, the undersigned delegates, by virtue of the power and authority to us given for that purpose, do by these presents, in the name and in behalf of our respective constituents, fully and entirely ratify and confirm each and every of the said Articles of Confederation and perpetual Union, and all and singular the matters and things therein contained: and we do further solemnly plight and engage the faith of our respective constituents that they shall abide by the determinations of the United States in Congress assembled, on all questions which by the said Confederation are submitted to them. And that the Articles thereof shall be inviolably observed by the States we respectively represent, and the Union shall be perpetual."

Dickinson had established his reputation as an expositor many years earlier when, as a member of the Stamp Act Congress, he was instrumental in producing the Declaration of Rights and Grievances delivered to the British Parliament protesting the Stamp Tax. Those documents, along with his other writings, earned him the title "Penman of the Revolution." Some historians have speculated that Dickinson, had he been convinced earlier in the period leading up to the Revolutionary War that armed conflict was the only way to throw off the ever-increasing economic shackles imposed on the colonies, which Edmund Burke called "a succession of Acts of Tyranny," might have been given the assignment of producing the Declaration of Independence rather than Thomas Jefferson.

He had, however, alienated many of the "patriots," as those who believed war was the only acceptable alternative were called, with his "Olive Branch Petition" to King George III and other written and spoken public utterances favoring reconciliation, if at all possible. His "A Farmer's Letters to the Inhabitants of the British Colonies" have been called "among the best expositions of colonial rights that had yet appeared." (1)

Dickinson was originally opposed to independence because of his concern that conflicts of interests between the states would destroy the union; he did not sign the Declaration of Independence. Many have also speculated that his family's Quaker roots and his being married to a Quaker, although he later in life was a member of the Episcopalian Church, may have influenced his views regarding armed conflict. Based on Matthew 5:39 ("Do not resist one who is evil"), orthodox Quakers believed there was no legitimate justification for war, even to the point of not resisting attacks against them.

The British, perhaps more than his own countrymen, recognized his prominence in generating the rebellion when they demonstrated their irritation and their understanding of his role by burning his house to the ground in 1776. A major source of their consternation was publication of the previously mentioned *Farmer's Letters* carried by influential newspapers.

Dickinson's initial draft of the Articles of Confederation was begun in June of 1776 and was presented to the Congress July 12, eight days after the Declaration of Independence was signed. The Declaration of Independence and the Articles of Confederation basically went hand in hand; the Articles empowered Congress to conduct foreign policy and to fight the war while pretty much leaving domestic matters, with a nod towards cooperation, to the states. While it wasn't officially adopted until 1781, the Articles provided, in the meantime, a basic framework and operating procedures for nuts and bolts government until George Washington was inaugurated as the first president of the United States under the present Constitution in March of 1788. Actually, the First and Second Congresses operated under an almost identical system from 1774 to 1776; for all practical purposes, the country was operated in a way compatible with the Articles of Confederation for fourteen years including the entire Revolutionary War period. (2)

While it served an important purpose, the Articles, which provided a loose unity among the not-so-united colonies/states, had weaknesses, the most glaring of which was the lack of a strong executive along with what turned out to be a major stumbling block to national unity set forth in Article Two: "Each State retains its sovereignty, freedom, and independence, and every power, jurisdiction, and right, which is not by the Confederacy expressly delegated to the United States in Congress assembled." Consistent and coherent foreign and domestic policies were difficult if not impossible to formulate with the Articles' very specific emphasis on each state's sovereign rights. Because of his efforts to find the most desirable balance point between states' rights and a strong national government, Dickinson was often misunderstood by his contemporaries and some historians. He advocated a careful and intelligent approach to independence, rather than an emotional one. In today's parlance, he might have warned against "throwing out the baby with the bathwater." The Articles of Confederation represented an attempt to find that balance point, but it soon became obvious the Articles didn't quite achieve that objective. It became a stepping stone to a more pragmatic solution.

The writers of the Microsoft Encarta Encyclopedia provided an excellent capsulization of the problems inherent with the Articles:

> *The greatest weakness of the federal government under the Articles of Confederation was its inability to regulate trade and levy taxes. Sometimes the states refused to give*

the government the money it needed, and they engaged in tariff wars with one another, almost paralyzing interstate commerce. The government could not pay off the debts it had incurred during the revolution, including paying soldiers who had fought in the war and citizens who had provided supplies to the cause. Congress could not pass needed measures because they lacked the nine-state majority required to become laws. The states largely ignored Congress, which was powerless to enforce cooperation, and it was therefore unable to carry out its duties.

Congress could not force the states to adhere to the terms of the Treaty of Paris of 1783 ending the American Revolution, which was humiliating to the new government, especially when some states started their own negotiations with foreign countries. In addition, the new nation was unable to defend its borders from British and Spanish encroachment because it could not pay for an army when the states would not contribute the necessary funds. Leaders like Alexander Hamilton of New York and James Madison of Virginia criticized the limits placed on the central government, and General George Washington is said to have complained that the federation was "little more than a shadow without substance."

When the practicalities of governing a growing country and operating as a sovereign nation in a naturally hostile world set in, the stage was set for the Constitutional Convention of 1787 to which Dickinson was appointed as a delegate from the state of Delaware. Eventually, Dickinson, speaking before Congress in 1776, made his support of the Revolution clearly known: "The happiness of these Colonies has been, during the whole course of this fatal controversy, our first wish; their reconciliation with Great Britain our next: ardently have we prayed for the accomplishment of both.

"But if we must renounce the one or the other, we humbly trust in the mercies of the Supreme Governor of the universe that we shall not stand condemned before His throne if our choice is determined by that law of self-preservation which his Divine wisdom has seen fit to implant in the hearts of His creatures." (3)

What we now routinely refer to as the Constitutional Convention of 1787 was originally presented as the Philadelphia Convention, ostensibly called "for the sole and express purpose of revising the Articles of Confederation." (4) Many historians speculate that a number of states would not have sent delegates had they known the actual purpose of the convention was to replace the Articles of Confederation with a new "federal" constitution. Once those in attendance, including Dickinson who played an important but low profile role, had completed their work, the next obvious step was to sell enough states on its' advantages to get the new Constitution ratified. Once again, John Dickinson's pen was a major factor in the process. Writing under the name of Fabius, he produced a series of essays that are credited with playing a vital role in securing approval by Pennsylvania and Delaware, the first two states to officially accept the Constitution, creating much-needed momentum for the ratification campaign. While the *Federalist Papers* are much more generally recognized for their role in getting the Constitution ratified, Dickinson's *Letters* have been compared favorably by many historians.

When seminal events were taking place and vital decisions were being made from 1765 'til the end of the century, John Dickinson's name is nearly always mentioned. Born in 1732 in Talbot County, Maryland, and raised in Kent County, Delaware, he was prepared early in life to be an attorney by his father, Judge Samuel Dickinson. According to M. E. Bradford, "he was first educated privately and then in the offices of John Moland, a leader of the Philadelphia bar. Young John finished this preliminary training in 1753 and was then dispatched to London and the Middle Temple for four years of the best of English legal preparation. On his return he established himself in his profession, eventually becoming one of the most respected American attorneys."

He was first elected to public office in 1760 as a member of the Delaware Assembly which led to his direct involvement in independence issues. In 1774, he was named chairman of the Philadelphia Committee of Correspondence and appointed a delegate to the Continental Congress. "For his colleagues in Congress, he wrote the

Declaration and Resolves of the First Continental Congress and the *Declaration of the Causes of Taking Up Arms.*" (5)

Dickinson was asked by Samuel Adams and James Otis to compose a freedom song to be sung at public demonstrations. Here is what he wrote:

> *Come join hand in hand, brave Americans all;*
> *And rouse your bold hearts at fair Liberty's call.*
> *No tyrannous acts shall suppress your just claim;*
> *Or stain with dishonor America's name.*
> (Chorus)
> *In freedom we're born and in freedom we'll live;*
> *Our purses are ready; Steady Friends, steady.*
> *Not as slaves, but as freemen our money we'll give.*
> *Then join in hand brave Americans all*
> *By uniting we stand, by dividing we fall.*
> *To die we can bear, but to serve we disdain.*
> *For shame is to freemen more dreadful than pain.* (6)

As a member of the Pennsylvania militia, Dickinson was involved in military action in Pennsylvania and New Jersey.

John Dickinson grew up during the time the "Great Awakening" (1740's) was at its' zenith in the Colonies and, many historians say, helped to establish an impetus towards national unity. That unity was a necessary factor in rallying the general population to the cause of independence. "From the start, religion had been an intellectual force; in the 18C [century], it exerted a renewed influence on the broadest class. America like England witnessed a resurgence of religious passion, which put forward old ideas: consciousness of sin and recognition of God's mercy; self-reform imperative to ensure grace and salvation. The movement was known in England as Methodism, in America as the Great Awakening. The appeal of the eloquent preachers—John and Charles Wesley in England, George Whitefield in America—produced the mass phenomenon called 'revival'; Whitefield was said able to address audibly crowds of 25,000". (7) Dickinson would have experienced the "national" revival at an impressionable age.

Many of Dickinson's pronouncements make it clear that he was a Christian and that he believed in the providential nature of the independence movement. "Kings or parliaments could not give the rights essential to happiness," Dickinson said. "We claim them from a higher source—from the King of kings, and Lord of all the earth. They are not annexed to us by parchments and seals. They are created in us by the decrees of Providence, which establish the laws of our nature. They are born with us; exist with us; and cannot be taken from us by any human power without taking our lives. In short, they are founded on the immutable maxims of reason and justice. It would be an insult on the Divine Majesty to say that he has given or allowed any man or body of men a right to make me miserable."

Dickinson believed that love of God and love of country were so closely intertwined as to be inseparable as he wrote in *Letters from a Pennsylvania Farmer*: "I pray GOD that he may be pleased to inspire you and your posterity, to the latest ages, with a spirit of which I have an idea, that I find a difficulty to express. To express it in the best manner I can, I mean a spirit that shall so guide you that it will be impossible to determine whether an *American's* character is most distinguishable for his loyalty to his Sovereign [God], his duty to his mother country, his love of freedom, or his affection for his native soil."

"But above all," he said, "let us implore the protection of that infinitely good and gracious being [Proverbs 8:15] 'by whom kings reign, and princes decree justice'." (8)

History revisionists intent on portraying the Founding Fathers as being much less honorable and much less Christian in their behavior than they have been proven to be almost always use the issue of slavery to make their point. They ignore the evidence and the words of many of the founders who made it clear that slavery would be eliminated as soon as politically possible. They first had to make the country free and that required unity. As the Civil War and events leading up to it later made clear, the issue of slavery was a highly divisive one. They understood they had to secure the Union first. Many founders spoke out against it, including Dickinson, who said, "As Congress is now to legislate for our extensive territory lately acquired, I pray to Heaven that they may build up the system of the government on the broad, strong, and sound principles of freedom. Curse not the inhabitants of those regions and of the United States in general, with a permission to introduce bondage [slavery]." (9)

Abolishing slavery in the United States took longer than the founders intended, but that issue wasn't theirs to decide. They created a system through which future generations could accomplish much needed reform the founders could not due to circumstances beyond their immediate control. George Washington, who was opposed to the idea of slavery, probably had that issue in mind when he said, "I wish the Constitution which is offered, had been made more perfect, but I sincerely believe it is the best that could be obtained at this time. And, as a constitutional door is opened for amendment hereafter, the adoption of it, under the present circumstances of the Union, is in my opinion desirable." After the Constitution was ratified, Washington freed his slaves.

John Dickinson lived and died according to his Christian faith. As part of his last will and testament, he wrote: "Rendering thanks to my Creator for my existence and station among His works, for my birth in a country enlightened by the Gospel and enjoying freedom, and for all His other kindnesses, to Him I resign myself, humbly confiding in His goodness and in His mercy through Jesus Christ for the events of eternity."

Chapter Thirteen

Benjamin Rush

*I do not believe that the Constitution
was the offspring of inspiration, but I am as
perfectly satisfied that the Union of the States
in its form and adoption is as much
the work of a Divine Providence as any
of the miracles recorded in the Old and New Testament
were the effects of Divine Power.*
-- **Benjamin Rush**

*In all the periods of his life,
he was remarkable for his attention to religious duties and his
reverence for the Holy Scriptures.
He urges, in all his writings, the excellency
of the Christian faith and its happy influence
upon the social habits of the country.* --
John Sanderson.

Benjamin Rush's status as an over-achiever throughout the course of his life was foreshadowed by his graduating from what is now Princeton University at the age of sixteen. He had been admitted to the prestigious school at the junior level two years earlier as a result of his entrance exam scores.

Beginning early in Rush's childhood, his widowed mother had placed a high priority on education, personal responsibility, and daily Bible-reading, all of which helped to "bend the twig" in a direction that greatly benefited the cause of American independence. "I have acquired and received nothing from the world," Rush said, "which I prize so highly as the religious principles I inherited from [my parents]; and I possess nothing that I value so much as the innocence and purity of their characters."

Historian and author David Barton, in his biography entitled *Benjamin Rush: Signer of the Declaration of Independence*, provides the following laudatory introduction to the life and works of this eminent founder:

> *At the time of his death in 1813, newspapers, Founding Fathers, and other leaders of the day heralded Benjamin Rush as one of America's three most notable individuals, ranking him with George Washington and Benjamin Franklin. The esteem he achieved was rightfully deserved as a result of his numerous accomplishments: he offered four decades of political service to his country; he was such an accomplished doctor that he has been titled "The Father of American Medicine"; he helped establish at least five universities, colleges, or academies; he formulated visionary educational policies and authored numerous textbooks; he pioneered educational opportunities for both women and Black-Americans; and he helped found and guide numerous societies—societies to end slavery, to promote science, to encourage Sunday schools, to distribute Bibles, to provide relief for the insane, etc.*
>
> *Dr. Rush's abilities were both broad and productive. As a statesman, his leadership was invaluable; as a physician, his discoveries benefited all of humanity; as a philanthropist,*

his generosity was unparalleled; as a reformer his efforts were tireless; and as a Christian, his zeal for the propagation of his faith was unrivaled.

If that weren't enough to validate his reputation as an over-achiever, Rush's resume also includes his having been a member of the Second Continental Congress and signer of the Declaration of Independence, service in three Presidential administrations (John Adams, Thomas Jefferson, and James Madison), Surgeon-General of the Middle Department of the Continental Army, Professor at the College of Philadelphia, Chairman of Theory and Practice of Medicine department at the University of Pennsylvania, Treasurer of the United States Mint, Vice-President of the American Philosophical Society, President of the Pennsylvania Society for Promoting the Abolition of Slavery, and author of more than twenty books dealing with medical and psychiatric subjects. He also was present as a physician in the battles of Princeton, Trenton, and others.

Benjamin Rush was an unabashed patriot and he believed all loyal citizens had duty to love and support their country and its general policy positions. "Patriotism," he said, "is as much a virtue as justice, and is as necessary for the support of societies as natural affection is for the support of families. The *amor patriae* (love of country) is both a moral and a religious duty. It comprehends not only the love of our neighbors but of millions of our fellow creatures, not only of the present but of future generations. This virtue we find constitutes a part of the first characters in history. The holy men of old in proportion as they possessed a religion were endowed with a public spirit. What did not Moses forsake and suffer for his countrymen! What shining examples of Patriotism do we behold in Joshua, Samuel, Maccabeus, and all the illustrious princes, captains, and prophets amongst the Jews! St. Paul almost wishes himself accursed for his countrymen and kinsmen after the flesh. Even our Savior himself gives a sanction to this virtue. He confined his miracles and gospel at first to his own country." (1)

In his *Lives of the Signers of the Declaration of Independence*, historian B. J. Lossing, writing in 1848, penned this tribute to

Rush, especially pointing to his Christian beliefs and how he lived according to them:

As a patriot, Doctor Rush was firm and inflexible; as a professional man he was skilful, candid, and honorable; as a thinker and writer, he was profound; as a Christian, zealous and consistent; and in his domestic relations, he was the centre of a circle of love and true affection. Through life the Bible was a "lamp to his feet" – his guide in all things appertaining to his duty toward God and man. Amid all his close and arduous pursuit of human knowledge, he never neglected to "search the Scriptures" for that knowledge which points the soul aright in its journey to the Spirit Land. His belief in revealed religion, and in the Divine inspiration of the Sacred Writers, is manifested in many of his scientific productions; and during that period, at the close of the last century, when the sentiments of infidel France were infused into the minds of men in high places here, Doctor Rush's principles stood firm, and his opinions never wavered.

Because of his pro-independence writings, he became known by others of like mind including many people who we now recognize as Founding Fathers. One of a series of Providential events happened in 1769 when, as part of his medical studies, Rush was studying under Sir John Pringle, the Royal Court Physician in London. While there, he unexpectedly formed a friendship with Benjamin Franklin, a friendship that gave him access to the inner circle of patriots, many of whom would become fellow signers of the Declaration of Independence.

That hand of Providence seems also to have been very much involved in two of Rush's most important, although indirect, contributions to the cause of independence: He played a role in convincing John Witherspoon to come to America for the purpose of becoming president of Princeton College and he recruited Thomas Paine to join him in writing articles and pamphlets designed to build support for independence. Witherspoon did come to America and became a powerful force in the independence movement as well as a signer of the Declaration of Independence, and Thomas Paine did join Rush in writing highly effective pieces that have been recognized as tipping the public scales in favor of independence. The most influential of Paine's writings, a soon-to-be famous pamphlet entitled *Common Sense,* was published January 10, 1776; more than 500,000 copies were eventually sold throughout the Colonies. George Washington credited it with having "worked a powerful change in the minds of many men." *Common Sense* is the manifestation of "the power of an idea whose time has come."

Paine captured the essence of the spirit of independence that was gaining momentum in this brief paragraph: "O ye that love mankind! Ye that dare oppose not only the tyranny but the tyrant, stand forth! Every spot of the Old World is overrun with oppression. Freedom has been hunted round the globe. Asia and Africa have long expelled her. Europe regards her like a stranger and England has given her warning to depart. O! receive the fugitive, and prepare in time an asylum for mankind."

Rush explained his role in the influential pamphlet with these words: "When the subject of American independence began to be agitated in conversation, I observed the public mind to be loaded with an immense mass of prejudice and error relative to it...At this time I called upon Mr. Paine and suggested to him the propriety of preparing our citizens for a perpetual separation of our country from Great Britain...He seized the idea with avidity and immediately began his famous pamphlet in favor of that measure. He read the sheets to me at my house as he composed them. When he had finished them, I advised him to put them into the hands of Dr. [Benjamin] Franklin, Samuel Adams, and the late Judge [James] Wilson, assuring him at the same time that they all held the same opinions that he had defended...A title only was wanted for this pamphlet before it was committed to the press. Mr. Paine proposed to call it 'Plain Truth.' I objected to it and suggested the title of 'Common Sense.' This was instantly adopted...and *Common Sense* burst from the press...in a few days." (2)

Less than six months after *Common Sense* was first published, the Declaration of Independence was approved.

After independence was won, Rush devoted his time and activities to the field of medicine along with his prodigious writings primarily on medical topics but also including many works advocating societal reforms he felt were needed. The issue he most strongly felt needed to be addressed was the abolition of slavery, an issue that had attracted his attention much earlier in his public life. His native state of Pennsylvania passed an anti-slavery law in 1773 which was vetoed, along with similar laws in other northern states, by King George III.

Writing in *The Role of Pastors & Christians in Civil Government*, historian and author David Barton points out facts little known to today's history students: "The King was pro-slavery; the British Empire practiced slavery; and as long as America was part of the British Empire, it too would practice slavery. . . Since the only way for America to end slavery was to separate from Great Britain, many founders believed that separation would be an appropriate course of action. . . Ending slavery was so important to so many of the founders that when America did separate from Great Britain in 1776, several states began abolishing slavery, including Pennsylvania, Massachusetts, Connecticut, Rhode Island, Vermont, New Hampshire, and New York." (3)

"Domestic slavery is repugnant to the principles of Christianity," Rush exclaimed. "It is rebellion against the authority of a common Father. It is a practical denial of the extent and efficacy of the death of a common Savior. It is an usurpation of the prerogatives of the great Sovereign of the universe who has solemnly claimed an exclusive property in the souls of men."

In 1774, Rush and Benjamin Franklin worked together to found the Pennsylvania Society for Promoting the Abolition of Slavery and the Relief of Free Negroes Unlawfully Held in Bondage. Rush had gone on record the previous year with a powerfully worded and well-reasoned pamphlet entitled *On Slavekeeping*. It generated acclaim from those who agreed and heavy criticism from those who differed. He wrote:

> *Ye men of sense and virtue—Ye advocates for American liberty, rouse up and espouse the cause of humanity and*

general liberty. Bear a testimony against a vice which degrades human nature, and dissolves that universal tie of benevolence which should connect all the children of men together in one great family. The plant of liberty is of so tender a nature, that it cannot thrive long in the neighbour-hood of slavery. Remember the eyes of all Europe are fixed upon you, to preserve an asylum for freedom in this country, after the last pillars of it are fallen in every other quarter of the globe.

But chiefly—ye ministers of the gospel, whose dominion over the principles and actions of men is so universally acknowledged and felt,--Ye who estimate the worth of your fellow creatures by their immortality, and therefore must look upon all mankind as equal;--let your zeal keep pace with your opportunities to put a stop to slavery. While you enforce the duties of "tithe and cumin," neglect not the weightier laws of justice and humanity. Slavery is an Hydra sin, and includes in it every violation of the precepts of the Law and the Gospel. In vain will you command your flocks to offer up the incense of faith and charity, while they continue to mingle the sweat and blood of Negro slaves with their sacrifices. –If the blood of Abel cried aloud for vengeance;--If, under the Jewish dispensation, cities of refuge could not screen the deliberate murderer—if even manslaughter required sacri-fices to expiate it,--and if a single murder so seldom escapes with impunity in any civilized country, what may you not say against that trade, or those manufactures—or laws which destroy the lives of so many thousands of our fellow-crea-tures every year?—If in the Old Testament "God swears by his holiness, and by the excellency of Jacob, that the earth shall tremble, and every one mourn that dwelleth therein for the inequity of those who oppress the poor and crush the needy, who buy the poor with silver, and the needy with a pair of shoes," what judgments may you not denounce upon those who continue to perpetrate these crimes, after the more full discovery which God has made of the law of equity in the New Testament. Put them in mind of the rod which was held

*over them a few years ago in the Stamp and Revenue Acts.
Remember that national crimes require national punishments, and without declaring what punishment awaits this
evil, you may venture to assure them, that it cannot pass with
impunity, unless God shall cease to be just or merciful. (4)*

No matter his subject matter, Rush's writings almost always
made a clear connection between Biblical precepts and correct governance. While there are hundreds of examples available included in
his writings, here is one, the meaning of which would be difficult
to misunderstand or misportray: "I fear all our attempts to procure
political happiness by the solitary influence of human reason will be
as fruitless as the search for the philosopher's stone. It seems to be
reserved to Christianity alone to produce universal, moral, political,
and physical happiness. Reason produces, it is true, great and popular
truths, but it affords motives too feeble to induce mankind to act
agreeably to them. Christianity unfolds the same truths and accom-
panies them with motives, agreeable, powerful, and irresistible. I
anticipate nothing but suffering to the human race while the present
systems of paganism, deism, and atheism prevail in the world. New
England may escape the storm which impends our globe, but, if she
does, it will only be by adhering to the religious [Biblical] principles
and moral habits of the first settlers of that country."

Another area in which Rush would find himself strongly at
odds with modern day pagans, deists, and atheists, many of whom
attempt to fly under the radar by labeling themselves as "moderates," whatever that really means, is the topic of Christianity and
the Bible in public education. "I lament that we waste so much time
and money in punishing crimes and take so little pains to prevent
them," Rush observed. "We neglect the only means of establishing
and perpetuating our republican form of government; that is, the
universal education of our youth in the principles of Christianity by
means of the Bible; for this Divine Book, above all others, constitutes the soul of republicanism." Obviously, Rush would not agree
with removing the Ten Commandments from our schools. Sounding
like a prophet, Rush also said, "The present fashionable practice
of rejecting the Bible from our schools, I suspect, has originated

with the Deists. They discover great ingenuity in this new mode of attacking Christianity. If they proceed in it, they will do more in half a century in extirpating our religion than Bolingbroke or Voltaire could have effected in a thousand years."

On another occasion, Rush wrote, "The only foundation for a useful education in a republic is to be laid in religion. Without this there can be no virtue, and without virtue there can be no liberty, and liberty is the object and life of all republican governments."

Anyone who has read anything regarding the life of this preeminent founder cannot doubt his reference to religion was always to the Judeo/Christian religion, as was this statement: "The great enemy of the salvation of man, in my opinion, never invented a more effectual means of extirpating Christianity from the world than by persuading mankind that it was improper to read the Bible at schools." Driving home his point, Rush also said, "Without the restraints of religion and social worship, men become savages." King Solomon had it right when he said there is nothing new under the Sun.

A man for his times, Rush was born December 24, 1745, on a farm near Berberry, Pennsylvania, a short distance from Philadelphia. Except for his travels to Europe as a student, his life was generally spent in that immediate area. In January of 1776, he married Julia Stockton, daughter of Richard Stockton, who, along with Rush, would sign the Declaration of Independence later that year. The Rush's had thirteen children, four of whom died in childbirth. Julia shared his strong Christian faith and, with some early reservations, his devotion to the cause of independence, as well. In a letter to John Adams, Rush included this informative comment: "My dear wife, who you know in the beginning of the war, had all the timidity of her sex as to the issue of the war and the fate of her husband, was one of the ladies employed to solicit benefactions for the army. She distinguished herself by her zeal and address in this business and is now so thoroughly enlisted in the cause of her country that she reproaches me with lukewarmness."

Rush's feelings regarding his wife, which, according to all accounts, were requited, are probably best illustrated by this poem he wrote in 1812 one year before his death

To Mrs. Julia Rush
When tossed upon the bed of pain,
And every healing art was vain,
Whose prayers brought back my life again?
My Julia's.
When shafts of scandal round me flew,
And ancient friends no longer knew,
My humble name, whose heart was true?
My Julia's
When falsehood aimed its poisoned dart,
And treachery pierced my bleeding heart,
Whose friendship did a cure impart?
My Julia's
When hope was weak, faith was dead,
And every earthly joy was fled,
Whose hand sustained my drooping head?
My Julia's
When worn by age, and sunk in years,
My shadow at full length appears,
Who shall participate my cares?
My Julia
When life's low wick shall feebly blaze,
And weeping children on me gaze,
Who shall assist my prayers & praise.
My Julia
And when my mortal part shall lay,
Waiting in hope, the final day,
Who shall mourn o're my sleeping clay,
My Julia
And when the stream of time shall end,
And the last trump, my grave shall rend,
Who shall with me to Heaven ascend?
My Julia (5)

To his wife just prior to his death, he wrote: "My excellent wife, I must leave you, but God will take care of you. By the mystery of Thy holy incarnation; by Thy holy nativity; by Thy baptism, fasting, and temptation; by Thine agony and bloody sweat; by Thy cross and passion; by Thy precious death and burial; by Thy glorious resurrection and ascension, and by the coming of the Holy Ghost, blessed Jesus, wash away all my impurities, and receive me into Thy everlasting kingdom."

Chapter Fourteen

Roger Sherman

Let us live no more to ourselves,
but to him who loved us and gave himself to die for us.
-- Roger Sherman

...an old Puritan, as honest as an angel and as firm
in the cause of American Independence as Mount Atlas.
-- Sherman as described by John Adams

Twistical. A friend of Roger Sherman's once used that whimsical word to describe him. Based upon Sherman's reputation as a skillful legislator, his friend was obviously referring to this influential founder's recognized ability to maneuver within whatever political landscape he found himself with instinctive skills that allowed him to accomplish his goals. His many years experience in the Connecticut legislature, the Connecticut Senate, and as a judge of the Connecticut Superior Court provided him with skills that served him and, eventually, the country well in helping to bring the Constitutional Convention to a successful conclusion.

Jeremiah Wadsworth, a friend who knew Sherman well, said he was "as cunning as the Devil."

Shepherding proposed legislation through the maze that is the political process in any existing representative government such as each state had prior to the Revolutionary War, was tough enough. When that proposed "legislation" has as its purpose establishing guidelines for subordinating a collection of state governments to one national in scope, the challenge was nearly impossible. Historians have given Roger Sherman credit as being one of the most effective members of the Constitutional Convention in moving the delegates to the accomplishment of what has often been recognized as the "Miracle of Philadelphia" where, although he was not known for his speaking ability, he is said to have spoken 138 times.

"He is no orator," said Rufus W. Griswold, "and yet not a speaker in the convention is more effective; the basis of his power is found, first in the thorough conviction of his *integrity*; his countrymen are satisfied that he is a *good man,* a real patriot, with no little or sinister or personal ends in view; next, he addresses the reason, with arguments, logically arrayed, so clear, so plain, so forcible, that, as they have convinced him, they carry conviction to others who are dispassionate." (1)

Some have referred to Sherman, along with, George Washington, Alexander Hamilton, Charles Cotesworth Pinckney, and James Madison as the "master-builders of the Constitution." (2)

Sherman, senior in age to every delegate to the Philadelphia Convention except for Benjamin Franklin, "was the only one of the Founding Fathers to sign all four of the major founding documents: *The Articles of Association,* 1774; *The Declaration of Independence,* 1776; *The Articles of Confederation,* 1777; and *The Constitution of the United States, 1787.*" (3)

The transformation from a group of loosely associated colonies to a united entity that would eventually become the United States of America took a great leap forward when the First Continental Congress produced *The Articles of Association* in 1774. Although the *Articles* were, in fact, a forerunner to the *Declaration of Independence,* that wasn't the original intent.

That document began with these words: "We, his majesty's most loyal subjects, the delegates of the several colonies of New Hampshire, Massachusetts-Bay, Rhode-Island, Connecticut, New-York, New-Jersey, Pennsylvania, the three lower counties of Newcastle, Kent and Sussex on Delaware, Maryland, Virginia, North-Carolina and South-Carolina, deputed to represent them in a continental Congress, held in the City of Philadelphia, on the 5th day of September, 1774, avowing our allegiance to his majesty, our affection and regard for our fellow-subjects in Great-Britain and elsewhere, affected with the deepest anxiety, and most alarming apprehensions, at those grievances and distresses with which his Majesty's American subjects are oppressed; and having taken under our most serious deliberations, the state of the whole continents, find, that the present unhappy situation of our affairs is occasioned by a ruinous system of colony administration, adopted by the British ministry about the year 1763, evidently calculated for enslaving these colonies, and with them, the British Empire."

The *Articles of Association*, which many believe set the colonies on the road to revolution, was intended only as a petition of grievances in response to the "Intolerable Acts" imposed by the British Parliament of the same year. Among other things, the grievances specifically mentioned were: the deprivation of the right to a jury trial; the prosecution in England for crimes committed in America; and the various penalizing Acts specifically targeted upon the citizens of Boston and the Massachusetts Bay Colony as a whole, the most egregious of which was the Massachusetts Government Act, which removed all local control over governance and the courts. (4)

Setting forth fourteen retaliatory economic acts to which the colonies had objected, the *Articles* concluded with this statement:

> *And we do solemnly bind ourselves and our constituents, under the ties aforesaid, to adhere to this association, until such parts of the several acts of parliament passed since the close of the last war, as impose or continue duties on tea, wine, molasses, syrups, paneles, coffee, sugar, pimento, indigo, foreign paper, glass, and painters colours, imported into America, and extend the powers of the admiralty courts*

beyond their ancient limits, deprive the American subject of trial by jury, authorize the judge's certificate to indemnify the prosecutor from damages, that he might otherwise be liable to from a trial by his peers, require oppressive security from a claimant of ships or goods seized, before he shall be allowed to defend his property, are repealed.-And until that part of the act of the 12 G. 3. ch. 24 entitled "An act for the better securing his majesty's dock-yards magazines, ships, ammunition, and stores," by which any persons charged with committing any of the offenses therein described, in America, may be tried in any shire, or county within the realm, is repealed-and until the four acts, passed the last session of parliament, viz. that for stopping the port and blocking up the harbour of Boston-that for altering the charter and government of the Massachusetts-Bay-and that which is entitled "An act for the better administration of justice, &c."-and that "for extending the limits of Quebec, &c." are repealed. And we recommend it to the provincial conventions, and to the committees in the respective colonies, to establish such farther regulations as they may think proper, for carrying into execution this association. The foregoing association being determined upon by the Congress, was ordered to be subscribed by the several members thereof; and thereupon, we have hereunto set our respective names accordingly.

IN CONGRESS, PHILADELPHIA, October 20, 1774.

While he was strongly opposed to British legislation designed to punish the colonies following the Boston Tea Party, Sherman was slow to accept the idea of armed resistance to the mother country. The occupation of Massachusetts by British troops and passage of the Intolerable Acts were the deciding events in putting Sherman firmly on the side of rebellion. He was also irrevocably opposed to the Declaratory Act of 1766 with which Parliament claimed the right to legislate for the colonies in all cases whatsoever. Sherman considered the idea ludicrous that the colonies were represented in Parliament.

Sherman's signature on the *Articles of Association* established his credentials as one of the more prominent Founding Fathers. Later, in recognition of his legislative abilities and common sense, he was selected as a member of the separate committees that produced both the Articles of Confederation and the Declaration of Independence. But many historians believe his single most important contribution to history was the role he played, as a delegate to the Constitutional Convention, in advancing what became known as The Connecticut Plan. Also known as The Great Compromise, and sometimes as The Sherman Compromise, it eventually became the basis of our bicameral legislature; equal representation in the U. S. Senate, and proportional representation in the U. S. House of Representatives. "Roger Sherman will ever be conspicuous", said Lewis Henry Boutrell, "as the statesman to whose wise and conciliatory spirit it was largely due that the Federal Convention was not held in vain."

The highly emotional and hotly discussed issue of how the states were to be represented in a national legislature had threatened to bring the Convention to an unsuccessful conclusion. Feeling the situation was hopeless, some delegates had already left Philadelphia. During a lengthy speech delivered at the height of the tension, Benjamin Franklin said, "We are sent here to consult, not to contend with each other; and declarations of a fixed opinion, and of determined resolution never to change it, neither enlighten nor convince us. Positiveness and warmth on one side naturally beget their like on the other; and tend to create and augment discord and division in a great concern, wherein harmony and union are extremely necessary to give weight to our councils, and render them effectual in promoting and securing the common good." (5) When Franklin had finished, calm was restored and the delegates moved forward to finish the business at hand. Sherman's name was linked with Franklin's earlier during the Convention when he seconded Franklin's motion to open each day of the Constitutional Convention with prayer. Sherman also shared the title of "Master Builder of the Constitution" with Franklin, as well as George Washington, Charles Cotesworth Pinckney, James Madison, and Alexander Hamilton, an all-star group of ever-honored memory.

Once the Constitution was finally put into final form and approved by the delegates, the next huge hurdle was to get it ratified by the required number of states. Sherman was instrumental in securing ratification by the influential state of Connecticut.

All of the Founding Fathers, including the Federalists and especially the luke-warm Federalists including Sherman, who had grave reservations regarding a central government, would be aghast, appalled, shocked, horrified, dismayed, astounded, disgusted, stunned – pick your favorite descriptive word – to see what the federal government has lately become! Some might call it Federalism gone berserk. Speaking as a prophet, Alexis de Tocqueville said, "America will last until the populace discovers it can vote itself largess from the public treasury." Can any intelligent person deny that the populace discovered that fact with a vengeance in the 1960s? Using the federal treasury as a source of funds with which to purchase blocks of votes was something most of the founders could hardly have imagined, but it has become standard operating procedure today.

Sherman finally, if reluctantly, decided that a central government was a necessary evil. "The great end of the federal government," Sherman had said, "is to protect the several states in the enjoyment of [such] rights [as concern local interests and customs] against foreign invasion, and to preserve peace and a beneficial intercourse among themselves; and to regulate and protect our commerce with foreign nations." (6)

A harsh reality finally set in: The United States of America could not be that in name only. The former colonies had become an important member of the international community and as such could only operate successfully as one united country rather than as a loosely-united group of individual sovereign states, any of which could go their own way regarding selected issues. The states had to speak with one voice in foreign policy and in matters related to international trade which they could not do without a national government. National defense required an effective military establishment. In order to support the military and other developmental needs, the states had to have a way to raise money through a national taxation vehicle. There had to be a responsible entity, that is, a national treasury, that could establish the new nation's financial creditability and there had to be a Federal agency with the authority to pay the country's bills.

Even though they were highly concerned about preserving states' rights, enough of the reluctant Federalists did eventually agree to the U. S. Constitution to approve it but the more conservative delegates managed to include enough restraints to make its approval possible. Sherman was adamant in his belief that it would not be acceptable for the Federal government to interfere with the government of individual states nor with the rights of individuals. "State declarations of Rights are not Repealed by this Constitution," Sherman said. He was instrumental in preventing a provision that would have allowed the Federal government to have veto power over state laws. Thomas Jefferson probably echoed the thoughts of Sherman as well as a majority of the Convention delegates when he said, "A government big enough to give you everything you want, is big enough to take everything you have."

In his 1848 book entitled *Lives of the Signers of the Declaration of Independence*, B. J. Lossing provides us with this glimpse into the formative years of the life and times of this exceptional founder:

> *One of the most remarkable men of the Revolution was Roger Sherman. He was born in Newton, Massachusetts, on the nineteenth of April, 1721. In 1723, the family moved to Stonington, in that State, where they lived until the death of Roger's father, in 1741. Roger was then only nineteen years of age, and the whole care and support of a large family devolved on him. He had been apprenticed to a shoemaker, but he now took charge of the small farm his father left. In 1744, they sold the farm, and moved to New Milford, in Connecticut, where an elder brother, who was married, resided. Roger performed the journey on foot, carrying his shoemaker's tools with him, and for some time he worked industriously at his trade there.*
>
> *Mr. Sherman's early education was exceedingly limited, but with a naturally strong and active mind, he acquired a large stock of knowledge from books, during his apprenticeship. It is said that while at work on his bench, he had a*

book so placed that he could read when it was not neces-
sary for his eyes to be upon his work. He thus acquired a
good knowledge of mathematics, and he made astronomical
calculations for an almanac that was published in New York,
when he was only twenty-seven years old. Not long after he
settled in New Milford, he formed a partnership with his
brother in a mercantile business, but all the while was very
studious. He turned his attention to the study of law, during
his leisure hours; and so proficient did he become in legal
knowledge, that he was admitted to the bar, in December,
1754. Mr. Sherman had no instructor or guide in the study of
the law neither had he any books but such as he borrowed,
yet he became one of the most profound jurists of his day.

Regarding Sherman's formal education or lack thereof, John
Adams said, "Destitute of all literary and scientific education, but
such as he acquired by his own exertions, he was one of the most
sensible men in the world. The clearest head and steadiest heart."
Such tributes to Sherman's character and devotion to perfection were
common among those who knew him well. The Rev. Ezra Stiles a
Congregational minister and president of Yale College from 1778
to 1795, said Sherman "had that Dignity which arises from doing
every Thing perfectly right. He was an extraordinary Man – a venerable uncorrupted Patriot."

Growing up in a Congregationalist church, whose doctrines were
rooted in English Puritanism, Sherman believed that piety and sound
morals are two pillars necessary to good individual citizenship and
that it is therefore altogether proper for the state to disseminate religious truth. At the same time, he was opposed to any kind of state
control over the church. That attitude of cooperation/separation
regarding the altogether proper and acceptable relationship between
church and state was generally accepted by most of the Founding
Fathers.

Many historians have concluded that Sherman was one of the most
devout of his contemporaries. In response to a request by members
of the White Haven Congregational Church, Sherman revised their
creed with which he obviously was in complete agreement:

I believe that there is one only living and true God, existing In three persons, the Father, the Son, and the Holy Ghost, the same in substance equal in power and glory. That the scriptures of the old and new testaments are a revelation from God and a complete rule to direct us how we may glorify and enjoy him.

That God has foreordained whatsoever comes to pass, so as thereby he is not the author or approver of sin.

That he creates all things, and preserves and govern all creatures and all their actions, in a manner perfectly consistent with the freedom of will in moral agents, and the usefulness of means.

That he made man at first perfectly holy, that the first man sinned, and as he was the public head of his posterity, they all became sinners in consequence of his first transgression, are wholly indisposed to that which is good and inclined to evil, and on account of sin are liable to all the miseries of this life, to death, and to the pains of hell forever.

I believe that God having elected some of mankind to eternal life, did send his own Son to become man, die in the room and stead of sinners and thus to lay a foundation for the offer of pardon and salvation to all mankind, so as all may be saved who are willing to accept the gospel offer.

Also by his special grace and spirit, to regenerate, sanctify and enable to persevere in holiness, all who shall be saved; and to procure in consequence of their repentance and faith in himself their justification by virtue of his atonement as the only meritorious cause.

I believe a visible church to be a congregation of those who make a credible profession of their faith in Christ, and obedience to him, joined by the bond of the covenant...

I believe that the souls of believers are at their death made perfectly holy, and immediately taken to glory: that at the end of this world there will be a resurrection of the dead, and a final judgment of all mankind, when the righteous shall be publicly acquitted by Christ the Judge and admitted to everlasting life and glory, and the wicked be sentenced to everlasting punishment. (7)

On Friday, September 25, 1789, the day after the first U. S. House of Representatives approved the First Amendment, Elias Boudinot proposed that Congress should request President George Washington issue a Thanksgiving proclamation for "the many signal favors of Almighty God." Boudinot said he "could not think of letting the session pass over without offering an opportunity to all the citizens of the United States of joining, with one voice, in returning to Almighty God their sincere thanks for the many blessings he had poured down upon them." (9) The resolution approved by both Houses of Congress and sent to the President reads as follows:

Resolved, That a joint committee of both Houses be directed to wait upon the President of the United States to request that he would recommend to the people of the United States a day of public thanksgiving and prayer, to be observed by acknowledging with grateful hearts the many signal favors of Almighty God, especially by affording them an opportunity peaceable to establish a Constitution of government for their safety and happiness. . .

Mr. [Roger] Sherman justified the practice of thanksgiving, on any signal event, not only as a laudable one in itself but as warranted by a number of precedents in Holy Writ: for instance, the solemn thanksgivings and rejoicings which took place in the time of Solomon after the building of the temple was a case in point. This example he thought worthy of Christian imitation on the present occasion; and he would agree with the gentleman who moved the resolution. Mr. Boudinot quoted further precedents from the practice of the last Congress and hoped the motion would meet a ready acquiescence [approval]. The question was not put on the resolution and it was carried in the affirmative. (10)

The president approved the Congressional resolution and issued the thanksgiving proclamation October 3, 1789.

In life and in death, Sherman bore witness to his strong and active Christian faith. The inscription on his tome reads:

IN MEMORY OF
THE HON. ROGER SHERMAN, ESQ.
MAYOR OF THE CITY OF NEW HAVEN,
AND SENATOR OF THE UNITED STATES.
HE WAS BORN AT NEWTOWN, IN MASSACHUSETTS,
APRIL 19th, 1721
AND DIED IN NEW HAVEN, JULY 23rd, A.D. 1793
AGED LXXII

...He ever adorned
the profession of Christianity
which he made in youth;
and, distinguished through life
for public usefulness,
and died in the prospect of a blessed immortality. (8)

Chapter Fifteen

George Mason

The laws of nature are the laws of God,
whose authority can be superseded by no power on earth.
(Later included in the Declaration of Independence as
"the laws of nature and nature's God.)
-- **George Mason**

It is tempting to label George Mason, an important but often over-looked Founding Father, as enigmatic. Although he had strong convictions regarding his vision for the new Republic he helped to establish, he harbored no ambitions where national offices were concerned, preferring the quiet life in his beloved Gunston Hall to a high profile political career in the new government. Highly esteemed by his contemporaries -- Thomas Jefferson referred to Mason as "the wisest man of his generation" and James Madison called him "the greatest debater" he ever knew -- George Mason seems lately to have been pushed into the shadows of early American history. He is difficult to pigeonhole as far as his social and political beliefs were concerned.

Mason was outspokenly anti-Federalist in that he did not trust in the basic concept of a strong central government, yet he understood that the fledgling nation he was helping to establish had to speak with one voice in its dealings with other nations. And, that voice, he understood, had to have substance behind it; the "big stick" as future president Theodore Roosevelt would eloquently enunciate the principle. The "big stick" could only be created and wielded effectively by a central government, one that could, for example, "raise taxes and wage war." With the establishment of a strong central government, Mason was highly concerned about maintaining states' rights: "The State Legislatures," he warned, "ought to have some means of defending themselves against encroachments of the National Government." Speaking prophetically, Mason wanted the states to be protected from the possibility of tyranny by federal courts.

He was unabashedly opposed to the institution of slavery: "Every master of slaves is born a petty tyrant," he said. "They bring the judgment of heaven upon a country. As nations cannot be rewarded or punished in the next world, they must be in this. By an inevitable chain of causes and effects, Providence punished national sins, by national calamities." Mason is said to have influenced Thomas Jefferson in drafting the Northwest Ordinance which included a prohibition against slavery in the new states. Mason also said, "As much as I value a union of all the States, I would not admit the Southern States into the Union unless they agree to the discontinuance of this disgraceful [slavery] trade."

He was quoted as saying he "wished to see all slaves freed," yet, he owned more than two hundred slaves himself. Like most of the northern delegates to the Constitutional Convention, he was opposed to the idea of slavery, but understood the necessity that the slavery issue, as important as it was, be subordinate to the finalization of a national constitution that could be ratified. The Ship of State had to be launched, shaken down, and securely afloat before other important issues could be addressed. Those men charged with that Herculean task had to buy some time.

In his excellent explanation of the dilemma with which the convention delegates, including Mason, were faced over the slavery issue, Paul Johnson wrote: "In August the Convention turned its attention to the knotty problem of slavery, which produced the second major compromise [of the convention]. The debating was complex, not to say convoluted, since the biggest slave-holder attending, George Mason, attacked the institution and especially the slave trade. Article I, section 9, grants Congress the power to regulate or ban the slave trade as of January 1, 1808. On slavery itself the Northerners were prepared to compromise because they knew they had no alternative. Indeed, as one historian of slavery has put it, 'It would have been impossible to establish a national government in the 18th century [in America] without recognizing slavery in some way.' The convention did this in three respects. First, it omitted any condemnation of slavery. Second, it adopted Madison's three-fifths rule, which gave the slave states the added power of counting the slaves as voters, on the basis that each slave counted as three-fifths of a freeman, while of course refusing them the vote as such – a masterly piece of humbug in itself. Third, the words 'slave' and 'slavery' were deliberately avoided in the text. As Madison himself said (on August 25), it would be wrong 'to admit in the Constitution the idea that there could be property in men'." (1)

Mason, described by some as "a flaming patriot," was said to be a "man of the people" because of his dedication to the inclusion of a Bill of Rights, yet he was reputedly the richest man in Virginia and fits the classical definition of an aristocrat. Unlike most citizens of the colonies, he owned 15,000 acres of land in Virginia, an additional 80,000 acres in Kentucky, and a large estate in Ohio. He owned or chartered a number of ships involved in transporting goods between the colonies, England, France, and the West Indies. Some historians consider him to be founder of the American Merchant Marine. (2)

M. E. Bradford gives us this insight into Mason's bloodlines: "George Mason of Gunston Hall was the fourth of his name and line to occupy a position of importance in the northern neck of Virginia. He was a direct descendant of Col. George Mason of Worcestershire, England, a substantial yeoman with aristocratic connections in the Vale of Evesham, who in 1651 migrated to the Potomac River valley in Virginia after service at Worcester in the ill-fated army of King Charles II. The Masons prospered in Virginia, and by the time of the birth of the fourth George Mason held some five thousand acres at

Dogue's Neck below Alexandria, plus sundry other plantations in Maryland and Virginia. George Mason IV was the son of George Mason III and Ann Thomson Mason. He was connected by marriage, business, political association, and friendship with the Mercers, the Lees, the Brents, the Fitzhughs, and other significant families." (3) Few people in the colonies could claim such a pedigree, but Mason established his reputation by working for the kind of individual freedoms from which everyone could benefit. Mason and all his fellow founders, having been born and raised enjoying the protections of The English Bill of Rights of 1689 were determined to preserve individual rights even though separating from the mother country.

"He was indeed the people's man in a people's government," wrote General Fitzhugh Lee. "The tent of his faith was pitched upon the bedrock of the freedom of the citizen. Great was his belief in the security of a purely Republican form of government. Sublime was his reliance in the power of the people. This life of George Mason is proper and opportune. A period in our history has been selected to which we should more frequently recur, by calling attention to the service of a man with whose career we should become more familiar. 'The people should control the government, not the government the people,' was his war cry." (4)

One of the more important but less well-known pre-Revolutionary War documents was primarily authored by Mason. The Fairfax Resolves were adopted July 8, 1774, at Mount Vernon, Virginia, during a convention chaired by George Washington. The resolution was an unambiguous statement of Colonial rights and a revolutionary call for the colonies to organize in protesting Parliament's anti-American actions following the Boston Tea Party. Article One in the Fairfax Resolves stated that "this Colony and Dominion of Virginia can not be considered as a conquered Country; and if it was, that the present Inhabitants are the Descendants not of the Conquered, but of the Conquerors." In other words, they demanded their right to be treated as fellow citizens rather than a foreign country recently placed under British control. Issues specifically mentioned included Colonial representation in Parliament, especially where taxation was concerned, control over military forces located within the colonies, judicial independence, and less British interference in commercial activities and policies. Unspecified actions to enforce American rights were strongly implied. In this document, the colonials served notice that they, while loyal subjects, were not going to be treated as second class citizens and that independence was an option. Once again, George Mason was a key player.

Because Mason was strongly opposed to a Virginia bill that would have taxed citizens "to pay the salaries of teachers who taught the Christian religion," he has been claimed by some as "patron saint of the American Civil Liberties Union," a stretch by just about anyone's standard. Often referred to as the "Father of the Bill of Rights," Mason is credited with producing the first ten amendments, commonly known as the Bill of Rights to the U. S. Constitution. Earlier, he had written "The Virginia Declaration of Rights" that was included in the Virginia Constitution.

> *A declaration of rights made by the Representatives of the good people of Virginia, assembled in full and free Convention; which rights do pertain to them and their posterity, as the basis and foundation of government.*
>
> *That all men are by nature equally free and independent, and have certain inherent rights, of which, when they enter into a state of society, they cannot, by any compact, deprive or divest their posterity; namely, the enjoyment of life and liberty, with the means of acquiring and possessing property, and pursuing and obtaining happiness and safety.*
>
> *That all power is vested in, and consequently derived from, the People; that magistrates are their trustees and servants, and at all times amenable to them.*
>
> *That government is, or ought to be, instituted for the common benefit, protection, and security of the people, nation, or community;--of all the various modes and forms of Government that is best which is capable of producing the greatest degree of happiness and safety, and is most effectually secured against the danger of mal-administration;--and that, whenever any Government shall be found inadequate or contrary to these purposes, a majority of the community hath an indubitable, unalienable, and indefeasible right, to*

reform, alter, or abolish it, in such manner as shall be judged most conducive to the publick weal.

That no man, or set of men, are entitled to exclusive or separate emoluments and privileges from the community, but in consideration of publick services; which, not being descendible, neither ought the offices of Magistrate, Legislator, or Judge, to be hereditary....

That no free Government, or the blessing of liberty, can be preserved to any people but by a firm adherence to justice, moderation, temperance, frugality, and virtue, and by frequent recurrence to fundamental principles.

That Religion, or the duty which we owe to our Creator, and the manner of discharging it, can be directed only by reason and conviction, not by force or violence; and, therefore, all men are equally entitled to the free exercise of religion, according to the dictates of conscience; and that it is the mutual duty of all to practice Christian forbearance, love, and charity, towards each other.

Mason's inclusion of a reference to "our Creator" and to "Christian forbearance" would, of course, put him at odds with the ACLU. A key and often overlooked phrase in the First Amendment to the U. S. Constitution, pointedly says, "Congress shall make no law respecting an establishment of religion, *or prohibiting the free exercise thereof.*" Prohibiting the free exercise of religion, especially the Christian religion, or at least confining it to the interior of churches or private homes, has become the primary business of the ACLU; George Mason would vehemently reject that notion as being exactly the opposite of his intent. The ACLU, aided and abetted by a few radical leftwing judges, has stood the First Amendment on its head using a perverted interpretation of it to "outlaw" Christian symbols in public places. Only in the agenda-driven minds of ACLU lawyers and radical judges can the appearance of a religious symbol be considered "an establishment of religion."

The weapon of choice of the ACLU is the judicial branch of the government because they understand they can't advance their secular humanist agenda through the electoral process. A vast majority of the American people simply does not agree with their agenda and they know it. Time after time in recent years, Congress, the people's elected representatives in government, have been over-ridden by a handful of unelected judges. James Mason would be totally aghast at that kind of perversion of his beliefs. He believed that the House of Representatives should be the most powerful part of the Federal government because the composition of the House is determined by each state's population. His worst fear was that the Federal government would someday trample states' rights and the ACLU/judiciary branch coalition is in the process of proving that his fears were legitimate.

Mason seems to have been envisioning the likelihood of an ACLU-type organization eventually emerging with this ominous observation: "When we reflect upon the insidious art of wicked and designing men, the various and plausible pretenses for continuing and increasing the inordinate lust of power in the few, we shall no longer be surprised that freeborn man hath been enslaved, and those very means which were contrived for his preservation [such as the First Amendment] have been perverted to his ruin." Referring to the powers proposed for the judicial branch, Mason warned, "There is no limitation. It goes to everything."

Those who are confused regarding the ACLU-promoted perver-sion of the term "separation of church and state" should think about this sentiment expressed by Mason and echoed by most of the Founding Fathers: "All men have an equal, natural and unalien-able right to the free exercise of religion, according to the dictates of conscience; and that no particular sect or society of Christianity ought to be favored or established by law in preference to others." In other words, there was to be no officially-sanctioned Christian denomination. The government should keep its hands off!

"The free exercise of religion" means that government, including the judicial branch which obviously is part of the federal govern-ment, is to have no control over anyone's right to participate in or promote his or her religion. Clearly, from Mason's own words, he wanted NO official, state controlled church, Christian or otherwise, but he didn't want any governmental intervention, either.

At the end of the Constitutional Convention, Mason refused to add his signature to the document because he believed that it gave the Federal government too much power at the expense of the individual states. The power given to the Federal judiciary was a specific issue with he strongly disagreed. He said the Constitution's power "is specifically calculated to annihilate totally the State Governments." Eventually, the required nine states, including his home state of Virginia, did ratify the Constitution, but many of the unfortunate trends Mason foresaw have proven his point as the central government has grown to gargantuan proportions while states' rights have been systematically reduced.. He would be unhappy to see how correct his misgivings were.

"We are now to rank among the nations of the world," Mason said, 'but whether our Independence shall prove a blessing or a curse must depend upon our own wisdom or folly, virtue or wickedness… Justice and virtue are the vital principles of republican government." Mason would also be unhappy regarding the accelerating decline in public morality, a condition he probably never visualized. The need for justice and public virtue were often mentioned by most of the founders.

Mason was born in Fairfax County, Virginia, in 1725, and he died there in 1792. A member of the Anglican Church, he, along with George Washington, was a vestryman of Truro Parish; Mason served for 35 years. He was described by those who knew him as knowing the Bible well and that he quoted from it often in his public speeches. In commenting on the Constitution, he paraphrased the Apostle Paul when he said, "They have done what they ought not to have done, and have left undone what they out to have done." He was talking about the "sea change" brought about by the transference of power from state governments to a huge national government. We can almost hear him say "I told you so," from his grave, especially where social and religious issues are concerned.

In his last will and testament, Mason left no doubt regarding his Christian beliefs:

I, George Mason, of 'Gunston Hall', in the parish of Truro and county of Fairfax, being of perfect and sound mind and memory and in good health, but mindful of the uncertainty of human life and the imprudence of man's leaving his affairs to be settled upon a deathbed, do make and appoint this my last Will and Testament.

My soul, I resign into the hands of my Almighty Creator, whose tender mercies are over all His works, who hateth nothing that He hath made and to the Justice and Wisdom of whose dispensation I willing and cheerfully submit, humbly hoping from His unbounded mercy and benevolence, through the merits of my blessed Savior, a remission of my sins.

Chapter Sixteen

John Jay

[John] Jay believed the Bible.
He knew every word of it to be completely and literally true. His
immense faith buoyed him up in every misfortune. His quiet piety
and radiant serenity impressed themselves upon all his
children. When Peter August, his eldest son, died in 1843 he
likewise admonished his children in these last words:
"My children, read the Bible and believe it."
-- Frank Monaghan

Providence has given to our people the choice of their rulers,
and it is the duty, as well as the privilege and interest of our
Christian nation to select and prefer Christians for their rulers.
-- John Jay, First Chief Justice of the U.S. Supreme Court

Technically, George Washington was the fifteenth President of the United States of America; John Jay was the fifth President, serving from December 10, 1778, to September 27, 1779.

"Washington was not inaugurated until April 30, 1789. And yet the United States continually had functioning governments from as early as September 5, 1774, and operated as a confederated nation from as early as July 4, 1776. During that nearly fifteen-year interval, Congress—first the Continental Congress and then the Confederation Congress—was always moderated by a duly elected president. As the chief executive officer of the government of the United States, the president was recognized as the head of state. Washington was thus the fifteenth in a long line of distinguished presidents; he just happened to be the first under the current constitution." (1)

Like Washington, Jay spoke and wrote frequently regarding his belief that a free and independent United States of America was providentially assured. Jay also shared Washington's belief that manners, morality, and virtue were to be cultivated as part of the national character in order for the country, and individuals, to remain in God's good graces. "Let a general reformation of manners take place—let universal charity, public-spirit, and private virtue be inculcated, encouraged, and practiced," Jay said. "Unite in preparing for a vigorous defence of your country, as if all depended on your own exertions. And when you have done all things, then rely upon the good Providence of Almighty God for success, in full confidence that without his blessings, all our efforts will inevitably fail." (2)

Jay was among those who were slow to come around to the realization that war with Great Britain was inevitable. Conservative in nature, well-mannered, and somewhat reserved in his rhetoric, he was highly respected by his fellow members of Congress. He has been called by some historians "the father of American conservatism."

Jay was a member of the First Continental Congress and the Second Continental Congress that produced the *Olive Branch Petition* July 8, 1775, which was a last ditch effort to avoid all-out war. Even though the Battles of Lexington and Concord had already been fought and the American militia had surrounded Boston, Congress decided to make one more attempt at reconciliation. Considering the situation, the petition was couched in remarkably conciliatory, some might say self-demeaning, language:

To the King's Most Excellent Majesty.

MOST GRACIOUS SOVEREIGN: We, your Majesty's faithful subjects of the Colonies of New-Hampshire, Massachusetts-Bay, Rhode-Island, New-Jersey, Pennsylvania, the Counties of Newcastle, Kent, and Sussex, on Delaware, Maryland, Virginia, North Carolina, and South Carolina, in behalf of ourselves and the inhabitants of these Colonies, who have deputed us to represent them in General Congress, entreat your Majesty's gracious attention to this our humble petition.

The union between our Mother Country and these Colonies, and the energy of mild and just Government, produce benefits so remarkably important, and afforded such an assurance of their permanency and increase, that the wonder and envy of other nations were excited, while they beheld Great Britain rising to a power the most extra-ordinary the world had ever known.

The petition went on to respectfully itemize the many colonial grievances and appealed for relief and for reason to override emotions on both sides. Maintaining its deferential parlance, the petition concluded:

We therefore beseech your Majesty, that your royal authority and influence may be graciously interposed to procure us relief from our afflicting fears and jealousies, occasioned by the system before-mentioned, and to settle peace through every part of our Dominions, with all humility submitting to your Majesty's wise consideration, whether it may not be expedient, for facilitating those important purposes, that your Majesty be pleased to direct some mode, by which the united applications of your faithful Colonists to the Throne, in pursuance of their common counsels, may be improved into a happy and permanent reconciliation; and that, in the mean time, measures may be taken for preventing the further destruction of the lives of your Majesty's subjects;

and that such statutes as more immediately distress any of your Majesty's Colonies may be repealed.

For such arrangements as your Majesty's wisdom can form for collecting the united sense of your American people, we are convinced your Majesty would receive such satisfactory proofs of the disposition of the Colonists towards their Sovereign and Parent State, that the wished for opportunity would soon be restored to them, of evincing the sincerity of their professions, by every testimony of devotion becoming the most dutiful subjects, and the most affectionate Colonists.

That your Majesty may enjoy long and prosperous reign, and that your descendants may govern your Dominions with honour to themselves and happiness to their subjects, is our sincere prayer. (3)

Shortly following delivery of the *Olive Branch Petition* to the King, the Continental Congress produced another much less conciliatory document entitled a *Declaration of the causes and necessity for taking up arms*. It began with this rebuke:

If it was possible for men, who exercise their reason to believe, that the divine Author of our existence intended a part of the human race to hold an absolute property in, and an unbounded power over others, marked out by his infinite goodness and wisdom, as the objects of a legal domination never rightfully resistible, however severe and oppressive, the inhabitants of these colonies might at least require from the parliament of Great-Britain some evidence, that this dreadful authority over them, has been granted to that body. But a reverence for our great Creator, principles of humanity, and the dictates of common sense, must convince all those who reflect upon the subject, that government was instituted to promote the welfare of mankind, and ought to be administered for the attainment of that end.

The legislature of Great-Britain, however, stimulated by an inordinate passion for a power not only unjustifiable, but which they know to be peculiarly reprobated by the very constitution of that kingdom, and desparate of success in any mode of contest, where regard should be had to truth, law, or right, have at length, deserting those, attempted to effect their cruel and impolitic purpose of enslaving these colonies by violence, and have thereby rendered it necessary for us to close with their last appeal from reason to arms. -- Yet, however blinded that assembly may be, by their intemperate rage for unlimited domination, so to slight justice and the opinion of mankind, we esteem ourselves bound by obligations of respect to the rest of the world, to make known the justice of our cause.

The Declaration continued to layout the colonies' case in much more forceful terminology and ended with these stern words:

Our cause is just. Our union is perfect. Our internal resources are great, and, if necessary, foreign assistance is undoubtably attainable. -- We gratefully acknowledge, as signal instances of the Divine favour towards us, that his Providence would not permit us to be called into this severe controversy, until we were grown up to our present strength, had been previously exercised in warlike operation, and possessed of the means of defending ourselves. With hearts fortified with these animating reflections, we most solemnly, before God and the world, declare, that exerting the utmost energy of those powers, which our beneficent Creator hath graciously bestowed upon us, the arms we have been compelled by our enemies to assume, we will, in defiance of every hazard, with unabating firmness and perseverence, employ for the preservation of our liberties; being with one mind resolved to die freemen rather than to live slaves.

Lest this declaration should disquiet the minds of our friends and fellow-subjects in any part of the empire, we assure them that we mean not to dissolve that union which has so long and so happily subsisted between us, and which we sincerely wish to see restored. -- Necessity has not yet driven us into that desperate measure, or induced us to excite any other nation to war against them. -- We have not raised armies with ambitious designs of separating from Great-Britain, and establishing independent states. We fight not for glory or for conquest. We exhibit to mankind the remarkable spectacle of a people attacked by unprovoked enemies, without any imputation or even suspicion of offence. They boast of their privileges and civilization, and yet proffer no milder conditions than servitude or death.

In our own native land, in defence of the freedom that is our birthright, and which we ever enjoyed till the late violation of it -- for the protection of our property, acquired solely by the honest industry of our fore-fathers and ourselves, against violence actually offered, we have taken up arms. We shall lay them down when hostilities shall cease on the part of the agressors, and all danger of their being renewed shall be removed, and not before.

With an humble confidence in the mercies of the supreme and impartial Judge and Ruler of the Universe, we most devoutly implore his divine goodness to protect us happily through this great conflict, to dispose our adversaries to reconciliation on reasonable terms, and thereby to relieve the empire from the calamities of civil war. (4)

On August 23, 1775, the British King ignored the American Congress' efforts to avoid war and declared the colonies to be in a state of rebellion. Later in 1775, the King issued a proclamation forbidding any commerce between Britain and the United States. At that point, the movement towards independence was formally set in motion although there were still many colonists who favored further efforts towards reconciliation. As a member of the Second Continental Congress, Jay signed off on both the *Olive Branch Petition* and the *Declaration of causes and necessity for taking up arms*; he was well on his way to becoming a staunch supporter of independence.

For all practical purposes, the Second Continental Congress functioned as the Revolutionary government of the United States. As previously mentioned, Jay served as President of Congress from December 10, 1778, to September 27, 1779. Recognized at a young age for his wisdom and clear thinking, Jay was given a major role in drafting the first constitution of the state of New York where he also served as Chief Justice of the state Supreme Court during the war for independence. He was also selected to serve as a roving ambassador to several European capitals with the purpose of securing allies and funding for the revolutionary cause. Along with Benjamin Franklin, Thomas Jefferson, John Adams, and Henry Laurens, Jay represented the United States in the peace negations that resulted in the 1783 Treaty of Paris officially ending the Revolutionary War. By terms of the treaty, Great Britain recognized the thirteen colonies as a free and sovereign country.

Jay returned from Europe in 1784 at which time he was appointed Secretary of State, a position then known as Secretary of Foreign Affairs, an appointment he held until 1789. It was while serving in this position that he became acutely aware of the inadequacy of the Articles of Confederation, especially where America's international interests were concerned. Jay was an early advocate of a new constitution rather than a revamping of the Articles of Confederation. He is credited with helping Alexander Hamilton found the Federalist Party.

Hamilton, Jay, and James Madison combined to author *The Federalist*, a series of 85 essays published between October, 1787, and April, 1788, that effectively explained the advantages of such a government, especially the protection it could provide in the area of international commerce. They argued that unified government was also a strong deterrent to localized anarchy. Originally published in New York newspapers, *The Federalist Papers* were instrumental in the state of New York's ratifying the Constitution in 1788.

New Hampshire ratified the Constitution June 21, 1788, becoming the ninth state to do so, thereby officially putting it into effect. Congress agreed that government would begin to operate under the newly ratified Constitution March 4 1789. George Washington was inaugurated as the first President of the United States, April 30, 1789. In forming his administration, Washington gave Jay his choice of two positions: Secretary of State or Chief Justice of the first Supreme Court of the United States. Jay chose to become the first Chief Justice.

It was in 1794 that Jay was entrusted by Washington to handle the national task for which he is best remembered, the treaty with Great Britain that became known as "Jay's Treaty." The primary benefit of Jay's negotiations in behalf of the United States was the avoidance of becoming involved in a looming war between France and England, which Washington thought could be disastrous, and the possibility of another war with Britain. Another provision of the treaty required the British to evacuate their outposts on America's northwest frontier, a British concession much desired by the President. Washington felt the treaty had accomplished his basic purposes and agreed with Jay's assessment that "to do more was not possible." As a result of the controversy surrounding the treaty, the movement toward two opposing political parties was propelled forward.

While in England, Jay sent his wife a letter in which he indicated his belief in God's providential care and direction where the affairs of America are concerned: "If it should please God to make me instrumental to the continuation of peace, and in preventing the effusion of blood and other evils and miseries incident to war, we shall both have reason to rejoice. Whatever may be the event, the endeavour will be virtuous, and consequently consolatory. Let us repose unlimited trust in our Maker; it is our business to adore and to obey."

Upon returning to the United States from London, Jay learned he had been elected governor of his home state of New York. He served two terms from 1795 to 1801, then retired from public service. As a result of his well-known interest in and devotion to the Bible in his daily life, he was elected president of the Westchester Bible Society in 1818, and president of the American Bible Society three years later. "The Bible," Jay said, "is the best of all books, for it is the word of God and teaches us the way to be happy in this world and in the next."

In a letter to historian and Congregational Pastor Jedidiah Morse, Jay expressed his belief in the historicity of the Bible along with his prophetic fear that false teachers would someday find ways to undermine its principles and doctrines in this statement: "...It is to be regretted, but so I believe the fact to be, that except the Bible there is not a true history in the world. Whatever may be the virtue, discernment, and industry of the writers, I am persuaded that truth and error (though in different degrees) will imperceptibly become and remain mixed and blended until they shall be separated forever by the great last refining fire."

Jay's commitment to orthodox Christian views was evident in this statement to the American Bible Society in which he expressed the need for active evangelism:

> *By conveying the Bible to people thus circumstanced [untaught heathens], we certainly do them a most interesting kindness. We thereby enable them to learn that man was originally created and placed in a state of happiness, but becoming disobedient, was subjected to the degradation and evils which he and his posterity have since experienced.*
>
> *The Bible will also inform them that our gracious Creator has provided for us a Redeemer, in whom all the nations of the earth shall be blessed; that his Redeemer has made atonement "for the sins of the whole world," and thereby reconciling the Divine justice with the Divine mercy has opened a way for our redemption and salvation; and that these inestimable benefits are of the free gift and grace of God, not of our deserving, nor in our power to deserve.*

"The most effectual means of securing the continuance of our civil and religious liberties," Jay preached, "is always to remember with reverence and gratitude the source from which they flow."

Born December 12, 1745 in New City into an orthodox Protestant family, Jay was home-schooled, learning Latin as a young child prior to attending grammar school in New Rochelle beginning at the age of eight. At the age of fourteen, he enrolled in King's College, now Columbia University. His father described him as having "a grave disposition" and as one "who takes to learning very well." His serious interest in learning served him and his country very well throughout his distinguished public career. Jay was guided from the beginning to the end of that illustrious career by his love for the Bible and his devotion to living out his religious beliefs in whatever role he found himself.

While he was adamantly opposed to any state involvement in religious matters, Jay believed the establishment of a free and independent United States of America had been ordained in heaven to be a Christian nation and that America was a nation of destiny, especially in proclaiming and spreading the Christian religion. That's a concept much in dispute today. There would have been no dispute among the Founding Fathers, especially John Jay.

Jay died May 17, 1829, a confident and fulfilled man, leaving this statement as his last will and testament: "Unto Him who is the author and giver of all good, I render sincere and humble thanks for His manifold and unmerited blessings, and especially for our redemption and salvation by His beloved Son. He has been pleased to bless me with excellent parents, with a virtuous wife, and with worthy children. His protection has accompanied me through many eventful years, faithfully employed in the service of my country; and his providence has not only conducted me to this tranquil situation, but also given me abundant reason to be contented and thankful. Blessed be His holy name. While my children lament my departure, let them recollect that in doing them good, I was only the agent of their Heavenly Father, and that he never withdraws his care and consolations from those who diligently seek him."

Chapter Seventeen

Gouverneur Morris

᪥

He winds through all the mazes of rhetoric
and throws around him such a glare [of lights]
that he charms captivates, and leads away the senses of all who
hear him... No man has more wit, -- nor can any one engage the
attention more than Mr. Morris.
-- **William Pierce**

Religion is the only solid basis of good morals;
therefore education should teach the precepts of religion,
and the duties of man toward God.
-- **Gouverneur Morris**

Often described as one of the most brilliant of the Founding Fathers, Gouverneur Morris was best known for his rhetorical skills which were very much on display during the Constitutional Convention held in Philadelphia in 1787. According to records of those proceedings, Morris spoke more often than any of his fellow delegates, delivering 173 speeches, many of them lengthy. Some

historians have speculated that Morris was one of the most conge-
nial and well-liked delegates at the Convention. He was also lionized
by his contemporaries for his writing ability which apparently was
equal to his talent for verbal persuasion. His friend William Pierce
described him as "one of those geniuses in whom every species of
talents combine to render him conspicuous and flourishing in public
debate."

While James Madison is credited with generating the underlying
ideas and thrust of the Constitution, and with preparing its first draft,
Morris put the document in final form as head of the Committee on
Style. He is commonly believed to have been the originator of the
famous phrase "We the people of the United States, in order to form a
more perfect union, establish justice, insure domestic tranquility..."

Many historians have included Morris among the most highly
influential of the Founding Fathers in the company of such consensus
greats as George Washington, Benjamin Franklin, James Madison,
Alexander Hamilton, George Mason, and Roger Sherman. Even
though he harbored some reservations, Morris was an early advocate
of independence once it became clear to his way of thinking that an
autonomous British America would be an unlikely outcome of the
growing conflict. He signed the Articles of Confederation and, later,
the U.S. Constitution, after becoming convinced of the need for a
stronger central government than was provided for in the Articles of
Confederation. He believed in preserving the states and that the individual states should retain many rights, but the rights of the national
government must always trump states' rights: "When the powers of
the national government clash with the states," he said, "only then
must the states yield." Historian David Muzzey said Morris "was
a nationalist before the birth of the nation." (1) He is said to have
provided strong impetus towards formation of the Federalist Party.

Although his inheritance had included slaves, he was opposed
to the institution of slavery and verbally attacked it during the
Constitutional Convention. "I will never concur in upholding
domestic slavery," he said. "It is the curse of heaven on the states
where it prevails," he stated, making himself highly unpopular among
delegates from the Southern states. Understanding the practicality of
the matter, he advocated a gradual elimination of the institution he

abhorred because to force the issue at that time would have created irreparable division at a time when unity was a national necessity.

Morris, described by some historians as having "aristocratic" tendencies, was, by birth, a member of the local gentry. He was a grandson of Lewis Morris I, and the youngest son of Lewis Morris II, "lords of the manor and justices of the King's Bench." Born January 31, 1752, at Morrisania, the family seat in Westchester County, New York, he was "of distinguished Dutch, Huguenot, Welsh, and English ancestry" and educated in a French school at New Rochelle, in the Academy of Philadelphia, at King's College, and in the law offices of William Smith. Morris was "destined by birth, training, and ability for a life of public service and political importance." At the age of 19, he was admitted to the bar. (2)

Morris' activities in support of the American Revolution began with his election to the New York Provincial Congress in 1775. In 1778, he was elected to a seat in the Continental Congress and, in 1779, became a delegate to the Constitutional Convention.

After playing a major role in the formulation and ratification of the Constitution, Morris spent nine years in Europe as both a private citizen conducting personal business and as an official envoy of the United States. As foreign minister to France, he became a close observer of French culture and French politics, for both of which he developed an active dislike. He was convinced the blood-drenched French Revolution of 1789 would lead to tyranny, which it did, and the reason he was convinced of the inevitability of that undesirable development was the notoriously low moral state of the French people.

"The materials for a revolution in this country (France)", Morris wrote, "are very indifferent. Everybody agrees that there is an utter prostration of morals; but this general proposition can never convey to an American mind the degree of depravity. It is not by any figure of rhetoric, or force of language, that the idea can be communicated. A hundred anecdotes, and a hundred thousand examples, are required to show the extreme rottenness of every member. There are men and women who are greatly and eminently virtuous. I have the pleasure to number many in my acquaintance; but they stand forward from a background deeply and darkly shaded. It is however, from such crumbling matter, that the great edifice of freedom is to be erected here. Perhaps, like the stratum of rock, which is spread under the whole surface of their country, it may harden when exposed to the air; but it seems quite as likely that it will fall and crush the builders. . . [T]here is one fatal principle which pervades all ranks. It is a perfect indifference to the violation of engagements. Inconstancy is so mingled in the blood, marrow, and very essence of this people that when a man of high rank and importance laughs today at what he seriously asserted yesterday, it is considered as in the natural order of things. Consistency is a phenomenon. Judge, then, what would be the value of association, should such a thing be proposed, and even adopted. The great mass of the common people have no religion but their priests, no law but their superiors, no morals but their interest. These are the creatures who, led by drunken curates, are now in the high road a la liberte, and the first use they make of it is to form insurrections everywhere for the want of bread." (3)

Morris was also convinced the French Revolution would not lead to the establishment of a sound or stable society because of the prevailing absence of religious principles, the underlying cause of their societal moral disorder, upon which such a society could be built. He saw no positive comparison between the American and French revolutions primarily because of the differences he perceived in the prevailing moral standards of the two countries. He blamed much of the French moral degradation on their secular humanist orientation which he related to their growing "Enlightenment" mentality. "A system of government that would work for a highly religious and moral people (as Morris Thought the Americans to be) would not work in an immoral society like France." (4)

Lasting liberty, he believed, could only be built on a foundation of morality and morality was built upon the principles and doctrines of the Judeo-Christian religion as contained in the Bible. While he rarely quoted Scripture directly, Morris made frequent references to biblical precepts and familiar Bible characters and events. He perceived an "open contempt of religion" in France that he was convinced would prevent the people from building an American-style system of government based on self-restraint and the rule of law.

In his *Notes on the Form of a Constitution for France,* Morris wrote, "Religion is the only solid basis of good morals; therefore education should teach the precepts of religion, and the duties of man toward God. These duties are, internally, love and adoration; externally, devotion and obedience; therefore provision should be made for maintaining divine worship as well as education."

By 1794, Morris had worn out his welcome in France. M. E. Bradford gives us this account: "During the dark days of the [Reign of] Terror, he was the only foreign minister who kept to this post in Paris. He had tried, while still a private citizen, to save the government and the life of Louis XVI. Morris was, in fact, entrusted with the king's private funds not long before his execution. And, as American minister, he made his house a refuge to a great many who had, in his presence, flirted with advanced [Enlightenment] ideas, which Morris had warned against. Morris was, as his valuable diary indicates, appalled by the fanatical ideology of the Jacobin republic. The French recognized this attitude, and, in consequence, requested his recall. His time in France made the gentleman from New York if anything more conservative than he had been before, and more appreciative of the stability of the new [American] government."

After his recall as Ambassador to France, Morris remained in Europe engaging in personal business and "adventures," He returned to America in 1798. Two years later, he was elected to the U. S. Senate where he gave his valuable support to the Louisiana Purchase. Failing to win re-election to the Senate, he returned to private life at Morrisania.

In 1810, he was called out of retirement to become chairman of a commission assigned the task of planning and building the Erie Canal, a major engineering feat that hastened westward expansion by linking the Great Lakes with the eastern seaboard.

M. E. Bradford called Morris "an eminently civilized American and a great patriot." He had a grand vision for "national greatness" which was the title of this essay:

Thus, then we have seen that a People may be numerous powerful wealthy free brave and inured to War without being Great, and by reflecting of the Reason why a Combination of those Qualities and Circumstances will not alone suffice. We are close to the true Source and Principle of national Greatness. It is in the national Spirit. It is in that high, haughty, generous and noble spirit which prizes Glory more than wealth and holds Honor dearer than Life. It is that Spirit, the inspiring Soul of Heroes which raised Men above the Level of Humanity. It is present with us when we read the Story of ancient Rome. It swells our Bosoms at the View of her gigantic Deeds and makes us feel that we must ever be irresistible while human Nature shall remain unchanged. I have called it a high haughty generous and noble Spirit. It is high—Elevated above all low and vulgar Considerations. It is haughty—Despising whatever is little and mean whether in Character Council or Conduct. It is generous—granting freely to the weak and to the Indigent Protection and Support. It is noble—Dreading Shame and Dishonor as the greatest Evil, esteeming Fame and Glory beyond all Things human.

When this Spirit prevails the government, whatever it's Form, will be wise and energetic because such Government alone will be borne by such Men. And such a Government seeing the true Interest of those over whom they preside will find it in the Establishment of a national Character becoming the Spirit by which the Nation is inspired, Foreign Powers will then k now that to withhold a due Respect and Deference is dangerous. That Wrongs may be forgiven but that Insults will be avenged. As a necessary Result every Member of the Society bears with him every where full Protection & when he appears his firm and manly Port mark him of a superior Order in the Race of Man. The Dignity of Sentiment which he has inhaled with his native Air gives to his Manner an Ease superior to the Politeness of Courts and a Grace unrivalled by the Majesty of Kings.

These are Blessings which march in the train of national Greatness and come on the Pinions of youthful Hope. I anticipate the Day when to command Respect in the remotest Regions it will be sufficient to say I am an American. Our Flag shall then wave in Glory over the Ocean and our

Commerce feel no Restraint but what our own Government may impose. Happy thrice happy Day. Thank God, to reach this envied State we need only to Will. Yes, my countrymen. Our Destiny depends on our Will. But if we would stand high on the Record of Time that Will must be inflexible. (5)

Again, speaking prophetically, Morris said, "The proudest empire in Europe is but a bauble compared to what America will be, must be, in the course of two centuries, perhaps of one! If, with a calm retrospect to the progress made within forty years, we stand on the firm ground of calculation, warranted by experience, and look forward to the end of a similar period, imagination shrinks from the magnitude of rational deduction." Looking back over 200 years of U. S. history, few would deny the accuracy of his prediction.

Because Morris did not refer directly to Jesus in his writings, some historians have concluded he was a deist because, when he did speak of the Almighty, he spoke of God and His providence. He did believe in the power of prayer which would separate him from deists who do not believe in an engaged God. Morris was a member of the Episcopal Church which believed in the Triune God of the Bible. It is safe to assume that he believed the doctrine of the denomination of which he was a member, i.e., Jesus is God.

Speaking of his religious beliefs, a friend said of Morris, "The idea of a Deity is always present, the habit of contemplating him in his works, of imitating his goodness, of submitting to his will, with that calm resignation which arises from a belief that God can will nothing but what is good; such is the fountain from which his soul derives a confidence full of serenity, a boundless charity, and a hope..."

That he had a Biblical view of the after life, Morris provided this confirmation before he died: "I descend towards the grave full of gratitude to the Giver of all good."

Chapter Eighteen

Charles Cotesworth Pinckney

*Without Charles Cotesworth Pinckney,
no Constitution could have been agreed upon
in Philadelphia or approved in the Lower South.*
-- **Dr. M. E. Bradford**

*Among the evidences of his [Pinckney's] piety,
might not his moral attainments with propriety be enumerated?
For let me ask in what irreligious man has the same assemblage of
virtues ever been found? In whom has the like degree of upright-
ness been discovered separate from religious principle? The irreligious may have a love of country, but it is not of the disinterested
self-denying ruling character which the Christian exercises.*
-- **Rev. Christopher Gadsen**

Many of the Founding Fathers had strong ties to England; Charles Cotesworth Pinckney of South Carolina was one of the more closely connected having links to the mother country by blood, education, business, and political/diplomatic considerations. His father was a high profile colonial lawyer, judge, and legislator.

The Pinckney's, labeled by historians as fully-vested members of the southern aristocracy, had been actively involved in the Royal colonial government until it became clear to them that independence from Great Britain was the only available course of action available to the colonies. Some students of early American history have called Pinckney the most important of the southern statesmen of his time.

When young Charles was seven years old, his father, also named Charles, moved the family to London where he had been appointed to act as South Carolina's lobbyist charged primarily with looking after the colony's commercial interests. At that young age, Charles took for granted the close personal and working relationships he observed between colonial leaders such as his father and their British counterparts. As a wealthy planter himself, the elder Charles' commercial interests, directly influenced by political activities of the British Parliament, paralleled those of South Carolina. He was well-qualified to represent his country's interests.

When the Pinckney's returned to South Carolina after five years in London, young Charles remained in England where he completed his education at Westminster preparatory school and Christ Church College at Oxford.

He studied law at Oxford under Sir William Blackstone, author of a four-volume work entitled *Commentaries on the Laws of England,* a body of legal writings published from 1765 to 1769. By 1775, more copies had been sold in America than in England. Because of their general acceptance in the colonies, Blackstone's *Commentaries* greatly influenced the Founding Fathers' as they began to formulate a legal system in the United States. When the first American law school was established at the College of William and Mary in 1779, Blackstone's *Commentaries* had already become an important legal resource in the United States. By the early 1800s, law schools had been established at Harvard, Yale, and the University of Virginia, among other lesser known colleges, all of which relied heavily on Blackstone's writings as teaching materials. His work is still highly regarded in legal education.

To Blackstone, it was a given that God's laws as written in Scripture were to be the basis of man's laws. Here are his thoughts in his own words:

Man, considered as a creature, must necessarily be subject to the laws of his Creator, for he is entirely a dependent being...And, consequently, as man depends absolutely upon his Maker for everything, it is necessary that he should in all points conform to his Maker's will...this will of his Maker is called the law of nature.

These laws laid down by God are the eternal immutable laws of good and evil...This law of nature dictated by God himself, is of course superior in obligation to any other. It is binding over all the globe, in all countries, and at all times: no human laws are of any validity if contrary to this. . . The doctrines thus delivered we call the revealed or divine law, and they are to be found only in the holy scriptures...[and] are found upon comparison to be really part of the original law of nature. Upon these two foundations, the law of nature and the law of revelation depend all human laws; that is to say, no human laws should be suffered to contradict these.

Blasphemy against the Almighty is denying his being or providence, or uttering contumelious reproaches on our Savior Christ. It is punished, at common law by fine and imprisonment, for Christianity is part of the laws of the land.

If [the legislature] will positively enact a thing to be done, the judges are not at liberty to reject it, for that were to set the judicial power above that of the legislature, which would be subversive of all government.

The preservation of Christianity as a national religion is abstracted from its own intrinsic truth, of the utmost consequence to the civil state, which a single instance will sufficiently demonstrate.

The belief of a future state of rewards and punishments, the entertaining just ideas of the main attributes of the Supreme Being, and a firm persuasion that He superintends and will finally compensate every action in human life (all which are revealed in the doctrines of our Savior, Christ), these are the grand foundations of all judicial oaths, which call God to witness the truth of those facts which perhaps may be only known to Him and the party attesting; all moral evidences, therefore, all confidence in human veracity, must be weakened by apostasy, and overthrown by total infidelity.

Wherefore, all affronts to Christianity, or endeavors to depreciate its efficacy, in those who have once professed it, are highly deserving of censure. (1)

To Charles Cotesworth Pinckney, there was nothing in Blackstone's statements with which he would have disagreed having been raised by devout Episcopalian parents Charles and Eliza Cotesworth. The Cotesworth children, according to Marvin Zahniser, "were required at an early age to listen for the sermon text and to find it in the Bible as soon as they returned home from service. They were also expected to memorize the collect for the day, a task that seemed truly formidable to them. This early religious training had a profound impact on the Pinckney children, perhaps more on Charles Cotesworth than on his brother and sister. In later life his piety never seemed labored but arose spontaneously from a mind and heart trained from childhood to love Christ and the church." (2)

Pinckney's father died while he and his brother were still in school in London. In his father's last will and testament, he left these instructions regarding his first-born son: "And to the end that my beloved son Charles Cotesworth may the better be enabled to become the head of his family, and prove not only of service and advantage to his country, but also an honour to his stock and kindred, my order and direction is that my said son be virtuously, religiously and liberally brought up so...that he will employ all his future abilities in the service of God and his country, in the cause of virtuous liberty, as well religious as civil, and in support of private right and justice between man and man."

According to his biographers, Pinckney remained true to his father's wishes and his Christian faith all his life in whatever role he found himself. More than fifty years later, Pinckney was instrumental in founding the Bible Society of Charleston which became part of the American Bible Society in 1817. Pinckney served as a national vice president of the ABS and headed up the Charleston Bible Society until his death in 1825.

At the age of 23, Pinckney had become a member of the English bar, the beginning of an illustrious, multifaceted career as an attorney, plantation owner, soldier, politician, statesman, and lay leader in his church. In 1804 and 1808, Pinckney was the Federalist Party's candidate for President of the United States, losing first to Thomas Jefferson and then to James Madison.

Following his graduation from Oxford, he attended the French Royal Military Academy, preparing him for extensive participation in the Revolutionary War as an army officer. Eventually, he was promoted to the rank of General. As a soldier, Pinckney participated in the battles of Brandywine, Germantown, Savannah, and Charleston. When the British captured Charleston in 1780, Pinckney became a prisoner of war where he remained until 1782. Fortunately, he was considered a POW rather than a traitor to the Crown. When his captors enticed him to become a turncoat, Pinckney rebuffed them, uttering a statement for which he became well known: "If I had a vein that did not beat with the love of my Country, I myself would open it. If I had a drop of blood that could flow dishonorable, I myself would let it out."

After being released by the British as part of a prisoner exchange, Pinckney remained on Army active duty until his unit was deactivated in November of 1783 at which time he returned to his plantation and his law practice. In addition to serving in the South Carolina legislature, he was active in the state militia.

While a member of the state legislature in 1778, Pinckney played a major role in writing a state constitution. That document contains the following provision: "That all persons and religious societies who acknowledge that there is one God, and a future state of rewards and punishments, and that God is publicly to be worshipped, shall be freely tolerated...That all denominations of Christian[s]...in this State, demeaning themselves peaceably and faithfully, shall enjoy equal religious and civil privileges." Pinckney agreed that all governments should be guided by Christian principles as did a vast majority of his fellow Founders. Most state constitutions contain similar wording, a fact that directly refutes many rulings by activist judges working hand-in-hand with the ACLU.

When the Constitutional Convention was called in 1787, Pinckney was selected to represent South Carolina in Philadelphia where he renewed an association with George Washington that traced back to the Pennsylvania campaign ten years earlier. That association and mutual respect increased over the years. When Pinckney's mother died in 1793, Washington, at his own request, was one of her pallbearers.

Pinckney's excellent law education, governmental background, first-hand experience in military service, and devotion to Biblical morality made him an important member of the Philadelphia Convention. Although his philosophy of government was that the "great art of government is not to govern too much," Pinckney was convinced that America's future greatness depended on an overarching unity of the states in order to protect their collective political, economic, and military interests. That overarching unity, he came to understand, required that the Articles of Confederation be replaced by a national government operating under a new constitution even though he had reservations regarding the differences in regional interests between the southern states and New England.

In his book entitled *Founding Fathers*, M. E. Bradford included this concise capsulation of Pinckney's philosophy regarding the need for a national government and his role in its formation.: "Pinckney brought to the Constitutional Convention no draft of a new compact, as did his youthful cousin Charles Pinckney III, but only his conviction, shaped in the crucible of the Revolution, that the United States should not fight another war without the concentrated strength necessary to defend itself, and the related conviction that a national policy concerning foreign trade, currency, and finance was needed to relieve the burden of debt that weighed upon South Carolina and the other states. He was, in other words, a moderate military Federalist, a soldier politician, in whom the lawyer had been submerged by the exigencies of war. In Philadelphia he spoke plainly and displayed for effect none of his considerable erudition. Neither did he claim any special authority from the distinction of his name. Instead he went to the heart of whatever question was before the house and in the debates continued in an effort begun when, in 1775, he sat in the provisional provincial congress and put on a uniform to assist in organizing the defenses of the southern coast."

As a moderate among a few more aggressive Federalists, Pinckney more openly espoused a point of balance between the interests of the individual states and the new national government. Because of the influence he was able to exert, many historians have included Pinckney in the group including Roger Sherman, George Washington, Alexander Hamilton, and James Madison who they labeled "master-builders of the Constitution." Pinckney signed the new Constitution and returned to Charleston where he played an active role in obtaining South Carolina's ratification of the new document.

In 1790, Pinckney officially retired from politics with the intention of devoting his time to civic, religious, and charitable activities, turning down a number of political appointments offered him by Washington. In 1796, he did agree to serve as an ambassador to France during a time of increasing dissension between the former allies. Rejecting a requested bribe from a member of the French government, an event that became know as the "XYZ Affair," Pinckney uttered the now famous phrase, "millions for defense, but not one cent for tribute." To shield the names of the offending French officials, the infamous event was always publicly referred to by the initials "XYZ." The international "affair" that could have resulted in war between the United States and France was defused when Napoleon overthrew the French Directory 1800.

As a true son of the pre-Revolutionary War south, Pinckney did not oppose slavery. Slave owners consider their slaves to be personal property and the right to own personal property was a basic tenet of the Revolution. He accepted the three-fifths rule on representation of slaves, the twenty-year extension of the slave trade, the prohibition of taxes on exports, and the unanimous agreement of all present that the Constitution provided no authority to touch slavery in the states that chose to have it. (3) Had he personally supported an anti-slavery provision in the Constitution, he knew South Carolina would never ratify any constitution that made such a provision part of the law of the land. Pinckney was quoted as saying that "even if he and his colleagues were to sign the Constitution and use their personal influence, it would be of no avail towards obtaining the assent of their constituents. South Carolina and Georgia cannot do without slaves." (3) The Charleston Bible Society, of which Pinckney was President, said it had "no doubts concerning the moral and Religious Right of holding Slaves, lawfully obtained, when they are treated with justice and humanity." Pinckney, though, was determined to Christianize slaves and used his own financial resources to provide Bibles and Christian instruction for them.

Today, we would nod our heads in agreement with William J. Bennett who recently said, "It is difficult for us living in twentieth-century America to understand why the Founders' love of liberty did not move them to give immediate freedom to the slaves. But as difficult as it is to imagine, we must recall how entrenched the institution of slavery was, how deep prejudice ran, and the hostility and fear between the two races. Many citizens viewed slaves as subhuman, as property. No one, no matter how obtuse, could be insensible to the slaves' anger and resentment at being denied justice."

Human beings, as we know, have an almost limitless capacity for rationalization using the flimsiest "evidence." Some are better at it than others, but most people can, using tortured logic, convince themselves of the correctness of their pet causes by "interpreting" just about anything, even Bible passages, to give credence to whatever they want to believe or point they want to make. The words *interpret* and *Bible*, in my opinion, should rarely if ever be used in the same sentence. The Bible says what it says. Interpretation is too often, in truth, "twistification" which is what the *Jesus Seminar* people do to the Bible and the ACLU does to the Constitution. They twist the meaning of words, principles, and concepts to make them conform to their agenda. The word *abortion* does not appear in the Bible which abortion advocates are eager to point out. However, the ancient Israelites and their ancestors understood perfectly that abortion is murder and therefore covered by the Sixth Commandment.

"Just as the Bible does not specifically condemn abortion, it does not specifically condemn the practice of slavery. While the Bible does give instructions on how slaves should be treated, many colonists conveniently saw the specific lack of condemnation as a condoning of the institution of slavery. The distinction most people don't make is that slavery in Bible times was completely different from the slavery that was practiced in the United States in the 1700's and 1800's. Slavery in the Bible was not based on race; people were not enslaved because of their nationality or the color of their skin. In Bible times, people sometimes sold *themselves* as slaves when they could not pay their debts or provide for their family. Some people chose to be slaves so as to have all their needs provided for by their master. European and American slavery was based on skin color. Black people were considered slaves because of their nationality and most slave owners truly believed black people to be 'inferior human beings' to white people. This is similar to the slavery the Jews experienced when they were in Egypt. The Jews were slaves, not by choice, but because they were Jews." (5)

Reverend Alexander Campbell said, "There is not one verse in the Bible inhibiting slavery, but many regulating it. It is not then, we conclude, immoral." The colonists, especially the Christian slave owners, should have understood that the Golden Rule would most certainly apply: Do to others as you would have them do to you.

Charles Cotesworth Pinckney died August 16, 1825 in his home-town of Charleston, South Carolina, and was buried in the church-yard of St. Michael's Church. The Reverend Gibbes, speaking at the time of Pinckney's death, said "It was evident to all of us, that his long and useful life was drawing to a close. He seemed to come among us to show that in his last hours the cause of the Bible was nearest his heart, to give us his blessing and to bid us farewell."

His friends paid him tribute with this eulogy:

To the memory of
General Charles Cotesworth Pinckney
One of the Founders of
The American Republic.
In War
He was the companion in arms
And the friend of Washington.
In Peace
He enjoyed his unchanging confidence
And maintained with enlightened zeal

The principles of his administration
And of the Constitution.
As a statesman
He bequeathed to his country the sentiment
Millions for defence
Not a cent for tribute.
As a lawyer,
His learning was various and profound
His principles pure. His practice liberal
With all the accomplishment of the Gentleman
He combined the virtues of the patriot
And the Piety of the Christian.
His name
Is recorded in the history of his country
Inscribed on the Charter of her liberties,
And cherished in the affections of her citizens.

Chapter Nineteen

Noah Webster

*The moral principles and precepts
contained in the Scriptures ought to form the basis
of all our civil constitutions and laws.
All the miseries and evils which men suffer from
vice, crime, ambition, injustice, oppression, slavery, and war,
proceed from their despising or neglecting
the precepts contained in the Bible.*
-- **Noah Webster**

*Webster's books were unlike texts seen today,
for they openly presented Biblical admonitions,
as well as principles of American government.
In one of his early editions of the "blue-backed speller"
appeared a* Moral Catechism *– rules upon which to base moral
conduct. Webster stated unequivocally, "God's Word,
contained in the Bible, has furnished all necessary
rules to direct our conduct."*
-- **Verna Hall**

When the Declaration of Independence was signed in 1776, Noah Webster was a few months shy of his eighteenth birthday. Although he was not a delegate to the Constitutional Convention of 1787, he is usually included among those colonists called Founding Fathers because of his active role in promoting ratification of the product that has often been called "The Miracle of Philadelphia." By the time the delegates had completed their work. Webster's writing ability had attracted the attention of influential members of the Constitutional Convention. As a result of their coaxing, he wrote *Examination of the Leading Principles of the Federal Constitution*, and *Sketches of American Policy*," pamphlets credited with generating much-needed support for ratification.

In addition to his involvement in the successful campaign to secure ratification of the Constitution, he is most remembered among historians for the paramount role he played in establishing the foundation of American education. Webster has been called "the Schoolmaster of the Nation," a title he earned as the most active of the Founding Fathers in emphasizing the importance of education.

Securing government funding for education was a major interest of Webster's because he believed it was a responsibility of state and local governments to "discipline our youth in early life in sound maxims of moral, political, and religious duties." Known and respected by his peers as "a brilliant scholar and dedicated Christian," Webster was especially convinced of the need for government-sponsored teaching of moral principles.

H. R. Warfel wrote: "Along with good habits of work, Webster wished students to acquire 'good principles,' a predisposition for a virtuous life. 'For this reason society requires that the education of youth should be watched with the most scrupulous attention. Education, in a great measure, forms the moral characters of men, and morals are the basis of government Education should therefore be the first care of a legislature; not merely the institution of schools, but the furnishing of them with the best men for teachers. A good system of education should be the first article in the code of political regulations; for it is much easier to introduce and establish an effectual system for preserving morals, than to correct by penal statues the ill effects of a bad system.' On this point Webster was emphatic;

he asserted: 'The goodness of a heart is of infinitely more consequence to society than an elegance of manners; nor will any super-
ficial accomplishments repair the want of principle in the mind. It is
always better to be *vulgarly* right than *politely* wrong. . . The education of youth [is] an employment of more consequence than making
laws and preaching the gospel, because it lays the foundation on
which both law and gospel rest for success'." (1)

Webster's first contribution to the field of elementary education
was his *American Spelling Book*, which included "an easy Standard
of Pronunciation," that first appeared in 1783. Commonly known
as "the blue-backed speller", it eventually became an all-time best
seller with over seventy-million copies sold by 1947. His pronunciation guide later became part of *A Grammatical Institute of the
English Language*, an important educational tool he began in 1783
and completed in 1785.

"Noah Webster's Speller," explained Verna Hall "was compatible with the hearthside of a log cabin in the wilderness, or a city
classroom. It traveled on the flatboats of the Ohio River, churned
down the Mississippi and creaked across the prairies of the far west
as pioneer mothers taught their children from covered wagons.
Wherever the individual wished to challenge his own ignorance or
quench his thirst for knowledge, there, along with the Holy Bible
and Shakespeare, were Noah Webster's slim and inexpensive
Spellers, Grammars, Readers and his *Elements of Useful Knowledge*
containing the history and geography of the United States. Webster's
books were unlike texts seen today, for they openly presented Biblical
admonitions, as well as principles of American government. In one
of his early editions of the "blue-backed speller" appeared a *Moral
Catechism* – rules upon which to base moral conduct. Webster stated
unequivocally, 'God's Word, contained in the Bible, has furnished
all necessary rules to direct our conduct'." (2)

Webster's definition for *religion,* for instance, was: "Includes
a belief in the being and perfections of God, in the revelation of
His will to man, in man's obligation to obey His commands, in a
state of reward and punishment, and in man's accountableness to
God; and also true godliness or piety of life, with the practice of all
moral duties." (3) He defined *marriage* as "The act of uniting a man

and woman for life; the legal union of a man and woman for life. Marriage is a contract both civil and religious, by which the parties engage to live together in mutual affection and fidelity, till death shall separate them. Marriage was instituted by God himself for the purpose of preventing the promiscuous intercourse of the sexes, for promoting domestic felicity, and for securing the maintenance and education of children." (4)

Words were a passion; language an obsession with Webster. At the age of 14, he began studying classic literature with the Reverend Nathan Perkins as his tutor. Two years later, he enrolled at Yale College where he gravitated toward lexicography and philology. He is said to have learned more than twenty languages. After leaving Yale, Webster studied law in his spare time and was admitted to the bar in 1781.

Webster produced a series of lectures that were published in 1789 under the title "Dissertations on the English Language." Pursuing his interest in journalism, Webster founded the *American Magazine* in New York in 1789, a daily newspaper, *The Minerva* (later *The Commercial Advertiser*), and a semiweekly, *The Herald* (later *The Spectator*) in New York in 1793. (5) In his *Rudiments of English Grammar*, published in 1790, Webster continued his campaign to draw lines of distinction between the American version of the English language and the established British version.

Someone once said England and America were two countries separated by a common language. Webster was influential in the difficult task of codifying many of the differences that had evolved in the colonies in the way the language was spoken, words were spelled and pronounced, and in the rules of grammar. "Now is the time," Webster said, "and this is the country, in which we may expect success, in attempting changes favorable to language, science and government." It was probably mostly due to the work of Webster that eighteenth century travelers to America "remarked on the purity of the American speech, its grammatical correctness, and the absence of local dialects," wrote Catherine Drinker Bowen. Some said the Americans spoke better English than the English. He was definitely a leader in identifying a culture distinctly different from the mother country.

Between 1806 and 1833, Webster produced, among other writings, *A Compendious Dictionary of the English Language, A Philosophical and Practical Grammar of the English Language, A Synopsis of Words in Twenty Languages, The American Dictionary,* and *An American Dictionary of the English Language* – with *pronouncing vocabularies of Scripture, classical and geographical names,* his *History of the United States,* and a Bible translation entitled *Common Version of the Holy Bible, containing the Old and New Testament, with Amendments of the Language.* In 1840, an expanded edition of his 1828 dictionary, defining some 70,000 words, was published

In the preface of each of his books, Webster included comments explaining his belief that the Christian religion in general and the Bible in particular were the bedrocks of American civilization and were the only safeguard against tyranny. This statement appearing in the preface of his Bible translation is typical of all his words of introduction:

> *The Bible is the Chief moral cause of all that is good, and the best corrector of all that is evil, in human society; the best book for regulating the temporal concerns of men, and the only book that can serve as an infallible guide to future felicity...It is extremely important to our nation, in a political as well as religious view, that all possible authority and influence should be given to the scriptures, for these furnish the best principles of civil liberty, and the most effectual support of republican government.*
>
> *The principles of genuine liberty, and of wise laws and administrations, are to be drawn from the Bible and sustained by its authority. The man, therefore, who weakens or destroys the divine authority of that Book, may be accessory to all the public disorders which society is doomed to suffer...*
>
> *There are two powers only, sufficient to control men and secure the rights of individuals and a peaceable administration; these are the combined force of religion and law, and the force or fear of the bayonet. (6)*

Webster included *Advice to the Young* in his *Value of the Bible and Excellence of the Christian Religion* written as a companion piece to his translation to the King James Bible. His advice is as timely and valuable today as it was in 1833:

> *When you become entitled to exercise the right of voting for public officers, let it be impressed on your mind that God commands you to choose for rulers, just men who will rule in the fear of God. The preservation of a republican government depends on the faithful discharge of this duty; if the citizens neglect their duty, and place unprincipled men in office, the government will soon be corrupted; laws will be made, not for the public good, so much as for selfish or local purposes; corrupt of incompetent men will be appointed to execute the laws; the public revenues will be squandered on unworthy men; and the rights of the citizens will be violated or disregarded. If a republican government fails to secure public prosperity and happiness, it must be because the citizens neglect the divine commands, and elect bad men to make and administer the laws. Intriguing men can never be safely trusted.*
>
> *For a knowledge of the human heart, and the characters of men, it is customary to resort to the writings of Shakespeare, and of other dramatic authors, and to biography, novels, tales, and fictitious narratives. But whatever amusement may be derived from such writings, they are not the best authorities for a knowledge of mankind. The most perfect maxims and examples for regulating your social conduct and domestic economy, as well as the best rules of morality and religion, are to be found in the Bible. The history of the Jews presents the true character of man in all its forms. All the traits of human character, good and bad, all the passions of the human heart; all the principles which guide and misguide men in society, are depicted in that short history, with an artless simplicity that has no parallel in modern writings. As to maxims of wisdom or prudence, the Proverbs of Solomon furnish a complete system, and suffi-*

*cient, if carefully observed, to make any man wise, pros-
perous, and happy. The observation, that "a soft answer
turneth away wrath," if strictly observed by men, would
prevent half the broils and contentions that inflict wretchedness on society and families.*

*But were we assured that there is to be no future life, and
that men are to perish at death like the beasts of the field;
the moral principles and precepts contained in the scriptures
ought to form the basis of all our civil constitutions and laws.
These principles and precepts have truth, immutable truth,
for their foundation; and they are adapted to the wants of
men in every condition of life. They are the best principles
and precepts, because they are exactly adapted to secure the
practice of universal justice and kindness among men; and
of course to prevent crimes, war, and disorders in society. No
human laws dictated by different principles from those in the
gospel, can ever secure these objects. All the miseries and
evils which men suffer from vice, crime, ambition, injustice,
oppression, slavery, and war, proceed from their despising
or neglecting the precepts contained in the Bible.*

*As the means of temporal happiness then the Christian
religion ought to be received, and maintained with firm and
cordial support. It is the real source of all genuine republican principles. It teaches the equality of men as to rights
and duties; and while it forbids all oppression, it commands
due subordination to law and rulers. It requires the young to
yield obedience to their parents, and enjoins upon men the
duty and wisdom, and real religion – "men who fear God
and hate covetousness." The ecclesiastical establishments
of Europe, which serve to support tyrannical governments,
are not the Christian religion, but abuses and corruptions
of it. The religion of Christ and his apostles, in its primitive
simplicity and purity, unencumbered with the trappings of
power and the pomp of ceremonies is the surest basis of a
republican government.*

*Never cease then to give to religion, to its institutions,
and to its ministers, your strenuous support. The clergy*

in this country are not possessed of rank and wealth; they depend for their influence on their talents and learning, on their private virtues and public services. They are the firm supporters of law and good order, the friends of peace, the expounders and teachers of Christian doctrines, the instructors of youth, the promoters of benevolence, of charity, and of all useful improvements. During the war of the revolution, the clergy were generally friendly to the cause of the country. The present generation can hardly have a tolerable idea of the influence of the New-England clergy, in discouragements of the war. The writer remembers their good offices of that respectable order, in this country, attempt to undermine the best supports of religion; and those who destroy the influence and authority of the Christian religion, sap the foundations of public order, of liberty, and of republican government.

For instruction then in social, religious, and civil duties, resort to the scriptures for the best precepts and most excellent examples for imitation. The example of unhesitating faith and obedience in Abraham, when he promptly prepared to offer his son Isaac, as a burnt offering, at the command of God, is a perfect model of that trust in God which becomes dependent beings. The history of Joseph furnishes one of the most charming examples of fraternal affection, and of filial duty and respect for a venerable father, ever exhibited in human life. Christ and his apostles presented, in their lives, the most perfect example of disinterested benevolence, unaffected kindness, humility, patience in adversity, forgiveness of injuries, love to God, and to all mankind. If men would universally cultivate these religious affections and virtuous dispositions, with as much diligence as they cultivate human science and refinement of manners, the world would soon become a terrestrial paradise. (7)

Based on his public pronouncements, there can be no doubt that Webster was a dedicated Christian. His description of his conversion to the Christian faith should serve as an important example and warning to young people today:

Being educated in a religious family under pious parents, I had in early life some religious impressions, but being too young to understand fully the doctrines of the Christian religion, and falling into vicious company at college, I lost those impressions. . . [I] fell into the common mistake of attending to the duties which man owes to man before I had learned the duties which we all owe to our Creator and Redeemer. . . I sheltered myself as well as I could from the attacks of conscience for neglect of duty under a species of skepticism, and endeavored to satisfy my mind that a profession of religion is not absolutely necessary to salvation. In this state of mind I place great reliance on good works or the performance of moral duties as the means of salvation. . . About a year ago, an unusual revival of religion took place in New Haven. . . and [I] was led by a spontaneous impulse to repentance, prayer, and entire submission and surrender of myself to my Maker and Redeemer. . . I now began to understand and relish many parts of the Scriptures which before appeared mysterious and unintelligible, or repugnant to my natural. . . In short, my view of the Scriptures, of religion, of the whole Christian scheme of salvation, and of God's moral government are very much changed, and my heart yields with delight and confidence to whatever appears to be the Divine will. (8)

Born in Hartford, Connecticut, October 16, 1758, Webster, on his father's side, was a fourth generation descendant of John Webster, one of the first settlers of Hartford, and, on his mother's side, a descendant of William Bradford a passenger on the Mayflower. Bradford, who was elected Governor of Plymouth Colony thirty times, also organized the first Thanksgiving Day celebration in New England.

In addition to his voluminous writings and his unmatched contributions to the nation's emerging Bible-based system of education, Webster's resume included the following: Member of the American Philosophical Society in Philadelphia; Fellow of the American Academy of Arts and Sciences in Massachusetts; Member of the Connecticut Academy of Arts and Sciences; Fellow of the Royal

Society of Northern Antiquaries in Copenhagen; Member of the Connecticut Historical Antiquaries in Copenhagen; Member of the Connecticut Historical Society; Corresponding Member of the Historical Societies in Massachusetts, New York and Georgia; of the Academy of Medicine in Philadelphia; and of the Columbian Institute in Washington; and Honorary Member of the Michigan Historical Society." (9) He had also served as a soldier in the Revolutionary War.

Webster died May 28, 1843 in New Haven. In his "Memoir of the Author," the editor of *The American Dictionary*, concluded, "It may be said that the name Noah Webster, from the wide circulation of some of his works, is known familiarly to a greater number of the inhabitants of the united States, than the name, probably, of any other individual except the father of the Country. Whatever influence he thus acquired was used at all time to promote the best interests of his fellowmen. His books, though read by millions, have made no man worse. To multitudes they have been of lasting benefit not by the course of early training they have furnished, but by those precepts of wisdom and virtue with which almost every page is stored. August, 1847" (10)

Like his fellow Founding Fathers, Noah Webster was a patriot. These stirring words of his need to be remembered today when patriotism is sometimes mocked by lesser men and women: "Our fathers were men – they were heroes and patriots – they fought – they conquered – and they bequeathed to us a rich inheritance of liberty and empire which we have no right to surrender...Yes, my fellow freemen, we have a rich and growing empire – we have a lucrative commerce to protect – we have indefeasible rights – we have an excellent system of religion and of government – we have wives and children and sisters to defend; and God forbid that the soil of America should sustain the wretch who [lacks] the will or the spirit to defend them. Let us then rally round the independence and Constitution of our country, resolved to a man that we will never lose by folly, disunion, or cowardice what has been planned by wisdom and purchased with blood."

Chapter Twenty

John Hancock

And for the support of this Declaration,
with a firm reliance on the protection of divine Providence,
we mutually pledge to each other our Lives,
our Fortunes and our sacred Honor.
-- The Declaration of Independence

There! His Majesty can now read my name without spectacles,
and can now double his reward of five hundred pounds
for my head. That is my defiance!
-- John Hancock, upon signing
The Declaration of Independence

W hen John Hancock, as president of the Second Continental Congress was first to sign *The Declaration of Independence*, he, along with all the others signers, was well aware that he may have just signed his own death warrant. After making his famous statement regarding the clarity of his signature on the Declaration, he went on to say, "There must be no pulling different ways; we must all hang together." Rarely one to pass up a good straight line, Benjamin Franklin equipped, "Yes. We must all hang together, or most assuredly we shall all hang separately." Stephen Hopkins' hand shook as he signed the historic document: "My hand trembles," he said, "but my heart does not." (1)

Such were the mixed feelings of the fifty-six men representing a fledgling nation that was now openly defying the most powerful nation on earth. That mixture of elation, joviality, hubris, confidence, wonder and trepidation was not confined to the room in which the members of Congress met to sign the document that would propel them on a course leading into unknown waters. Among the colonists, there may have been a consensus of sorts for independence, but it was far from unanimous.

Until the Boston Massacre of 1770, Hancock himself had been of more loyalist persuasion than rebellious even though he had been involved in protesting most of Parliament's provocations which had begun in 1765 with passage of the Stamp Act. Rather than a rebellion, the colonists had seen themselves in a struggle to maintain their rights as British citizens. To King George III, it was viewed almost from the initial signs of resistance to his authority as a rebellion.

Seizure by the British of one of Hancock's ships over a tax issue in 1768 added to his feelings that independence was an option the colonies must seriously consider. After "the massacre" during which three Americans were killed and two others died later of their wounds, he became a member of the committee that demanded British troops be removed from Boston. From that point on, he became more and more involved with the independence movement. Hancock's name became closely associated with that of firebrand Samuel Adams, who many believe was first to call the 1770 conflict a "massacre." The two were recognized as leaders of the Whig (Patriot) Party in Massachusetts.

Hancock and Adams began to attract the personal attention of King George. In better times, Hancock had attended the 1760 coronation of George as King of the British Empire. A few years later the British king offered amnesty to all revolutionary leaders except for "arch rebels" Hancock and Adams. British officials were aware that Hancock, along with John Adams and Elbridge Gerry, was known to have been responsible for Colonial military preparations, including the establishment of an arsenal at Concord. Confiscation of those weapons was one of the reasons for the British decision to launch their attacks on Lexington and Concord. April 19, 1775 became famous as the day "the shot heard 'round the world" was fired.

According to historian B. J. Lossing, British Governor Thomas Gage dispatched his soldiers with orders to confiscate or destroy the arsenal and to arrest Hancock and Adams on April 18, 1775, the night before the opening battles of the Revolutionary War. The two famous rebels were said to have escaped, after having been warned by Paul Revere, out one door as the soldiers entered through another. Three days earlier as a result of his growing conviction that war was inevitable, Hancock, son and grandson of influential protestant pastors, had called his fellow citizens of Massachusetts to a day of prayer and fasting, writing:

In circumstances dark as these, it becomes us as men and Christians to reflect that whilst every prudent measure should be taken to ward off the impending judgments...all confidence must be withheld from the means we use and reposed only on that God who rules in the armies of heaven and without whose blessing the best human councils are but foolishness and all created power vanity.

It is the happiness of his church that when the powers of earth and hell combine against it...then the throne of grace is on the easiest access and its appeal thither is graciously invited by that Father of mercies who has assured it that when His children ask bread He will not give them a stone...

That it be, and hereby is, recommended to the good people of this colony...as a day of public humiliation, fasting and prayer...to confess the sins...to implore the forgiveness of all our transgressions...and especially that the union of the American colonies in defence of their rights, for which, hitherto, we desire to thank Almighty God, may be preserved and confirmed...and that America may soon behold a gracious interposition of Heaven. (2)

Considered one of the richest men in America, Hancock inherited the business and personal wealth of his uncle and guardian Thomas Hancock in 1764, ten years after his graduation from Harvard at the age of seventeen. Working with his uncle, Hancock had learned the various family businesses which included importing/exporting, shipping, retailing, investment banking, and real estate investing. Being preeminent among the merchants and shippers in America's most important city and port of its day generated profits that later were often used to finance military equipment and operations.

Hancock was also was the principal financial backer of the Sons of Liberty, a secret patriotic society organized in 1765 to oppose the Stamp Act. After the act was repealed in 1766, the society, which consisted of numerous local chapters, formed Committees of Correspondence to foster resistance to other oppressive British economic and political actions. The Sons of Liberty also helped enforce the policy of nonimportation, by which American merchants refused to import goods carried in British ships, and in 1774 it took part in convoking the Continental Congress. (3)

Spawned by the Sons of Liberty, Committees of Safety began to be formed in the colonies with Massachusetts thought to have been the first to do so in 1774 when Hancock was president of the Provincial Congress of Massachusetts. That committee was to act as an executive board for the colony, especially where matters pertaining to the mother country were concerned. One of its most important responsibilities was to supply the Continental Army with men and equipment.

Another offshoot from the Sons of Liberty was the formation throughout the colonies of Committees of Correspondence that were helpful in establishing much-needed lines of communication. The first such committee was formed in Boston with the support and participation of Hancock and others including Sam Adams and fellow Founding Father James Otis, who James Adams once described as "a flame of fire." Otis's writings and speeches are laced with refer- ences to God as the only "king" of the colonies. [For government to] "have any solid foundation," he said, "it must be planted in the unchangeable will of God, the author of nature, whose laws never vary."

Otis and Hancock were in agreement regarding the kingship of the colonies. They described the policies of the king and Parliament toward the colonies as tyrannical. "Tyranny of all kinds," Otis said," is to be abhorred, whether it be in the hands of one, or of the few, or of the any...The power of God Almighty is the only power that can properly and strictly be called supreme and absolute. In order of nature immediately under Him comes the power of simple democracy or the power of the whole over the whole. Subordinate to both these are all other political powers."

That's a pretty good summation regarding the fundamental beliefs of the men who provided us with our independence and our form of government. They believed that God's precepts as recorded in the Bible provided the only secure guidelines and foundational supports for government and that Americans wanted to be guided by God's precepts rather than the fallibility and wishy-washy precepts of secular-thinking men. Because of their affluence and power, the British Government had become self centered rather than God-centered. The Founding Fathers had no intention of letting that happen to them. "The Declaration of Independence," said historian David Barton, "was actually a dual declaration: A Declaration of *Independence from Britain* and a Declaration of *Dependence on God.*"

In a resolution distributed by the Massachusetts Committee of Correspondence, produced under the direction of Hancock, their purpose was "to defend the rights of colonists, and of this province in particular, as men, as Christians, and as subjects; to communicate then publish the same to the several towns in this province and the world as to the sense of this town...also requesting each town provide a free communication of their sentiments on this subject." (4)

With Committees of Correspondence soon established in nearly every town, and with Parliament issuing more and more legislation deemed to be oppressive by the colonists, momentum was building for separation from the mother country. "Our mother should remember we are children, not slaves," said the Presbyterians. "If the colonist is taxed without his consent, he will perhaps seek change," warned a New York newspaper. "The ways of Heaven are inscrutable," said Richard Henry Lee. "This step of the mother country, though intended to secure our dependence, may produce a fatal resentment and be subversive of that end," he concluded. In a speech following Parliament's passage of the Stamp Act in 1765, Otis observed, "One single act of Parliament we find has set people a thinking in six months more than they had done in their whole lives before." (5)

Soon pastors were delivering fiery sermons and newspapers throughout New England were contributing to the din. The colonies had found their voice. A vocal crescendo was building to which the British, in their arrogance, responded with more oppressive measures. British General Thomas Gage put voice to British arrogance and intransigence when he said, "Let's squash this spirit at a blow." Although it would take a few more years, the die was cast and confidence was building among the colonists.

In a speech delivered March 5, 1774, commemorating the Boston Massacre of 1770, Hancock said, "I have the most animating confidence that the present noble struggle for liberty will terminate gloriously for America. And let us play the man for our God, and for the cities of our God; whilst we are using the means in our power, let us humbly commit our righteous cause to the great Lord of the Universe, who loveth righteousness and hateth iniquity. And having secured the approbation of our hearts by a faithful and unwearied discharge of our duty to our country, let us joyfully leave our concerns in the hands of Him who raiseth up and pulleth down the empires and kingdoms of the world as He pleases; and with cheerful submission to His sovereign will, devoutly say, 'Although the fig tree shall not blossom neither shall fruit be in the vines, the labor of the olive shall fair and the field shall yield not meat, the flock shall be cut off from the fold and there shall be no herd in the stalls, yet we will rejoice in the Lord, we will joy in the God of our salvation.' [Habakkuk 3:17-18]." (6)

Days of fasting and prayer became common in Massachusetts and throughout New England. Hancock was outspoken regarding his Christian beliefs, especially the need for inclusion of Christian principles in governance. "Sensible of the importance of Christian piety and virtue to the order and happiness of a state, I cannot but earnestly commend to you every measure for their support and encouragement...Manners, by which not only the freedom but the very existence of the republic are greatly affected, depend much upon the public institutions of religion."

Because of Boston's importance as a commercial port, many of Parliament's "Intolerable Acts" increasingly had a negative effect upon the citizens of Massachusetts. As president of the Second Continental Congress, Hancock signed a *Declaration of the Causes and Necessity of Taking up Arms* July 6, 1775, in which many references to the colonists' belief in divine support for their cause were included. The lengthy declarations which amounted to a bill of particular complaints included these excerpts:

If it was possible for men, who exercise their reason to believe, that the divine Author of our existence intended a part of the human race to hold an absolute property in, and an unbounded power over others, marked out by his infinite goodness and wisdom, as the objects of a legal domination never rightfully resistible, however severe and oppressive, the inhabitants of these colonies might at least require from the parliament of Great Britain some evidence, that this dreadful authority over them, has been granted to that body. But a reverence for our great Creator, principles of humanity, and the dictates of common sense, must convince all those who reflect upon the subject, that government was instituted to promote the welfare of mankind, and ought to be administered for the attainment of that end.

The legislature of Great Britain, however, stimulated by an inordinate passion for a power not only unjustifiable, but which they know to be peculiarly reprobated by the very constitution of that kingdom, and desparate of success in any mode of contest, where regard should be had to truth, law, or right, have at length, deserting those, attempted to effect their cruel and impolitic purpose of enslaving these colonies by violence, and have thereby rendered it necessary for us to close with their last appeal from reason to arms.

...Our cause is just. Our union is perfect. Our internal resources are great, and, if necessary, foreign assistance in undoubtably attainable. – We gratefully acknowledge, as

signal instances of the Divine favour towards us, that his Providence would not permit us to be called into this severe controversy, until we were grown up to our present strength, had been previously exercised in warlike operation, and possessed of the means of defending ourselves.

. . . fortified with these animating reflections, we most solemnly, before God and the world, declare, that exerting the utmost energy of those powers, which our beneficent Creator hath graciously bestowed upon us, the arms we have been compelled by our enemies to assume, we will, in defiance of every hazard, with unabating firmness and perseverance, employ for the preservation of our liberties; being with one mind resolved to die freemen rather than to live slaves . . .

With an humble confidence in the mercies of the supreme and impartial Judge and Ruler of the Universe, we most devoutly implore his divine goodness to protect us happily through this great conflict, to dispose our adversaries to reconciliation on reasonable terms, and thereby to relieve the empire from the calamities of civil war.

At least partly due to health problems, Hancock resigned from Congress in 1777 with the intention of returning to private life, but was soon after elected a member of a body formed to produce a Constitution for the state of Massachusetts. In 1780, he was elected as the first governor of Massachusetts, a position he held until 1785. He was elected governor again in 1789. While governor, he helped win ratification of the U. S. Constitution in 1788.

In his official capacity of Governor in 1788, Hancock is remembered for issuing *A Proclamation for a Day of Thanksgiving* to celebrate the colonies victory in the Revolutionary War in which he makes specific reference to his belief in God's role in that victory. The proclamation reads as follows:

Whereas...these United States are not only happily rescued from the Danger and Calamities to which they have been so long exposed, but their Freedom, Sovereignty and Independence ultimately acknowledged.

And whereas…the Interposition of Divine Providence in our Favor hath been most abundantly and most graciously manifested, and the Citizens of these United States have every Reason for Praise and Gratitude to the God of their salvation. Impressed therefore with an exalted Sense of the Blessings by which we are surrounded, and of our entire Dependence on that Almighty Being from whose Goodness and Bounty they are derived;

I do by and with the Advice of the Council appoint Thursday the Eleventh Day of December next (the Day recommended by the Congress to all the States) to be religiously observed as a Day of Thanksgiving and Prayer, that all the People may then assemble to celebrate…that he hath been pleased to continue to us the Light of the Blessed Gospel;…That we also offer up fervent Supplications to cause pure Religion and Virtue to flourish…and to fill the World with his glory.

John Hancock, Esquire
Governor of the Commonwealth of Massachusetts (7)

In a speech delivered February 27, 1788, Hancock said the Lord gave this country "a name and a standing among the nations of the world…I hope and pray that the gratitude of their hearts may be expressed by proper use of those inestimable blessings, by the greatest exertions of patriotism, by forming and supporting institutions for cultivating the human understanding, & for the greatest progress of the Arts and Sciences, by establishing laws for the support of piety, religion, and morality…and by exhibiting on the great theater of the world those social, public and private virtues which give more dignity to a people, possessing their own sovereignty than the crown and diadems afford to sovereign princes." (8)

According to B. J. Lossing in his 1848 *Lives of the Signers of the Declaration of Independence*, John Hancock "was beloved by all his contemporaries, and posterity venerates his name, as a benefactor of his country. He died on the eighth of October, 1793, in the fifty-fifth year of his age."

Epilogue

Christianity is the
predominant religion in America.
We all know that's an incontrovertible fact.
The media always refer to the Jewish state of Israel.
They talk about the Muslim country of Saudi Arabia, of Iran, of
Iraq. We all talk about the Hindu nation of India.
America is not a nothing country. It's a Christian Country.
-- **Kirk Fordice**

A contempt of the monuments and wisdom of the past
may be justly reckoned one of the reigning follies of these days to
which pride and idleness have equally contributed.
-- **Samuel Johnson**

Patriotism, to me, is as natural as breathing. Patriots love this country because of the freedoms, especially the freedom to worship without fear of oppression or persecution, and the opportunities we enjoy that make it possible for us to live fulfilling lives. We are free to choose how we will live, free to pursue our dreams. Woodrow Wilson described that concept well: "America lives in the heart of every man everywhere who wishes to find a region where he will be free to work out his destiny as he chooses."

The freedoms we enjoy are based on biblical concepts. We have those freedoms because the Founding Fathers were, far and away, Bible-believing Christians who built this nation on a foundation of Christian precepts. The Founding Fathers are my heroes. I love the United States of America and all it stands for, or used to stand for before the silly incorrectness of "political correctness" gained some measure of public acceptance. That acceptance has been generated by those with an inordinate power to influence public opinion. An unholy trinity made up of the traditional news media, the entertainment industry, and academia, all tightly controlled for most of the second half of the twentieth century by pseudo-sophisticated modern-day neo-liberals, has generated a campaign to lead us down the deceptively attractive (to some) road to their idea of man-made Utopia. Their Utopia has little or no room for God; love of God and country are beneath their dignity. Faith in God and love of country apparently are, in their elevated opinions of themselves, antiquated ideas offensive to their self-proclaimed superior intellect and advanced state of sophistication. I might suggest they could benefit from a re-reading of *The Emperor's New Clothes*, but they wouldn't get it.

The self-absorption of *our* times is an unintended consequence of the self-government and free enterprise systems established by our Founding Fathers who made it clear that these systems would only work as intended as long as citizens exercised self control and when they recognized their personal accountability to God. Self control, personal responsibility, and accountability are precepts seemingly practiced less and less in the U. S. today because they are biblical precepts that are considered to be outmoded. The Bible and its teachings are under attack by the secular humanists who are especially offended by use of the word *sin*. Christopher Lasch hit that nail squarely on the head when he said, "The vacuum left by secularization has been filled by a permissive culture that replaces the concept of sin with the concept of sickness. We much prefer terms like sociopath and psychopath, addict and compulsive to just plain sinner."

Many of the freedoms the founders provided have been used of late to permit licentious behavior protected by their blatant subversion of the First Amendment. To the ACLU, all the perversities and self-indulgences practiced by the most prurient and self-centered members of our society are freedom of speech issues. They pretty much know which dim-witted judges generally accept such nonsense as having legal standing.

The widespread affluence we enjoy today along with the fairly recent embracing of tenets of secular humanism by many who should know better has produced a result that hardly resembles the vision the founders had for the future of their country. The combination of affluence and secular humanism has produced pandemic hedonism, nihilism, irresponsibility, self-centeredness, greed, immoral behavior, and Godlessness the likes of which are rare in human history for a civilized society. Johann Schiller warned that "Genuine morality is preserved only in the school of adversity; a state of continuous prosperity may easily prove a quicksand to virtue." As the inevitable results of such behavior by a large percentage of the population became apparent, a counter movement began and has gained a sizeable number of adherents resulting in what has come to be known as the culture war.

In his excellent book entitled *How to Win the Culture War*, Peter Kreeft decries the fact that too many people don't seem to understand the concept of a culture war let alone concede the fact that we are in one. Kreeft's book is a call to battle which he calls "an ugly, blaring trumpet.' On a battlefield, Kreeft points out, "a trumpet works better than a violin." He goes on to explain you can't win any kind of war without knowing nine necessary things:

1. that you are at war
2. who your enemy is
3. what kind of war you are in
4. what the basic principle of this kind of war is
5. what the enemy's strategy is
6. where the main battle field is
7. what weapon will defeat the enemy
8. how to acquire this weapon
9. why you will win "

You cannot win a war," Kreeft says

1. if you blissfully sew peace banners on a battlefield
2. if you do not know who you are fighting
3. if you do not know what kind of war you are fighting
4. if you do not know the basic rules of battle
5. if you do not know your enemy's battle plan
6. if you send your troops to the wrong battlefield
7. if you use the wrong weapons
8. if you don't know how to get the right weapon
9. if you are not confident of your inevitable victory

The culture war didn't begin in the 1960s, but conditions necessary to its advancement surfaced. That decade was described by Robert Bork in *Slouching Toward Gomorrah* as "unlike any previous decade in American experience."

According to Bork, with whom I wholeheartedly agree, "the Sixties combined domestic disruption and violence with an explosion of drug use and sexual promiscuity; it was a decade of hedonism and narcissism; it was a decade in which popular culture reached new lows of vulgarity. The Sixties generation combined moral relativism with political absolutism. And it was the decade in which the Establishment not only collapsed but began to endorse the most outrageous behavior and indictment of America by young radicals. It was the decade that saw victories for the civil rights movement, but it was also the decade in which much of America's best educated and most pampered youth refused to serve the country in war, disguising self-indulgence and hatred of the United States as idealism. What W. H. Auden said of the 1930's was even more true of the 1960's: It was a 'low and dishonest decade'."

The radical's bases of operations were the universities where they were given aid and comfort by the administrations who were "soft, alienated from the surrounding society, without belief in themselves and the worth of what they did," according to Bork. "The Sixties students did not create the emptiness of the universities; they simply exploited it," Bork observed. The universities were empty of resolve because of their having adopted the tenets of secular humanism and its "no absolutes" corollary. That, of course, would have been anathema to the 56 framers of the Constitution, 24 of whom had seminary degrees, and 54 of whom were members of Christian denominations when Christians believed in the inerrancy of the Bible which teaches that there are, indeed, absolutes. Bork points out that "the great majority of that generation was not radical or hippie," but with their allies in the press, the radicals unfairly put their imprimatur on their contemporaries."

The late Bill Bright, founder of Campus Crusade for Christ International pointed out that "...without question, the greatest difference between the America of 1776 and the America of 2003 is the banishment of the God of the Bible – the God of Abraham, Isaac, and Jacob; the God and Father of our Lord Jesus Christ – from the public square.

"To that fundamental flaw in the fabric of our modern culture can be traced the weakening of every moral seam since. Only by restoring God to His rightful place as the central issue in all of human life – political, spiritual, moral, economic, philosophical – will there be sufficient motivation and reason to correct what ails America."

Bright goes on to say, "As a nation, our spiritual blood has been poisoned, yet we are merely treating the boils that have resulted. In order to cure a sick culture, we must attack the root cause: the exclusion of God from American culture. We need not settle for a 'post-Christian America,' or yield to the relentless onslaught against the God whose followers were instrumental in founding this great nation. As Ezekiel saw the dry bones of Israel come back to life before his eyes, we can see the soul of America revived by restoring God to His rightful place in our land – in our hearts, on our lips, in our homes, in the boardroom, in the classroom, in the marketplace, in the public square, and in the halls of government."

Speaking on the same subject, author Andrew M. Allison observed, "The nation these men [the Founding Fathers] built is now in the throes of a political, economic, social and spiritual crisis that has driven many to an almost frantic search for "modern solutions." Ironically, the solutions have been readily available for nearly two hundred years in the writings of our Founding Fathers. An honest examination of twentieth-century American history reveals that virtually every serious problem which has developed in our society can be traced to an ill-conceived departure from the sound principles taught by these great men. The citizen of today who turns back to the founders' writings is often surprised by their timeless relevance – and perhaps equally dismayed that we have permitted ourselves to stray so far from such obvious truths."

Many have warned of the inevitability of decay in democratic systems. John Adams said, "Remember democracy never lasts long. It soon wastes, exhausts, and murders itself. There never was a democracy yet that did not commit suicide. . . Democracy will soon degenerate into an anarchy, such an anarchy that every man will do what is right in his own eyes and no man's life or property or reputation or liberty will be secure, and every one of these will soon mould itself into a system of subordination of all the moral virtues and intellectual abilities, all the powers of wealth, beauty, wit and science, to the wanton pleasures, the capricious will, and the execrable cruelty of one or a very few." Do Adams' words describe American society today? I think they do.

The anti-Christian, secular humanist left seems to be saying, so, what's wrong with wanton pleasure and capricious will? "If it feels good, do it" is their axiom. None are so blind as those who will not see.

Alexander Tyler, a Scottish history professor at the University of Edinborough wrote in 1787, "A democracy is always temporary in nature; it simply cannot exist as a permanent form of government. A democracy will continue to exist up until the time that voters discover they can vote themselves generous gifts from the public treasury. From that moment on, the majority always votes for the candidates who promise the most benefits from the public treasury, with the result that every democracy will finally collapse due to loose fiscal policy, always followed by a dictatorship. The average age of the world's greatest civilizations from the beginning of history, has been abut 200 years. During those 200 years, these nations always progressed through the following sequence:

From bondage to faith;
From spiritual faith to great courage;
From courage to liberty;

From liberty to abundance;
From abundance to complacency;
From complacency to apathy;
From apathy to dependence;
From dependence back into bondage."

A realistic reading of Tyler's list should be sobering to thoughtful people, most of whom will realize we could locate our current condition somewhere on that scale between abundance and dependence, depending on your degree of pessimism. So, should we shrug our shoulders and say we may as well surrender to the inevitable? If we have any of the character of the Founding Fathers remaining in us, we will not surrender to those who want to separate us from our Christian heritage. We will heed the call of Peter Kreeft's trumpet and join the battle. "All that is necessary for evil to triumph is for good people to do nothing." Edmund Burke warned. Every responsible citizen needs to ask himself what he is doing to oppose the forces of evil.

Soren Kierkegaard could have been speaking to us today: "As soon as Christ's kingdom comes to terms with the world, Christianity is abolished." If Christianity is abolished, we will have hell on earth because, "If there is no God," Fyodor Dostoyevsky correctly pointed out, "everything is permissible." Judge Roy Moore reminds us that "The nation that forgets God is in absolute trouble." Can anyone who reads a newspaper doubt that we are already a long way down that road?

So, the answer is obvious: Take a stand, Christian! What the Founding Fathers fought for, we cannot simply give away. John Quincy Adams had a word for us: "Posterity – you will never know how much it has cost my generation to preserve your freedom. I hope you will make good use of it." Adams was a devout Christian as were his parents, John and Abigail. He was talking about all of our freedoms, especially our freedom of religion by which he meant the Christian religion. At the time of the Revolutionary War, it was estimated that 99% of the colonists were Christians.

Speeches and writings of our Founding Fathers and more recent presidents and public figures abound with statements regarding the importance of the Christian religion to our continued well being as a nation. Here are a few of their thoughts:

George Washington: "No Country upon Earth ever had it more in its power to attain these blessings...Much to be regretted indeed would it be, were we to neglect the means and depart from the road which Providence has pointed us to, so plainly; I cannot believe it will ever come to pass. The Great Governor of the Universe has led us too long and too far...to forsake us in the midst of it...We may, now and then, get bewildered; but I hope and trust that there is good sense and virtue enough left to recover the right path."

Jedediah Morse: "To the kindly influence of Christianity we owe that degree of civil freedom, and political and social happiness which mankind now enjoys. In proportion as the genuine effects of Christianity are diminished in any nation, either through unbelief, or the corruption of its doctrines, or the neglect of its institutions; in the same proportion will the people of that nation recede from the blessings of genuine freedom, and approximate the miseries of complete despotism."

"All efforts to destroy the foundations of our holy religion ultimately tend to the subversion also of our political freedom and happiness."

"Whenever the pillars of Christianity shall be overthrown, our present republican form of government, and all the blessings which flow from them, must fall with them."

Justice Joseph Story: "Let the American youth never forget, that they possess a noble inheritance, bought by the toils and sufferings and blood of their ancestors; and capacity, if wisely improved, and faithfully guarded, of transmitting to their latest posterity all the substantial blessings of life, the peaceful enjoyment of liberty, property, religion, and independence."

Abraham Lincoln: "We have been the recipients of the choicest bounties of heaven. We have been preserved, these many years, in peace and prosperity. We have grown in numbers, wealth and power, as no other nation has ever grown. But we have forgotten God. We have forgotten the gracious hand which preserved us in peace, and multiplied and enriched and strengthened us; and we have vainly imagined, in the deceitfulness of our hearts, that all these blessings were produced by some superior wisdom and virtue of our own. Intoxicated with unbroken success, we have become too self-sufficient to feel the necessity of redeeming and preserving grace, too proud to pray to the God that made us! It behooves us, then to humble ourselves before the offended Power, to confess our national sins, and to pray for clemency and forgiveness."

Calvin Coolidge: "A spring will cease to flow if its source be dried up; a tree will wither if its roots be destroyed. In its main features the Declaration of Independence is a great spiritual document. It is a declaration not of material but of spiritual concepts. Equality, liberty, popular sovereignty, the rights of man – these are not elements which we can see and touch. They are ideals. They have their source and their roots in religious convictions. They belong to the unseen world. Unless the faith of the American people in these religious convictions is to endure, the principles of our declaration will perish. We cannot continue to enjoy the result if we neglect and abandon the cause."

Ronald Reagan: "While never willing to bow to a tyrant, our forefathers were always willing to get to their knees before God. When catastrophe threatened, they turned to God for deliverance. When the harvest was bountiful, the first thought, was thanksgiving to God. Prayer is today as powerful a force in our nation as it has ever been. We as a nation should never forget this source of strength. Through the storms of Revolution, Civil War, and the great World Wars, as well as during times of disillusionment and disarray, the nation has turned to God in prayer for deliverance. We thank Him for answering our call, for, surely, He has. As a nation, we have been richly blessed with His love and generosity."

1892 U. S. Supreme Court Ruling: "Our laws and our institutions must necessarily be based upon the teachings of the Redeemer of Mankind. It is impossible that it should be otherwise; and, in this sense, and to this extent, our civilization and our institutions are emphatically Christian."

I could fill volumes with quotations by prominent Americans regarding the importance of the Judeo/Christian God and the Bible, but let's see what a prominent European writer/philosopher said about America's spiritual condition. Alexis de Tocqueville was intrigued by America because he recognized the uniqueness of the new nation. In 1832, he wrote, "I sought for the greatness and genius of America in her commodious harbors and her ample rivers, and it was not there; in her fertile fields and boundless prairies, and it was not there; in her rich mines and her vast world commerce and it was not there. Not until I went to the churches of America and heard her pulpits aflame with righteousness did I understand the secret of her genius and power. America is great because she is good and if America ever ceases to be good, America will cease to be great."

Tocqueville recognized something too many modern day Christians seem to have forgotten or have discounted in the face of an orchestrated campaign to marginalize the religion upon which our laws, ethics, moral codes, and traditions were inspired. America will continue to be good and therefore great as long as our culture is based on biblical precepts. The future well-being of America will be best served by restoring the Bible to its rightful place of honor and authority in our society, not by kicking the Bible and other Christian symbols out of public schools and the public square.

The secular humanists have nothing to offer but an accelerated increase in moral laxity and a lessening belief in our accountability to God. Even H. J. Blackman, Director of the Humanist Institute, ruefully admitted the truth about humanism: "The most potent objection to humanism is it's just too bad to be true." Contrast that with Christianity which is sometimes described as "too good to be true." That makes one wonder why anyone is attracted to humanism if a prominent secular humanist could make a statement like Blackman's.

It's way past time for Christians to wake up. Rudyard Kipling defined the problem for us many years ago:

For all we have and are,
For all our children's fate,
Stand up and take the war.
The Hun is at the gate!

It's time to reclaim our identity as a nation established on Judeo/ Christian principles and doctrines. It's time to say Enough! to those who would marginalize Christianity and separate us from our Judeo/ Christian roots.

We would do well to remember King David's admonition in Psalm 33: *Blessed is the nation whose God is the Lord...*

END NOTES

Authors are listed along with book titles in *For Further Reading*.

CHAPTER ONE
1. Quoted in *Understanding the Times*, pg. 14
2. *Slouching Toward Gomorrah*, pg. 35
3. Quoted in *America's God and Country*, pg. 153
4. Quoted in *America's Christian History: The Untold Story*, pg. 1
5. Coral Ridge Ministries sermon transcript
6. Quoted from *The Rewriting of America's History*, pg. 111
7. Ibid.
8. *Conspiracy of Ignorance*, pgs. 3-4
9. *None Dare Call It Education*, pg. 41
10. *God and Caesar: Biblical Faith and Political Action* by John Eidsmoe
11. *Christianity and the Constitution*, pgs 72-73
12. *Original Intent*, by David Barton, pg. 146

CHAPTER TWO
1. Quoted in *The Rewriting of America's History*, pg. 6
2. Quoted in *America's God And Country Encyclopedia of Quotations*, pg. 113
3. Ibid, pg. 114
4. Ibid, pg. 119
5. Quoted in *The Rewriting of America's History*, pg. 3
6. Quoted in *America's God And Country*, pg 119

7. Quoted in *America's Christian History*, pg. 52
8. Ibid, pgs. 54-55
9. Ibid, pg. 57
10. Ibid, pg. 56
11. Quoted in *Christianity and the Constitution,* pgs. 29-30
12. Quoted in *America's Christian History*, pg. 58
13. Ibid, pg. 59
14. Ibid.

CHAPTER THREE
1. Quoted in *Founding Fathers* , pg. 126
2. *America's God and Country*, pg. 636
3. Ibid.
4. Ibid, pgs. 636-637
5. Ibid, pg. 637
6. Quoted in *Christianity and the Constitution,* pg. 116
7. Ibid.
8. Quoted in *America's God and Country*, pg. 643
9. Ibid.
10. Quoted in *Miracle at Philadelphia*, pg. 29
11. Quoted in *America's God and Country*, pg. 651
12. Ibid, pg. 652
13. *Christianity and the Constitution*, pg. 118
14. *America's God and Country* pg. 647
15. Ibid pg .664
16. Ibid pg. 641
17. Quoted in America's God and Country pg 664
18. *The Rewriting of American History* pg. 61
19. *Christianity and the Constitution*, pg. 142

CHAPTER FOUR
1. Quoted in *America's Christian History*, pgs. 4-5
2. *They Preached Liberty*, pgs. 11-12
3. Quoted in *America's Christian History*, pg. 5
4. *John Witherspoon: Parson, Politician, Patriot*, pg. 32
5. *Original Intent*, pg. 83
6. *The Patriot's Handbook*, pg. 114

7. *Original Intent*, pg. 98
8. *Lives of the Signers of the Declaration of Independence*, pg. 84

CHAPTER FIVE
1. Quoted in *The Rewriting of America's History*, pg. 77
2. Quoted in *The Founders Almanac*, pg 63
3. Quoted in *America's God and Country*, pg. 2
4. Ibid, pg. 3
5. *The Rewriting of America's History*, pg 83
6. Microsoft Encarta, 1993-2002
7. *The Founders' Almanac,* pg. 66
8. Ibid, pg. 67
9. Quoted in *America's Christian History*
10. Quoted in *Original Intent*, pg. 162
11. Ibid.
12. Ibid. pg. 128
13. Ibid. pg. 103
14. Ibid. pg. 184
15. Quoted in *The Rewriting of America's History*, pgs. 83-84
16. *America's God an Country*, page 14

CHAPTER SIX
1. Quoted in *The Rewriting of America's History*, pg. 92
2. Ibid., pgs 327-328 (Prayer for Peace)
3. Quoted in *America's God and Country*, page 331
4. Quoted in *The Role of Pastors & Christians in Civil Government*, pg 24
5. Quoted in *Faith & Freedom*, pg 349
6. Quoted in *Christianity and the Constitution*, pg. 243
7. Quoted in *Christianity and the Constitution, pg. 244*
8. Quoted in *The Real Thomas Jefferson, pgs 319 – 323*
9. Ibid., pgs. 227-229
10. Ibid., pg 234
11. Ibid., pg 231

CHAPTER SEVEN
1. Quoted in *Founding Fathers*, pg. 141

2. Quoted in *Miracle at Philadelphia*, pg. 30
3. Ibid.
4. *The Rewriting of America's History*, pgs. 113 - 114

CHAPTER EIGHT
   1. The Biblical Basis for Our Constitution, by D. James Kennedy, Pg. 1
   2. Quoted in *Original Intent, pgs. 130-131*
   3. Quoted in *America's God and Country*, pg. 253
   4. Quoted in *AG&C*, pg. 252
   5. Patriot's Handbook by George Grant, pgs. 239-240

CHAPTER NINE
   1. Quoted in *The Spirit of America*, pg 56
   2. Ibid, pgs. 56-57
   3. The Myth of Separation, pg. 93
   4. Quoted in *America's God and Country*, pg. 22
   5. Microsoft Encarta Encyclopedia, 2003
   6. Lives of the Signers of the Declaration of Independence, originally published in 1848 and reprinted by WallBuilder Press, pg. 36
7.Ibid., pgs. 34-35
8.Quoted in *America's God and Country*, pg. 23

CHAPTER TEN
   1. Quoted in *The Founders' Almanac*, pg. 229
   2. Quoted in *The Spirit of America*, pg. 354
   3. Christianity and the Constitution, pg. 298

CHAPTER ELEVEN
   1. Microsoft Encarta Encyclopedia 2003
   2. In God We Trust, by Norman Cousins, pg. 327
   3. Founding Fathers, by M. E. Bradford, pg. 40
   4. The Founders' Almanac, Edited by Matthew Spalding, pg 95
   5. Quoted in *A Basic History of the United States*, Vol. 2, Pg 78
   6. Quoted in *The Founders' Almanac*, pg 99
   7. A Basic History of the United States, Vol. 2, pg s 124-125

8. Ibid., pgs 129-130
9. *Founding Fathers*, pg 48
10. *The Patriot's Handbook, pg. 242*

CHAPTER TWELVE
1. Quoted in *Faith & Freedom*, pg 250
2. *A Patriot's History of the United States*, pg. 92-93
3. Quoted in *America's God & Country*, pg. 213
4. *Miracle at Philadelphia*, pg. 4
5. *Founding Fathers* by, pg. 100
6. Quoted in *Faith & Freedom*, pg. 254
7. *From Dawn to Decadence*, pg. 404 – 405
8. Quoted in *Faith of our Founding Fathers*, pg. 156
9. Quoted in *Original Intent*, pg. 291

CHAPTER THIRTEEN
1. Quoted in *The Spirit of America*, pg. 41
2. Quoted in *Benjamin Bush*, pgs. 16-17
3. Quoted in *The Role of Pastors & Christians In Civil Government*, pgs. 5-6
4. Quoted in *The Spirit of America*, pgs. 376-377
5. Quoted in *Benjamin Rush*, pgs. 211-212

CHAPTER FOURTEEN
1. Quoted in *Christianity and the Constitution*, pg.319
2. Quoted in *Original Intent*, pg. 204
3. *America's God and Country*, by pg. 55
4. *Wikipedia* on-line encyclopedia
5. *Miracle at Philadelphia*, pg. 95
6. Quoted in *Founding Fathers*, pg. 25
7. Quoted in *America's God and Country*, pg. 560
8. Quoted in *Faith of our Founding Fathers*, pg. 134
9. Quoted in *America's Christian History*, pg. 203
10. Quoted in *Original Intent*, pg. 115

CHAPTER FIFTEEN
1. *A History of the American People,* pg. 188
2. *The Rewriting of American History*, pg. 143
3. *Founding Fathers*, pg. 149
4. *The Rewriting of American History* , pg. 143
5. Quoted in *America's God and Country*, pg. 424

CHAPTER SIXTEEN
1. *The Patriot's Handbook*, pg. 225
2. *Christianity and the Constitution*, pg. 166
3. *Microsoft Encarta*
4. *Wikipedia On-Line Encyclopedia*
5. *Christianity and the Constitution*, pg. 165

CHAPTER SEVENTEEN
1. Quoted in *The Patriot's Handbook*, pg. 248
2. *Founding Fathers*, pg. 74
3. Quoted in *Christianity and the Constitution*, pg. 186
4. Ibid., pg. 187
5. Quoted in *The Spirit of America*, pg. 86

CHAPTER EIGHTEEN
1. Quoted in *America's God and Country*, pgs. 52 – 53
2. Quoted in *Christianity and the Constitution*, pg. 330
3. *Founding Fathers*, pg. 196
4. Quoted in *Christianity and the Constitution*, pg. 336
5. *Hard Sayings of the Bible*

CHAPTER NINETEEN
1. Quoted in *Faith of Our Founding Fathers*, pg. 76
2. Ibid., pg. 77
3. Quoted in *Original Intent*, pg. 313
4. Microsoft Encarta Encyclopedia 2003
5. Quoted in *None Dare Call It Education*, pg. 43
6. Quoted in *America's God and Country*, pg. 679
7. Quoted in *The Spirit of America*, pg. 396
8. Quoted in *Original Intent*, pg. 342

9. Quoted in *The Rewriting of America's History*, Pg. 154
10. Ibid.

CHAPTER TWENTY
1. Quoted in *Greatness to Spare*, pgs. 18-19
2. Quoted in *Original Intent*, pg. 96
3. Microsoft Encarta Encyclopedia 2003.
4. Quoted in *Faith & Freedom*, pg. 258
5. Ibid., pg 246-247
6. Quoted in *Original Intent*, pg. 91
7. Quoted in *America's God and Country Encyclopedia*, pg. 276
8. Quoted in *The Spirit of America*, pg. 17

Further Reading

The following list of books proved to be an excellent source of background information on the individuals and events featured in this book and the times in which they occupied center stage in the formation of the unique Republic the Founding Fathers created for us. For readers interested in a more in-depth study of early American history, this list will be a valuable resource. It is my hope and expectation that *In Their Own Words* will whet the public intellectual appetite for extended reading and study of our valuable heritage. Hopefully, it will also help to motivate concerned citizens to become involved in the vital issues being publicly debated and contested today. In order to cast an intelligent vote, each citizen must become an informed voter. Our founders would heartily agree; they intended that citizens of the Republic they created would involve themselves in public issues and that they would take responsibility for their own enlightenment rather than relying upon questionable news media/ entertainment sources to guide their thinking. They would have especially expected that kind of behavior of Christians just as they would have expected them to vote in every election.

John Adams said, "Liberty must at all hazards be supported. We have a right to it, derived from our Maker. But if we had not, our fathers have earned and bought it for us, at the expense of their ease, their estates, their pleasure, and their blood."

The very least we can do is to make a sincere effort to become thoroughly informed citizens and to cast intelligent votes based on the well-documented Christian precepts passed down to us from our

Founding Fathers. First, we must understand those precepts so that we can practice them and pass them along to our future generations. We all have a responsibility to do that. We can't leave all the teaching to others.

A Basic History of the United States, Volume 2 by Clarence B. Carson

A History of the American People by Paul Johnson

America: A call to Greatness by John W. Chalfant

America's Christian History by Gary DeMar

America's God and Country by William J. Federer

A Nation Conceived and Dedicated by Corinne Hoexter and Ira Peck

A Patriot's History of the United States by Larry Schweikart and Michael Allen

Christianity and Liberalism by J. Gresham Machen

Christianity and the Constitution by John Eidsmoe

Christianity in the Constitution by Archie Preston Jones, Ph.D.

Edmund Burke: A Genius Reconsidered By Russell Kirk

Faith & Freedom by Benjamin Hart

Faith of Our Founding Fathers by Tim LaHaye

Founding Brothers by Joseph J. Ellis

Founding Fathers by M. E. Bradford

From Dawn to Decadence by Jacques Barzun

From Union to Empire by Clyde N. Wilson

God and the Constitution by Paul Marshall

Great Books of the Western World, American State Papers (#43)

Greatness to Spare by T. R. Fehrenbach

How to Win the Culture War by Peter Kreeft

In God We Trust by Norman Cousins

Intellectual Morons by Daniel Flynn

Lives of the Signers of the Declaration of Independence by B. J. Lossing

Miracle at Philadelphia by Catherine Drinker Bowen

National Review's American Classics (Historical Colonial Documents)

None Dare Call It Education by John A. Stormer

Not Our America...The ACLU Exposed! by Daniel J. Popeo

One Nation, Two Cultures by Gertrude Himmelfarb

Original Intent by David Barton

Reclaiming the Lost Legacy by D. James Kennedy

Roots of Freedom by John W. Danford

Slouching Towards Gomorrah by Robert H. Bork

The ACLU vs. America by Alan Sears and Craig Osten

The American Tradition by Clarence B. Carson

The Antifederalists by David J. Siemers

The Christian and American Law by H. Wayne House, General Editor

The Clash of Orthodoxies by Robert P. George

The Death of Truth edited by Dennis McCallum

The Founders' Almanac edited by Matthew Spalding

The Look-It-Up Book of Presidents by Wyatt Blassingame

The Myth of Separation by David Barton

The Patriot's Handbook **by** George Grant

The Politically Incorrect Guide to American History by Thomas E. Woods, Jr.

The Real Thomas Jefferson by Andrew M. Allison

The Rewriting of America's History by Catherine Millard

The Spirit of America Edited by William J. Bennett

The Story of In God We Trust by John Hudson Tiner

The Story of The Pledge of Allegiance by John Hudson Tiner

The Naked Square by Richard John Neuhaus

Tipping the Scales Coral Ridge Ministries

Understanding the Times by David A. Noebel

What Is A Man? edited by Waller R. Newell

What They Believed by D. James Kennedy

What If America Were A Christian Nation Again? by D. James Kennedy

CPSIA information can be obtained at www.ICGtesting.com
Printed in the USA
BVOW08s0210280116

434493BV00050B/78/P